T0320143

Sustainable Growth Through Strategic Innovation

To my family

Sustainable Growth Through Strategic Innovation

Driving Congruence in Capabilities

Mitsuru Kodama

Professor of Innovation and Technology Management, College of Commerce and Graduate School of Business Administration, Nihon University at Tokyo, Japan

Edward Elgar
PUBLISHING

Cheltenham, UK • Northampton, MA, USA

Published by
Edward Elgar Publishing Limited
The Lypiatts
15 Lansdown Road
Cheltenham
Glos GL50 2JA
UK

Edward Elgar Publishing, Inc.
William Pratt House
9 Dewey Court
Northampton
Massachusetts 01060
USA

A catalogue record for this book
is available from the British Library

Library of Congress Control Number: 2017950456

This book is available electronically in the **Elgar**online
Business subject collection
DOI 10.4337/9781785366383

MIX
Paper from
responsible sources
FSC® C013056

ISBN 978 1 78536 637 6 (cased)
ISBN 978 1 78536 638 3 (eBook)

Typeset by Servis Filmsetting Ltd, Stockport, Cheshire
Printed and bound in Great Britain by TJ International Ltd, Padstow

Contents

Figures

Boxes

Preface and acknowledgments

This is the third book I have published as a single author through Edward Elgar Publishing. The book discusses strategic management and innovation activities in corporations from the perspective of the capabilities of individuals, groups and organizations. This book is the result of substantive observations made over a long period of time by me in the business workplace, and analysis of those observations. The industries I selected for this research are those in primarily high-tech areas such as ICT. The reason for selecting this field from among the many industries is because it has the most intense changes in business models due to the particularly dynamic evolution of the capabilities in it.

Over 21 years, I experienced the exciting business of mainly company-internal ventures and the development of new products, services and businesses in the rapidly changing ICT field. Through past business experience, I found that a driving force supporting learning and innovation in companies is capabilities, and that these are dynamic elements that are constantly changing. I found that these capabilities evolve by the orchestration (or integration) of the assets (knowledge) of people and groups, the leadership of top and middle management, and staff, and dynamic process to achieve real business. The asset orchestration, leadership, and dynamic process dynamically formulate and implement strategy in corporate organizations. An important aspect of the evolution of capabilities is the theoretical perspective on dynamic capabilities. At the micro level, practitioners either consciously or unconsciously, and dynamically network assets (knowledge) to bring about continuous strategic innovation and sustainable growth.

The purpose of this book is to extract micro level theoretical frameworks (capabilities congruence, strategic innovation capabilities, strategic innovation loop, strategic innovation system, sustaining strategic innovation model) for companies to bring about new assets (knowledge) and strategic innovation with a realistic view of organizational and strategic dynamic processes in industries that are constantly changing through time such as the fast-moving ICT field. As a researcher of business persons and in the field of business and management studies, the most important objective of this book is how to bridge theory and practice. For this reason,

I have immersed myself deeply in organizations and closely observed and analyzed the thinking and actions of many practitioners including those in their partnered corporations and their customers. Hence, I performed an in-depth qualitative study pursuing the research issues of how practitioners actually dynamically set down and execute strategy both inside and outside of companies, and how they restructure organizations to acquire and demonstrate new capabilities. Accordingly the research methodologies I employed are primarily in-depth case studies centered on participant observation and ethnography.

In this long-term field research, I was giving much encouragement and valuable insights into practitioners' creation of the businesses of the future and achievement of visions in exciting business environments through practical hands-on activities as their way of lives. However, there is also drama in business activity (macro and micro, and in both cases of success and failure), and it's the subjectivity and values as beliefs and thoughts of practitioners that achieve strategy and acquire capabilities.

This book could not be completed without the thorough and strict interaction that I have had with many practitioners. I would like to extend my gratitude to these practitioners that are of a number too great to count. Concerning the publication of this book, I wish to extend my appreciation to Ms Francine O'Sullivan, Senior Commissioning Editor in Edward Elgar, who provided tremendous support.

I am also deeply grateful for the valuable comments offered by the two reviewers of the proposal for this book. Lastly I would like to express my deep gratitude to Nihon University's College of Commerce, my workplace which has provided me with the comforts of a day-to-day research environment.

Mitsuru Kodama

1. Strategic innovation for sustainable growth: reviews of existing capabilities theories, and new propositions

Strategic innovation dynamically brings about strategic positioning through new products, services and business models, and is a dynamic view of strategy that enables a large corporation to maintain its competitiveness and establish sustainable growth. For these reasons, large corporations have to be innovators that can reinforce their existing positions (businesses) through incremental innovation, while at the same time constantly renew or destroy existing business through radical innovation.

From detailed reviews of existing capabilities theories (resource-based theory of the firm and dynamic capabilities, and so on), and further theories deeply related to the characteristics of corporate or organizational capabilities and field data on sustainable growth of global corporations, this chapter presents the concept of a "Capabilities Map" derived from existing research into the characteristics of dynamic capabilities responding to environmental conditions such as dynamic temporal shifts and factors of uncertainty.

1.1 SUSTAINABLE GROWTH THROUGH RADICAL AND INCREMENTAL INNOVATION

Here in the 21st century, changes in business circumstances surrounding large corporations are becoming more pronounced. Managers and business leaders face a wide range of challenges as businesses globalize and increasingly operate in emerging markets, as technologies innovate rapidly, networking permeates throughout societies and markets mature, as well as price wars and environmental problems. Obviously, a large corporation must continuously create new products, services and business models to maintain sustainable competitiveness and growth over the long term.

The creation of new business models that change existing rules and radically revamp conventional products and services trigger major trans-formations in the corporate strategy of large corporations. For example, new value chains and business ecosystems in the ICT industry that origi-nated in the United States with the creation of a new music distribution system and smartphones with Apple's iPhone, iPod and iTunes music store caused major shakeups in both the music and mobile phone industries.

The collection of innovation research of recent years into radical inno-vation (e.g., Leifer et al., 2000), breakthrough innovation (e.g., O'Connor et al., 2008; Hargadon, 2003), discontinuous innovation (e.g., Kaplan et al., 2003) and disruptive innovation (Christensen, 1997) has offered both theoretical and practical pointers for transforming strategies in large corporations to advance technologies and create new markets. The impor-tant implications put forth by existing research suggest it is not enough to just be able to respond quickly to environmental changes – companies also need to acquire capabilities to develop business and create new environ-ments (markets).

Thus, to swiftly respond to changing circumstances, companies have to continually polish their existing capabilities to fortify their main busi-nesses. Incremental innovation (e.g., Ettlie, et al., 1984; Dewar and Dutton, 1986) through strengthening and utilization of company capabilities through regular, continuous and cumulative upgrade and improvement activities is important. At the same time, to drive business for radical innovation to create new environments (markets) (e.g., Henderson, 1993; McDermott and O'Connor, 2002), it's also necessary to seek out or create never-before-seen capabilities to drive business development. In these two innovation processes – incremental (exploitation) and radical (exploration) innovation – it's the former that entails strengthening and utilizing capa-bilities for a company's existing business (its main business) and pursuing greater operational efficiency. In contrast, it's the latter that involves a large corporation searching out or building new capabilities in pursuit of the creativity needed to pioneer new business models and the new busi-nesses of the future. However, large corporations have to manage these two totally different innovation processes simultaneously and incorporate both of them into the nuclei of their corporate strategies.

The traditional large corporations of the past found great competitive-ness in reinforcing and utilizing their path-dependent capabilities to incre-mentally innovate their existing products and profit by releasing newer versions of them. In contrast, radical or breakthrough innovations result in paradigm shifts accompanied by new markets and technologies that bring big increases in product functionality, radical changes to existing markets, the creation of new markets and substantial cost reductions (Leifer et al., 2000; O'Connor and Rice, 2001). In this way, as new breakthroughs, radical innovations are different in character to the incremental and path-dependent innovations of the large corporations of the past. To achieve radical innovation, large corporations need to seek out and create new capabilities that are different from their existing skills and know-how (e.g., Dewar and Dutton, 1986; Ettlie et al., 1984; Green et al., 1995).

However, corporations taking on radical innovation and various projects within themselves must face uncertainties and discontinuities in areas such as markets, technologies, organizations and resources. Hence, while it may be possible for some projects to overcome these hurdles, many projects lose momentum and fail (e.g., Leifer et al., 2000). To seek out and create new capabilities for radical innovation, large corporations must engage in management activities that are not the same as reinforcing and utilizing the capabilities they have nurtured through their incremental innovation histories (the business elements of strategy, organizations, resources, technologies processes and leadership) (e.g., Kodama, 2003; O'Reilly and Tushman, 2004; Vanhaverbeke and Peeters, 2005).

There is a dynamic relationship between the creation and utilization of these capabilities. Since strengthening and utilizing existing capabilities for incremental innovation means fostering and accumulating technical know-how and personnel skills within companies, these capabilities can trigger the achievement of radical innovation through the searching and creation of new capabilities. Therefore, large corporations must understand their desired level (optimal level) of balance between creating and utilizing capabilities, and must intentionally manage them. Companies face new challenges regarding the creativity and efficiency of their capabilities, in other words "the combination of exploration and exploitation," to bring about radical innovation by seeking out and creating new capabilities, while at the same time maintaining their competitiveness through incremental innovation in their main businesses by strengthening and utilizing existing capabilities (March, 1991).

Thus, leaders and managers of large corporations need a perspective on seeking out and creating new capabilities to pioneer new business and create new markets while strengthening and utilizing capabilities to maintain their core businesses. Simultaneously executing and combining these two substantially different innovation processes entails the pursuit and pioneering of new and highly individualized strategic positions, and is thus a superior corporate strategy that also leads to the achievement of sustainable competitiveness and growth (e.g., Markides, 1999; Kodama, 2006).

In this book, the strategic activities or innovation processes that achieve a combination of radical and incremental innovation, or in other words combine the exploration and exploitation mentioned earlier, the author calls "strategic innovation." It's this strategic innovation that achieves sustainable growth in large corporations. Nevertheless, the questions remain – how do large corporations bring about strategic innovation, and what kind of strategic management in (and between) leading companies is needed to achieve sustainable growth? This book answers these holistic research questions from the perspective of academic research into strategic management and innovation.

1.2   DYNAMIC CAPABILITIES AND STRATEGIC INNOVATION

Markides (1997) defined strategic innovation as the dynamic creation of creative strategic positioning from new products, services, and business models, and emphasized that this framework was a dynamic view of strategy by which a company establishes sustained competitive excellence. To achieve this, companies must not adhere to existing positioning (existing business), but must always innovate in ways that destroy this positioning. Moreover, Govindarajan and Trimble (2005) defined it as realizing strategically innovative new business models (including new products and services). This strategic innovation refers to business innovation that transforms the established into new business and has a major impact on corporate performance, and is different in essence from incremental innovation.

Nevertheless, it goes without saying that incremental innovation drives existing business, and is a business activity crucial to making gains in the visible near term, but from there, companies must also keep an eye on initiatives to achieve radical innovation to secure sustainable growth into the future while investing their acquired short-term profits in new R&D activities. In other words, companies have to strengthen their incremental innovation activities, while simultaneously directing themselves toward the challenge of radical innovation (e.g., Christensen, 1997; Goold and Cambell, 2002; Heller, 1999; Kodama, 2003, 2004; Tushman and O'Reilly, 1997; O'Reilly and Tushman, 2004). Thus, in this perspective, both incremental innovation and radical innovation must be simultaneously pursued in the strategic innovation implied by Markides (1997) and Govindarajan and Trimble (2005).

Based on a number of major studies, in particular those done on dynamic capabilities (Teece, 2007, 2014), this chapter clarifies the dynamic innovation processes of companies for establishing strategic innovation (incremental innovation and radical innovation) for sustainable growth. The characteristics of the capabilities that corporations use to handle such externalities as the fast environmental changes and uncertainties they face are described by the Capabilities Map concept (as the four capabilities domains).

1.3 CAPABILITIES THEORY – DISCUSSIONS FOCUSING ON DYNAMIC CAPABILITIES

The resource-based theories that focused on independent capabilities for companies and organizations (e.g., Penrose, 1959; Richardson, 1972; Wernerfelt, 1984; Rumelt, 1984; Barney, 1991) became strategic theory frameworks from the viewpoints of microeconomics and organizational economics. These resource-based theories and Porter's (1980) competition strategy theory enable a detailed analysis of strategic positioning and the relationship between competitive excellence and internal resources already owned by companies in slowly changing environments and industries. However, it is difficult to analyze how companies create new competitive excellence in rapidly changing high-tech industries in competitive environments such as the ICT and digital sectors.

In recent years, the theory of dynamic capabilities (DC hereinafter) (e.g., Teece et al., 1997; Teece, 2007, 2014) has been developed and refined, and has become a fundamental theory that clarifies the mechanisms for sustainable growth through corporate strategic innovation. Teece et al. (1997, p.516) define DC as the firm's ability to integrate, build, and reconfigure internal and external competences to address rapidly changing environments, Thus, they assert that DC reflect an organization's ability to achieve new and innovative forms of competitive advantage given its path dependencies and market positions (Leonard-Barton, 1992). Moreover, Teece (2014, p.332) also asserts that strong DC help enable an enterprise to profitably build and renew resources and assets that lie both within and beyond its boundaries, reconfiguring them as needed to innovate and respond to (or bring about) changes in the market and in the business environment more generally.

As core, micro level functions, DC can usefully be broken down into three primary clusters: (1) identification, development, co-development, and assessment of technological opportunities in relationship to customer needs (sensing); (2) mobilization of resources to address needs and opportunities, and to capture value by taking opportunities (seizing); and (3) continued renewal (transforming). Engagement in continuous or semi-continuous sensing, seizing, and transforming is essential if a company is to sustain itself as customers, competitors, and technologies change (Teece, 2007, 2014).

Regarding the area in which DC are applied, Teece et al. (1997)

claimed that DC are important for sustainable company-level competitive advantage, especially in high-velocity markets. As well as that, strong DC enable an enterprise and its top management to develop assumptions about the evolution of consumer preferences, business problems and technology, validate and fine-tune them, and then act on them by realigning assets and activities to enable continuous innovation and change (Teece, 2014).

In this perspective, DC can be thought of as a dynamic business process that should be demonstrated in business environments that are changing rapidly, and/or in business environments that have high levels of uncertainty. It is especially important to demonstrate this DC in Domains I, II, III in the Capabilities Map in Figure 1.1 (business environments that are changing rapidly, and/or business environments that have high levels of uncertainty) discussed later.

In the dynamic environments of "hypercompetition" (D'Aveni, 1994) or "next-generation competition" (Teece, 2012a) gaining attention in recent years, the theoretical concept of DC has become crucial for companies to drive "ecosystem strategies" (Teece, 2014). Moreover, asset orchestration (Teece, 2007), a core function of DC, is reinforced by the organizational processes of (1) coordination/integration, (2) learning, and (3) reconfiguration (Teece et al., 1997). Affecting performance in the individual domains in the Capabilities Map (Figure 1.1) (discussed later), asset organization also has a profound relationship with the core theoretical "capabilities congruence" framework of this book (discussed in Chapter 3).

Teece (2007, 2014) clearly distinguishes these DC from "ordinary capabilities" (OC hereinafter). Teece (2014, p.330) states:

> Ordinary capabilities have also been called static (Collis, 1994), zero-level (Winter, 2003), first order (Danneels, 2002), and substantive (Zahra, Sapienza, and Davidsson, 2006). The zero-, first-, and second- typology is used by Easterby-Smith and Prieto (2008) and Schilke (2014). The more common usage seems to be equating first-order with ordinary.

These OC generally fall into three categories: administration, operations, and governance. In describing specific details of corporate activity, OC enable a firm to perform activities on an ongoing basis using more or less the same techniques on the same scale to support existing products and services for the same customer population. Such capabilities can be said to be ordinary in the sense of maintaining the *status quo* (that is, not out of the ordinary; Winter, 2003) (Helfat and Winter, 2011).

Nevertheless, in the pursuit of efficiency in terms of a company's best practices and "doing things right," OC are not to be underestimated – they are often fundamental and can support competitive advantage for decade-long periods (Teece, 2014). In other words, in relatively stable environments where environmental change is gradual and there are low levels of uncertainty, OC function usefully in business, but don't secure corporate sustainable growth over the long term. However, in traditional large corporations engaging in wide-ranging business activities, there are always some business domains in which OC must be demonstrated – these OC are critical for business in slow or relatively stable environments of low uncertainty, and are particularly important in Domain IV in Figure 1.1 (low uncertainty, slow environmental change), as discussed later.

Therefore, companies apply OC and systematically and analytically formulate and implement strategies under relatively stable or slow-moving conditions with little business uncertainty. "Learning before doing" (Pisano, 1994), that is, formulating and implementing detailed strategy planning and policies, is a key element of OC in market structures with clear corporate boundaries and where there is a good grasp of the players in value chains.

In contrast, DC have been reinterpreted by a number of researchers, and among those, Eisenhardt and Martin (2000) have been quoted in many papers (Web of Science: 2451, as of 2015). They express DC as "The firm's processes that use resources – specifically the processes to integrate, reconfigure, gain and release resources – to match and even create market change. Dynamic capabilities thus are the organizational and strategic routines by which firms achieve new resource configurations as markets emerge, collide, split, evolve, and die" (Eisenhardt and Martin, 2000, p.1107) and recursively extract the concept of corporate DC required in both slow and fast-moving business environments. They emphasize "learning by doing" with simple rules focusing on results rather than prior training and implementation processes, especially in fast-moving environments, where uncertainty rises and an industry's corporate borders become vague (Eisenhardt and Sull, 2001). However, Eisenhardt and Martin (2000) claimed that DC are inherently unsuited to creating sustainable advantage and that they are likely to break down in high-velocity markets.

In contrast to this assertion by Eisenhardt and Martin (2000) that "dynamic capabilities would break down in high-velocity environments because of the instability of the simple rules (basically, semi-improvised managerial actions)," Teece (2014, p.339) states that:

> In high-velocity environments, the business enterprise may well be particularly reliant on the sensing and seizing instincts and actions of the CEO and the top management team. To the extent that this is so, the capabilities will, of course suffer from a degree of instability because their longevity depends logically on the tenure of entrepreneurs/managers/leaders.

Viewed from the perspective of a practitioner, Teece's comments (2014, p.339) can be seen as more rational reasoning that captures the real business environment. Moreover, considering the author's experience of having worked on a number of product planning projects to date, DC are also the quick-wittedness required by the dynamic spiral thinking and action (simultaneously both deliberate and emergent) of regular trial and error of project leaders and team members on the front line of new processes for building new business, and are not just the attributes of top management in high-speed, rapidly changing environments. The author doesn't negate the idea of simple rules, although it should be one standard of judgment that practitioners use in complex and dynamic business processes in response to certain situations (not all situations).

In contrast to the discussions of Eisenhardt and Martin (2000), Teece (2014, p.332) asserts that:

> Eisenhardt and Martin's (2000) article misinterpreted (or reframed) the DC framework by claiming that all capabilities, including DC, can ultimately be characterized by best practice and hence imitated. In essence, Eisenhardt and Martin conflated two concepts that benefit from being analytically separated, namely OC and DC. OC and DC are quite distinct, both analytically and in practice.

Hence, it appears different researchers have different positions on the interpretation of DC.

Nevertheless, through some other researchers, this interest in strategy theory has evolved toward a dynamic structure that reflects current corporate activity. For example, O'Connor (2008) respects the DC theory of Eisenhardt and Martin (2000), and mentions that a large number of major innovations (MI) (included in the concept of strategic innovation in this book), including radical innovations, developed gradually from slow (or very slow) market environments, and were implemented over a period of several years to several decades. Thus, the concept of DC is described as a theory that can be evaluated and applied around the axes of both market speed and business uncertainty (including risk), and is characterized by strategic innovation.

In addition, O'Connor (2008) used the term "MI dynamic capability" for the capability that promotes the "exploration" process (March, 1991) and realizes strategic innovation under conditions of uncertainty and high risk. MI dynamic capability differs from the capability theory (e.g., King and Tucci, 2002; Nelson and Winter, 1982; Winter, 2000) that emphasizes the evolution of the original "exploitation" (March, 1991) activity process. MI dynamic capability responds to highly uncertain situations, regardless of the speed of market movement, and embraces the concept of DC in the high-speed (and highly uncertain) markets mentioned by Eisenhardt and Martin (2000).

Realistically speaking (including the author's practical experiences), many strategic innovations are established through discovery or invention in slow – and very slow-moving basic scientific research and technological development environments. Later, the developed core technologies and provisional business models based on discovered or invented ideas are adopted and exploited in products and services through improvisation and trial-and-error processes (including the weeding-out process) involving trial manufacture, experiment, and incubation. Product and service markets are gradually established. Then, new products and services antici-pated or forecast for growth spurn competitive markets involving other companies (just when other companies enter the market depends on indi-vidual businesses). These market environments become fast-moving, and companies accelerate their investment in necessary resources.

O'Connor and DeMartino (2006) undertook long-term observation and analysis of radical innovation in major US corporations, and identified the importance of three-phase management (discovery, incubation, and accel-eration) as a radical innovation (part of strategic innovation) development framework. They then named the ability to implement these processes the "breakthrough innovation capability," and suggested that building this capability into a company is a key managerial approach that can lead to successful radical innovation (O'Connor et al., 2008).

This three-phase management (discovery, incubation, and acceleration) is used in projects in large corporations (and venture enterprises) to develop various new products, services, and businesses. Different practitioner (and organizations such as project teams) capabilities are required in the individ-ual business processes in each of the three phases, depending on the degree of business uncertainty and environmental changes being faced. As mentioned, DC robustly function in response to these externalities (uncertainty and environmental change), and are also a framework for demonstrating diffi-cult-to-imitate competitiveness. Therefore, the three phases of Breakthrough Innovation Capability (O'Connor et al., 2008) (discovery, incubation, and acceleration) or MI dynamic capability (major innovation) (O'Connor, 2008) can be described as the three DC functions (sensing, seizing, trans-forming) which can be applied in high-speed and uncertain environments, and even in its theoretical concepts, DC can also be said to include the frameworks for Breakthrough Innovation Capability (discovery, incubation, and acceleration) and MI dynamic capability (major innovation).

Previous research, such as Teece's DC framework and MI innovation capability, is positioned around the two axes of uncertainty and change and led to the situation illustrated in the Capability Map in Figure 1.1,

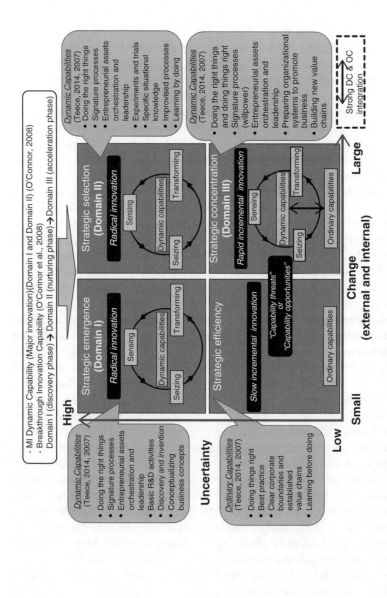

Figure 1.1 Capabilities Map, dynamic capabilities and ordinary capabilities

which shows the relationship between those previous researches and the three development phases of O'Connor and DeMartino (2006) mentioned above. As mentioned, three-phase management (discovery, incubation, and acceleration) entails moving in order through Domain I, Domain II and Domain III, from business conception or invention to practical realization, which are fields of business in which DC are demonstrated (and OC in Domain III as discussed later). In contrast, it is OC that function in pursuit of best practices (Teece, 2007, 2014) in slow and stable environments with low uncertainty and change (Domain IV). Here, strategic uncertainty beyond the four elements of markets, technology, organization and resources mentioned by Leifer et al. (2000) also exists, and change is not limited to the external elements of market or industrial technology speeds, but also corresponds to the internal elements of a company's own strategy – organization (organizational revamping), technology, operation and leadership (described in detail in Chapter 3). The following describes the characteristics of capabilities in each Domain.

1.4 THE CAPABILITIES MAP – THEORETICAL FRAMEWORKS

Based in the theoretical concepts of the exiting research described above, this book analyses the capabilities required by the various organizations in large corporations (organization charged with R&D and new business development, project teams, and existing traditional organizations, and so on) in the various business contexts that they regularly face, and provides a new theoretical framework.

1.4.1 DC in Domain I

Slow or very slow environmental change with a highly uncertain domain (Domain I) observed at the initial stage of strategic innovation is the technology creation stage arising from new ideas, business concepts, discoveries, and invention, and corresponds to the "discovery phase" described by O'Connor and DeMartino (2006). In this domain, the exploration process advances through the MI dynamic (or breakthrough innovation) capability mentioned above. The role of sensing is important in DC. In R&D organizations in major corporations (laboratories, development centers, and so on) R&D organizations set down and execute mid- to long-term plans either continuously or semi-continuously, which entails seizing and transforming processes while searching out and detecting latent new markets through sensing to achieve radical innovation.

The basic research and creation of ideas that are the source of new strategic innovation require (depending on the field) a longer period of time as the ratio of scientific elements and the degree of technological difficulty rises. In this domain, achievements are often the result of the creative thinking and actions of middle managers and staff in company R&D departments and business development divisions, but there is also substantial commitment and strategic contribution made by top management and upper level managers based on the policies of "doing the right things"(Teece, 2014). Moreover, there are important "signature processes" (Bruch and Ghoshal, 2004) in large traditional (leading) corporations that are difficult for other companies to copy, which are processes that raise the quality of R&D. The author calls this domain the "strategic emergence" domain.

In the asset orchestration process in this domain, practitioners have to pursue reconfiguration and transformation through coordination and integration of various intangible assets as well as engage in learning as hypothetical testing tailored to the their R&D aims. There are a variety of asset orchestration patterns, and there are still many cases in many traditional large companies under conventional hierarchical systems of closed innovation centered on internal laboratories and development divisions (Japanese manufacturing is a typical example). To develop incremental innovation or sustain innovation through accumulated path-dependent knowledge (Christensen, 1997), closed innovation is still an important process. Closed innovation plays a critical role in traditional high-tech fields such as the heavy electrical, nuclear power generation, aviation, vehicle equipment, machine tool, medical and semiconductor machinery industries. In contrast, in industries in which technologies are rapidly advancing such as ICT, the best technical achievements and know-how are becoming increasingly spread out across the globe. In these fast-moving environments, open innovation is adopted (Chesbrough, 2003), partial core intangible assets are incorporated from externalities, and hence processes to merge and integrate intangible assets both within and from the outside of companies become critical. Here, of particular importance are the processes of coordination and integration in asset orchestration of various resources performed by top and middle managers in an entrepreneurial fashion.

In Domain I, companies must consider what business models they are seeking. Should a company adopt a vertical integration model with the aim of finally bringing about completed parts, products and services, and so on, or adopt horizontal integration to focus on the company's particular area of expertise? Should a company reinforce its technologies while searching out strategic alliances (strong or weak ties) with other companies? Should a company build new value chains through coordination and integration of intangible assets, which means using the strengths of the company and other companies forged though strategic collaboration across different types of business. Thus, in allowing for expanded diversification of asset orchestration, practitioners have to concentrate on learning through trial and error, experiments and trial activities.

In strategic emergence in Domain I, companies have to hypothetically test their corporate boundaries in response to strategic objectives or business environments and make attempts at reconfiguration/transformation of diverse entrepreneurial asset orchestration through processes of trial and error. If it's advantageous to develop or manufacture in-house, then it's better to configure a vertical value chain model with a focus on creativity (Kodama, 2009a). In contrast, if another company has achieved more with its developments than those in-house, there are many cases in which a company should abandon its development efforts, and focus on efficiency not only through strategic outsourcing but also through strategic alliances, joint developments and M&A to access and acquire external intangible assets. The important factor of this asset orchestration process is the "co-specialization" described in Chapter 3. Co-specialization is the way the levels of synergies of technologies and so forth are raised in business, and the process of co-specialized assets orchestration is an important factor in raising a company's "dynamic internal and external congruence in capabilities."

1.4.2   DC in Domain II

Next, with rapid changing of in-house (or occasionally external) human resources and maintenance and upgrading of organizations oriented to business incubation, core technologies and business concepts migrate from the slow-moving environment of Domain I to a dramatically transforming Domain II environment that is full of rapid change and uncertainty. In this domain, the exploration processes arising from DC (MI dynamic or breakthrough innovation) described by O'Connor (2008) are promoted. This domain corresponds to the incubation phase of hypothetical setups, experiments, and assessments mentioned by O'Connor and DeMartino (2006). Learning through trials and experiments also leads to less risk and uncertainty with markets and technologies and greater probability of success for incubations aimed at realizing strategic innovation (O'Connor et al., 2008). Then, top and middle management can make decisions to select and bring to market rigorously tested products, service, and business models.

In Domain II (the incubation phase), the role of seizing is important in commercial development divisions on the business side to achieve radical innovation. Commercial development divisions "sense" matches between the market and technical innovations while seizing and transforming for radical innovation as the commercial development of new processes, new technologies and new businesses. Thus, practitioners pursue entrepreneurial strategies, demonstrate commitment and make strategic contributions based on the basic policy of "doing the right things." Moreover, the quality of the signature processes unique to a company that were required in Domain I are more strongly reflected in this domain. This is because there exist serious hurdles called the "valley of death" (Kodama, 2011) between R&D and commercialization of its achievements, and the ability to surmount these hurdles largely comes down to these rarified signature processes unique to companies.

O'Connor et al. (2008) confine this incubation domain to trials and assessment models, but in many cases current business activities go beyond trials in uncertain and dramatically changing, fast-moving environments to the launch of commercial businesses, where companies might boldly undertake risks. In this domain, there are numerous cases of excessive trust and commitment of leaders and managers leads toward strategic activity based on the creation of business through trial and error, although whether newly developed ideas and prototypes are capable of becoming new business models and value chains might still remain to be seen. These enterprises are typical of the new online business world where products are both trialed and launched in dramatically changing, risky and uncertain domains. The key here is being able to select and implement promising, valuable businesses, which is why the author calls this domain the "strategic selection" domain.

In this domain, the asset orchestration process entails selection and narrowing down and refining the diverse intangible and tangible assets trialed and experimented on in the strategic emergence domain. Following, the level of completeness of asset orchestration as products, services and business models is raised through the processes of (1) coordination/integration, (2) learning, and (3) reconfiguration. Hence, depending on circumstances, there are cases where a corporation has to rethink its corporate boundaries (both vertical and horizontal) or its relationships such as partnerships with other companies, and realign or reconfigure its assets.

1.4.3   DC and OC in Domain III

New businesses (including new products and services) chosen through strategic selection in Domain II that have future prospects and somewhat reduced uncertainty shift to the more certain Domain III, although external (environmental) and internal change continues. In Domain III, the strategic innovation incubated (or partially commercialized) in Domain II enters a growth trajectory which corresponds to the "acceleration phase" discussed by O'Connor and DeMartino (2006). According to O'Connor et al. (2008), this is where the exploitation process is promoted by Breakthrough Innovation Capability. Hence, this is the domain where building and optimization of processes and value chains for selected new businesses is achieved.

These new business functions are wholly or partially transferred to the appropriate business divisions to accelerate commercialization (or new business divisions are established, or made independent as external ventures), and further resources are intensively invested through "doing the right things" and the strategic commitment of top and middle management. Hence, the author calls this domain the "strategic concentration" domain. In the past, a large number of product and service development projects for major corporations (e.g., Kodama, 2005; 2007d) invested management resources through asset orchestration in commercialization through this shift from strategic selection to strategic concentration.

In Domain III, a domain in which the pace of environmental change is fast and competition with other companies is fierce, "transforming" on the business side plays an important role. With the passing of time, newly developed products and businesses will burst into the competitive environments with other companies at the stage of shifting into Domain III. Nevertheless, the shift to a competitive environment depends on the industry or the features of a product, and in this sense the birth of a competitive market means that uncertainty lowers in the environment, in other words the market. In contrast, divisions such as product planning and technical development positioned on the upstream of the value chain at the business side (sales HQ and sales divisions, and so on), also function to sense and detect changes in the market that have been newly brought about, and establish robust value chains through seizing and transforming for upgrades and improvements by rapidly and incrementally innovating new products and services (sustainably advancing the technologies) that have been successfully commercialized. For this reason, practitioners pursue entrepreneurial strategies here (including deliberate and emergent strategies), and demonstrate commitment and strategic contribution based on the basic policy of "doing the right things."

Moreover, in Domain III, there is a significant dependence on the "willpower" (Bruch and Ghoshal, 2004) of the unique signature processes of a company to win out over the competition. Willpower is the energy and concentration of the thinking and action that accompany a sense of purpose. Energy means vigor, and concentration directs this vigor toward a particular goal. Practitioners paint a clear picture of their intended strategy in their minds, with the most important factor being that they consciously dedicate themselves to planning to bring their intended strategy into being in the midst of stiff competition. Moreover, in this domain, it's the willpower in the unique and highly rarefied signature processes of a company that carries much of the burden. Just as Teece (2014, p.341) argues, a strategy can be defined as "a coherent set of analyses, concepts, policies, arguments, and actions that respond to a high-stakes challenge" (Rumelt, 2011, p.6). The best strategies require (1) a diagnosis, (2) a guiding policy, and (3) coherent action brought about by the unique signature processes of a company based on willpower (Rumelt, 2011). Currently, the smartphone industry is in this Domain III stage.

In Domain III, the completion level of products and services is raised through upgrades and improvements for rapid incremental innovation following commercialization, through the processes of asset orchestration promoted and concentrated to complete value chains. Through trial and error, although the changes in factors of the asset orchestration process are lower than the strategic selection in Domain II, the most important issue is overall optimization (external and internal congruence in capabilities) of the corporate system, as described in Chapter 3.

However, in Domain III, to get new products, services and businesses off the ground and win out over the competition, robust value chains must be configured. As mentioned, organization supervisors and staff in product planning and technical development divisions on the business side upstream in the value chain must demonstrate strong DC, however in contrast, staff and leaders in routine divisions on the downstream in the value chain (sales, technical management, procurement, manufacturing and after support etc.) need thoroughly reinforced operations management enabled through strong OC. These downstream organizations invest in current products (and their successor upgraded and improved versions), and require strong OC to win out amid stiff competition and turn a profit. Thus, the characteristics of the capabilities required to promote business in Domain III are not the same as those in Domains I and II, and have a particularly strong focus on integration of DC and OC (see Figure 1.1).

1.4.4   OC in Domain IV

A great deal of existing business is positioned in Domain IV, in slow-moving market environments with low uncertainty and a low rate of change. Here, incremental innovation is promoted to systematically enhancing business efficiency through the exploitation process, which entails activities to improve existing business using mainstream organizations that demonstrate inherent OC (Teece, 2007, 2014).

In Domain IV, the weight on DC diminishes, and the focus shifts to the demonstration of best practices through OC. Existing traditional organizations (business divisions, and so on) detect slow changes in existing markets, and execute existing operations at formal organizations through strict top-down centralized leadership (Kodama, 2004), path-dependent planning in business divisions and well thought-out deliberate strategies. In Domain IV, high performance must be brought about by evolving routines through higher-order learning to generate short-term profits in response to internal and external changes, and to drive slow incremental innovation through strengthened OC (King and Tucci, 2002; Benner and Tushman, 2003; Winter, 2000; Amburgey et al., 1993; Nelson and Winter, 1982). Promoting this Domain IV process management accelerates an organization's speed of response to achieve incremental innovation (Benner and Tushman, 2003). However, as discussed later in Chapter 2, there is always a danger that product lineups in this Domain could be threatened by emergent technical innovations. The author calls this domain the "strategic efficiency" domain.

Most of the businesses in Domain IV (products and services) are survivors from the competitive environment in Domain III that have moved into Domain IV, a domain that entails shifting from old to new business over long periods of time (Markides, 2001). In other words, existing business in the strategic efficiency Domain IV might be subjected to this old-new business conversion into a new strategic concentration (Domain III) business as a path newly created through strategic innovation (Domain I → Domain II → Domain III). Markides' (2001) discussion of simultaneously managing existing and new strategic positions implies the combination of Domains IV and III respectively, and that the shift from an old position to a new one implies (all) existing business in Domain IV can shift to accelerate and grow as new business in Domain III.

As above, in describing the dynamics of the shifts between domains in the Capabilities Map, of particular importance are the strategic actions in Domains III and IV that aim for sustainable growth through ongoing corporate strategic innovation. According to the "Capabilities Lifecycles" framework of Helfat and Peteraf (2003) (described in section 2.3 in Chapter 2), to achieve further strategic innovation, companies have to uncover "capability opportunities" and sometimes deal with "capability threats" by driving new DC in Domains III and IV, which hinges on the shift to Domain I (see Figure 1.1). In short, through dynamic interaction with environmental changes, leading major corporations engage in spiraling strategic activities between these four domains to achieve strategic innovations (Domain I → Domain II → Domain III → Domain IV → Domain I and/or Domain III → Domain I → and so on) (discussed in detail in Chapter 2).

1.5   CHAPTER SUMMARY

This chapter presents the concept of a Capabilities Map derived from existing research into the characteristics of DC responding to environmental conditions such as dynamic temporal shifts and factors of uncertainty (see the four capability domains in Figure 1.1).

However, increasingly important is research from a strategic and organizational perspective on capabilities needed to achieve sustainable growth through continuous strategic innovation – the systematic incremental and radical innovation in large corporations which does not depend on black box capabilities or the capabilities of certain practitioners. Compared to startups and venture companies, large corporations have greater wherewithal for new routines and learning through experiment or trial and error (Floyd and Wooldridge, 1999; Kogut and Zander, 1992). However, not much theoretical or empirical research into continuously and systematically bringing about strategic innovation (incremental and radical innovation) to achieve sustainable growth in large corporations exists. For this reason, research must be promoted from the perspective of corporate and management systems that achieve sustainable growth.

Following, Chapter 2 discusses capability factors needed for sustainable growth through the continuous execution of radical and incremental innovation (strategic innovation).

2. Dynamic capabilities, ordinary capabilities and strategic innovation capabilities: a dynamic view of capabilities theory

This chapter clarifies the differences between the two types of capabilities indispensable to companies, "dynamic capabilities" and "ordinary capabilities," by focusing on the dynamically changing characteristics of the boundaries of informal organizations. The chapter also clarifies the dynamic innovation process that companies need to achieve strategic innovation (incremental innovation and radical innovation) to grow sustainably. In addition, the chapter extracts the factors of capabilities (strategic innovation capabilities) required for sustainable growth through the continued execution of corporate incremental and radical innovation. The chapter presents the important "strategic innovation capabilities" of leading companies that entail the dynamic spiral of the two distinct types of capabilities on the time axis – the dynamic and ordinary capabilities on the Capabilities Map – which are skillfully used appropriately or combined to achieve fast or slow incremental innovation for exploitation and radical innovation for exploration.

2.1 THE DIFFERENCES BETWEEN DYNAMIC CAPABILITIES AND ORDINARY CAPABILITIES, AND THE CAPABILITIES FOR THEIR DYNAMIC COMBINATION (INTEGRATION)

As described by the Capabilities Map (Figure 1.1) in Chapter 1, demonstrating dynamic capabilities (DC) in Domains I, II, III (business environments where there is rapid change and/or high uncertainty) is crucial, whereas it's important to demonstrate ordinary capabilities (OC) in Domain IV (where there is low uncertainty, and environmental change is gentle). However as mentioned, not only must strong DC be demonstrated in Domain III to expand sales of newly commercialized products, services and business and subsequently upgrade and improve them to respond to rapidly changing market environments, but strong OC must also be demonstrated to properly manage operations such as production, sales and support. However, this does not mean that only DC are enacted in Domains I and II, but that OC are also required in these domains as well (discussed later). In particular, the author believes DC and OC can be clearly separated and interpreted similar to the views of Teece (2007, 2014).

In organizations in Domain I such as those involved in basic research or R&D centers, there are planning departments to manage R&D funding and expenses, and R&D progress, departments that order and procure materials for R&D as well as general affairs and accounting departments involved in these processes. These departments don't need DC – OC will always suffice. DC are required by top managers of R&D departments and research division directors as well as project leaders and staff involved in R&D activities (knowledge creation activities), and the same goes for business units in Domain II. In organizations involved in business, there are finance and planning departments that manage business incubation, commercialization planning and development expenses, departments involved in ordering and procuring materials for prototyping, and also general affairs or accounting departments involved in these processes. Moreover, with existing business units, there are departments set up to drive current enterprises (value chains consisting of sales, technologies, procurement, manufacturing and support divisions), while new business development units are set up alongside. Of course, the supervisors and staff of these existing businesses don't require DC, because OC will suffice. DC is required by leaders of departments planning new products to create new business, business incubations units, and commercial development departments and the directors of all these departments, as well as project leaders and staff involved in actual business and product development.

The characteristics of capabilities required in business departments affected by the rapidly changing environments of Domain III are slightly different. Companies in the smartphone business are good examples of this. Once a newly developed product or service is launched, it must be constantly improved and upgraded to win out in the competition against rival companies (high-speed incremental innovation), which means that directors and staff in organizations upstream in the values chain on the business side such as product planning and technical development units in particular need to demonstrate strong DC. In contrast to the necessity for DC, staff and supervisors in all departments downstream in the values chain where routines dominate (sales, technical management, procurement, aftercare and support and so forth) require strong OC to comprehensively manage operations such as efficient product manufacture, quality and stock control and further expansion of sales. These downstream organizations require strong OC to invest in current products (and their successor upgrades and improved versions), win out amid stiff competition and turn a profit in current and near term. In contrast, project leaders and staff involved with product planning and development activities in fiercely competitive environments require strong DC. Thus, Domain III is not the same as Domains I and II, and has a particular focus on strong integration of DC and OC (see Figure 1.1).

However as mentioned, in Domain IV, the weight on DC becomes smaller, and the demonstration of best practices through OC plays the main role. Directors and staff in traditional existing organizations (business units, and so on) detect gentle changes in existing markets and manufacture and sell their existing product lineups through slow incremental innovation. Here, operations (technology management, sales, production, technical support, and so on) are executed in accordance with planned and thought-out deliberate strategies based on the path dependencies in business units. In Domain IV, strong OC are required for a company to turn a stable profit (short-term profits, not guaranteed long-term profits).

There are many of these Capabilities Maps in large corporations, and naturally, it is the CEO who is responsible for these Capabilities Maps and domains. As well as that, senior executive vice presidents have responsibilities for multiple Capabilities Maps and domains in large bundles of business units. Therefore, people in top management have to demonstrate both strong DC and OC. Put differently, top management in a large corporation comes face-to-face with the business issue of combining exploration and exploitation, or combining incremental innovation (upgrades and improvements to existing products) and radical innovation (generating new business), to combine current and future businesses. Certainly, there are many cases of large corporations that carefully engage in these combinations.

Future growth is not determined by OC, although OC are indispensable for generating profit in the short term. Companies must demonstrate strong OC not only to maintain existing business (whole value chains) through gentle incremental innovation in stable environments where change is slow (Domain IV) (downstream in the value chain), but also to maintain swift incremental innovation by thoroughly reinforced operations management (downstream in the value chain) for strong selling products in rapidly changing competitive environments (Domain III). In contrast, strong DC is essential for the challenge of future radical innovation (Domains I and II) as well as for survival in fast-moving competitive environments (Domain III) and sustainable growth. In this book, the capabilities of a corporation to demonstrate strong DC and OC dynamically and asynchronously or synchronously, are called "strategic innovation capabilities (SIC)" (discussed later).

In existing research on the interpretation of DC and OC, Collis (1994) asserts that competitive advantage boils down to learning how to learn. If a rival appears who is good at learning how to learn, one's own advantage will be lost, hence, if that rival meets a rival who is better at learning how to learn . . . and so on. Thus, this process represents an infinite regression to even higher-order capabilities. Accordingly, regardless of the level of capabilities reached, Collis asserts that it's impossible to acquire a permanent advantage. Distinguishing OC as lower-order capabilities and DC as higher-order meta-capabilities to reform OC capabilities, corporations always require even better higher-order DC, and are thus drawn toward an infinite regression in pursuit of those meta-capabilities. Accordingly, Collis (1994) argues that a company can never acquire ultimate DC. Similarly, Zollo and Winter (2002) mainly focused on first- and second-order capabilities, although they stated that in fast-changing and unpredictable contexts, companies must constantly upgrade the higher-order learning approaches, which also implies infinite regression.

As put by Helfat and Winter (2011, p.1245) below, it's also impossible to draw a clear line between the two types of capabilities (DC and OC):

> It is impossible to draw a bright line between these two sorts of capabilities because: 1) change is always occurring to at least some extent; 2) we cannot distinguish dynamic from operational (ordinary) capabilities based on whether they support what is perceived as radical versus non-radical change, or new versus existing businesses; and 3) some capabilities can be used for both operational (ordinary) and dynamic purposes.

In relation to (1), they point out that:

> Because things are always changing at least some extent, identifying a precise threshold level of change that separates an operational capability from a dynamic one is likely to be fruitless, or to produce answers that vary erratically across cases. Instead, it may be more useful to assess the nature and speed of change that a capability enables.

Thus, to clarify the roles and positioning of DC and OC, the author presents the different capabilities in the four general domains (the Capabilities Map in Figure 1.1) for the speed of environmental change (markets, competition, and so on) (including the speed of change within a company) or uncertainty of environment (uncertainties and risks such as level of acceptance of new products by potential customers, business risks associated with R&D, and so on) surrounding corporations. Hence in this sense, as mentioned, the author has clarified the application of OC and DC, and presented how they are integrated.

For example, the case of the Intel chip development described by Helfat and Winter (2011) corresponds to the high-speed incremental innovation in Domain III, in which Intel executed ongoing business as incremental innovation or sustaining innovation (Christensen, 1997) of its chips as it worked unceasingly with Moore's law, by demonstrating strong DC and OC. Also, in cases where new chips are developed with new materials and radical new architecture (new physical structures or design concepts), and there is a long-term risk involved with development (and development costs), semiconductor companies have to demonstrate strong DC in such uncertain business environments (ones particularly uncertain about future demand for new chips) (in other words, in Domains I and II). For example, the high-function Cell processor development by IBM, Sony and Toshiba for the PlayStation 3 (e.g., Kodama, 2007c) is a case of huge and risky capital investments in chip developments with new architecture and radical innovation by the Domain I → Domain II → Domain III shift.

Also, in cases described by Helfat and Winter (2011) of Intel, the upstream oil industry, and Starbucks/Walmart, they state that "As these examples illustrate, capabilities that support existing businesses or seemingly non-radical change may have important dynamic attributes. These capabilities also entail costs to develop and maintain the capability, and to obtain the requisite inputs or resources." Thus, from the Capabilities Map in Figure 1.1, it can be interpreted that these DC are not restricted to new-to-the-world businesses (Domain I or Domain II) or fast-paced environments (Domain II or Domain III) or what is perceived as radical change (Domain I or Domain II).

On the other hand, in the cases of Starbucks and Walmart, Helfat and Winter (2011) say that the outlet proliferation occurred in a gradual fashion in a relatively placid external environment, yet the eventual outcomes irrevocably altered the scale and scope of company resources as well as the ecosystems of the industries involved and the environments of many communities. With a focus on marketing, these can be interpreted as cases of companies that have arrived in Domain III after spending time on trials and testing of new business models in pursuit of new customer value (that is, Domain I → Domain II). Starbucks and Walmart developed their businesses "in a gradual fashion in a relatively placid external environment," although these businesses are now mainly positioned in Domain III. This is because business speed perceived by the staff and organizations within these companies is inferred from the high rate of development accompanying global business expansion and diversification of customer needs (including geographical characteristics).

Thus, from a practical perspective, or the perspective of practitioners, how can companies achieve sustainable growth? How does a company succeed with continuous strategic innovation? What sort of strategies, organizations, technologies, operations and leadership are required? These issues are not only the responsibility of managers, but are always things that motivated practitioners always face. Thus, for serious practitioners, it seems no mistake that the differences (in capabilities or performance, and so on) between companies are at least something other than differences of routines or money (of course, as OC, the quality of routines is critical, but most practitioners do not think it's possible to produce excellent products or businesses that will change the world just with money or good routines – many business administrators question what these differences are and also question whether they can be acquired by their own companies).

While Teece (2014, p.338) states "First, I reject the notion that dynamic capabilities reside *only* in high-level routines," he also states that "creative managerial and entrepreneurial acts (e.g., creating new markets) are, by their nature, often non-routine." In the same vein, Teece (2014, p.332) quotes Steve Jobs, the late CEO of Apple, who said "Innovation has nothing to do with how many R&D dollars you have. When Apple came up with the Mac, IBM was spending at least one hundred times more on R&D. It's . . . about . . . how much you get it."

In an interview about product development at Apple (Burrows, 2004), Jobs described it as a blend of routine and creative acts:

> Apple is a very disciplined company, and we have great processes. But that's not what it's about. Process makes you more efficient. But innovation comes from people meeting up in the hallways or calling each other at 10:30 at night with a new idea, or because they realized something that shoots holes in how we've been thinking about a problem.

In other words, the acts of creativity at Apple born of various non-routines offer hints about unlocking the secrets of what Jobs described as "get it."

From the research done by the author into organizations that have achieved new innovations as new business or product developments (including business that the author was directly or indirectly involved with), the author wants to emphasize that DC are mainly demonstrated by practitioners through strategic non-routine business by mainly setting up informal organizations or networks, whereas OC are demonstrated by practitioners in business mainly in formal organizations and routines. Also, with 21 years of experience as a business person (involved in product planning and development and planning management in business units and company headquarters in major Japanese telecommunications carriers

NTT, NTT DOCOMO and KDDI), the author has first-hand experience of a variety of businesses, in particular the strategic shift from the telephone to Internet services, product planning and development for third generation mobile telephone services and strategic partnering and joint ventures with American companies. Hence, the author has developed a deep appreciation for the sorts of businesses and situations in which DC are or should be demonstrated, and the sorts of businesses and situations in which OC are or should be demonstrated. The findings of field research enabled by these practical experiences (in new business, product and service development, and so on) have been published in western academic journals (for example, *Organizational Studies, Journal of Management Studies, Long Range Planning, Research-Technology Management, Journal of Engineering and Technology Management, Technovation, Behavioral Science, International Journal of Project Management, International Journal of Human Resource Management*).

The clear point the author has uncovered through this accumulation of research is that the boundaries within and between organizations (or between practitioners at the micro level) change with changes in business characteristics and environmental conditions and it makes the form of informal organizations and their characteristics change. Hence, in this chapter, as a new perspective, the author would like to discuss how practitioners intentionally form informal organizations and networks called collectivities of practice (Col.oP) (Lindkvist, 2005) and teams of boundaries (ToB) (Kodama, 2007c) (the author calls these two informal organizations "Strategic Communities" (SC) (Kodama, 2005)), and through strategic non-routine activities mainly in these SC, proactively demonstrate DC. In contrast, the author will also present how OC are purposefully demonstrated in the formal organizations defined by corporate top management or organizational supervisors and the communities of practice (CoP) (Wenger, 1998) that practitioners form consciously or unconsciously for maintaining and strengthening routine activities. Although CoP are informal organizations, their purpose is mainly to reinforce routines through best practices.

Accordingly, dependent on the building abilities or characteristics of the SC that practitioners intentionally form, DC are not processes linked to infinite regression toward higher-order capabilities mainly based on routines, as argued by Collis (1994) (see above). Additionally, the author believes it's possible to clearly distinguish DC and OC focusing on dynamic differences in the characteristics of organizational boundaries involving informal strategic non-routines and formal routines respectively. Below, the author describes these organizational characteristics.

2.2 DYNAMIC INFORMAL ORGANIZATIONS THAT BRING ABOUT DYNAMIC CAPABILITIES AND ORDINARY CAPABILITIES

2.2.1 Sensing and Boundaries

In the knowledge economy, diverse human assets are the source of competitive and valuable products, services and business models. Through convergence across different technologies and diverse industries, asset orchestration with DC raises the potential to produce value chains for new products, services and business models, and new strategic models that span wide-ranging boundaries. Accordingly, for companies to configure new businesses, it's necessary for companies to freshly recognize the process business perspective of transcending the organizational boundaries both in and between companies to dynamically share and integrate the intangible assets of people, groups and organizations, and to create new intangible assets. Thus, dynamic asset orchestration is an important consideration on multiple organizational boundaries.

To achieve this, the capability that practitioners need is "sensing." Here, sensing functions to explore, filter and analyze business opportunities, and is heavily dependent on the abilities of individual practitioners, such as members of leader organizations in management layers. In particular, in the processes of R&D and selecting new technologies for radical innovation, the ability of those in management layers to recognize environments in which there are business opportunities is of critical importance. Furthermore, as well as upper management, the role of the recognition abilities and intuition of senior and middle management is also significant, and the awareness and inspiration that comes from recognition capability and intuition is brought about by interactions with various stakeholders (customers, business partners, and so on) (e.g., Kodama, 2007a, 2014).

To demonstrate recognition capability and intuition, practitioners must have the capability of boundaries vision (Kodama, 2011) to be able to acquire new insights from complex and diverse boundaries. Boundaries vision is a new proposition that entails dissimilar knowledge integration capability – the ability to orchestrate different intangible assets, boundaries architecture – the ability to achieve corporate design for new business models by defining new corporate boundaries by integrating dissimilar boundaries, and boundaries innovation – the process of innovation across the boundaries between companies and industries (Kodama, 2009a) and so forth.

Practitioners have to face these issues in their strategic thinking and actions focusing on wide-ranging boundaries to orchestrate different intangible assets (and co-specialized assets) to bring about innovations. Recently, the best core technologies of the world's cutting-edge businesses have become dispersed around the globe and are innovated all over the world. Accordingly, going forward in this era of convergence, in which valuable co-specialized assets bring about wealth, management that integrates multi-perspective intangible assets (asset orchestration) in open systems dispersed within and outside of organizations, and with customers, will become increasingly important. Thus, the concept of open innovation (Chesbrough, 2003) and hybrid innovation (Kodama, 2011) to create new products, services, and business models by developing and accumulating competitive intangible assets in a company through internal capabilities networks, at the same time, acquiring intangible assets outside of the company through external capabilities networks, and orchestrating one's company's intangible assets (and co-specialized assets) with those of other companies are of major importance in the knowledge economy.

Thus, sensing is particularly important in the aforementioned Domains I, II and III, and hence, practitioners must form informal networks (informal organizations) that span formal organizations to discover and absorb new information and intangible assets. For this, it is necessary to demonstrate strong DC in strategic high-quality (innovation-achieving) non-routine practice in informal networks consisting of the informal organizations of SC and networked SC discussed later (networked SC are also called boundary networks). The following describes the informal organizations in which strategic non-routine practice is executed.

2.2.2 Boundary Characteristics and Organizational Systems

Business people are aware of a range of boundaries in their daily business activities. These boundaries are as follows: First, there are organizational boundaries between official organizations within a corporation. These are examples of the organizational boundaries that formally exist between different business areas and functions such as research, development, manufacturing and sales. Based on the limitations and nature of their occupations, practitioners perform their daily business while adhering to the rules of their individual places of work. Formal organizational boundaries serve to delineate the territory for a business person's job, and in time, these formal organizational boundaries also transform into CoP (Lave and Wenger, 1990; Brown and Duguid, 1991; Orr, 1996) that correspond to the nature of the work and function of the business within those boundaries.

The second type of boundary is related to the first type, and is a boundary that sets out the hierarchical authoritative structure for the organization. In this type of boundary, official positions of authority are assigned to individual business people within an organization, and boundaries emerge as hierarchies of the powers held by those individuals (Thompson, 1967; Pfeffer and Salancik, 1978).

The third type of boundary is also related to the official positions in the first type, and is rooted in the specializations of business people involved in areas such as research, layout, manufacturing, product planning design and so forth. These boundaries can be called "knowledge boundaries." Knowledge boundaries separate the unique "thought worlds" or mental models of individual business people, and are the borders that define uniform opinions about various issues and serve to establish domains for occupations and tasks. Confrontation between marketers who focus on marketing, and engineers who concentrate on technologies occurs along these knowledge boundaries.[1]

As well as these boundaries, there are also a range of boundaries that exist between different corporations. Apart from the organizational and knowledge boundaries among business people, there are for instance, boundaries that are inherent in the various customs and practices of different types of businesses or business functions, as well as knowledge boundaries that are rooted in the individual strategic intentions of different corporations.

In the mass production model, organizational and knowledge boundaries promote efficiency in stable business environments, and provide an effective framework for business people to carry out their routine occupational functions within the individual official organizations in which they have been granted authority. In hierarchical (or bureaucratic) organizations, business people have clear boundaries defined for them in advance, and managers place importance on top-down leadership for their strategic planning. Thus, the mass production model demands systematic efficiency to meet central operating targets for product commercialization through routine business processes that have already been decided via hierarchical organizational structures and established development and manufacturing methods. The main purpose of these individual boundaries (organizational, hierarchical, knowledge) is to bring about efficient and productive business processes with a focus on rules, regulations and company procedures such as business and operation manuals for information dissemination and business interaction between organizations. Boundaries like this, which require business people to follow procedures for transferring knowledge and information among themselves have been called "syntactic or information-processing boundaries" (Carlile, 2002, 2004).

By contrast, in organizations that have responded to fluctuating market and business circumstances (but not high-speed environments), a different sort of boundary to these syntactic boundaries arises among business people. These different boundaries are formed among players to enable new ways for knowledge to be interpreted and new meanings to be created, and are called "semantic boundaries" (Shannon and Weaver, 1949; Jantsch, 1980; Carlile, 2002, 2004). Semantic boundaries serve to promote actions to gradually (incrementally) improve and reform existing business processes as well as development and manufacturing methods. Semantic boundaries focus on rules and regulations and company procedures in the same way as syntactic boundaries, but also promote ongoing organizational learning to advance a company's best practice, Total Quality Management (TQM) and so forth for corporate reform and improvement.

As previously mentioned, the formation of a "CoP" brings about the creation and sharing of new meanings among business people along semantic boundaries to promote organizational learning and best practices. Founded on the sharing, empathy and resonance of values among members, CoP promote mutual learning along semantic boundaries as business people deepen their understanding of each other's contexts and values, and thus bring about the sustained creation of new knowledge. As the membership of business people active on these semantic boundaries gradually becomes more established, there is increasing impetus for organizational learning to give birth to new contexts for their targets and missions.

Formal organizations that have these kinds of syntactic boundary characteristics and CoP that have semantic boundary characteristics raise the level of their personal and organizational capabilities for their regular routines and the higher-order routines discussed by Collis (1994) (which correspond to overall factors in value chains in Domain IV, and partial factors downstream in value chains in Domain III). These are the so-called "ordinary capabilities" (OC).

These semantic boundaries promote organizational learning, and are the first foundations on which teams of boundaries (ToB) and collectivities of practice (Col.oP) are formed, discussed in more detail below.

2.2.3   Col.oP and ToB – Pragmatic Organizational Systems

Innovation boundaries (new product, service and business model developments, and so on) with a high degree of novelty, or boundaries (also accompanying high-speed environments) (typical of the aforementioned Domains I, II and III) where uncertainty arises, demand the creation of new knowledge and exchange of existing knowledge that goes beyond the organizational learning and creation of new meaning in CoP with their shared contexts. These kinds of boundaries are called "pragmatic boundaries" (Shannon and Weaver 1949; Jantsch 1980; Carlile 2002, 2004), and are areas in which completely unconventional business concepts are realized, such as products and services developed with new business models, new component and technological architecture and big changes in rules that accompany new developments and manufacturing methods. Hence, as a source of innovation, there is high potential for new knowledge to be born along these pragmatic boundaries.[2]

Various frictions and conflicts occur at pragmatic boundaries. To achieve new and unconventional targets and solve problems as they arise, business people take action to advance existing knowledge through the conflicts and frictions among themselves and political leverage in these communities. Because these three types of boundaries are mutually dependent upon each other, their characteristics can change drastically with changing circumstances (customer needs, market competitiveness, and so on), the emergence of uncertainties, and the interests and intentions of the people involved. Especially with innovation and corporate reform, with changing circumstances and people's intentions working even stronger, a shift toward these pragmatic boundaries occurs in the relationships between business people (syntactic boundaries → semantic boundaries → pragmatic boundaries) (see Figure 2.1).

All kinds of conflicts, frictions and contradictions arise among business people working along pragmatic boundaries. Not only is this due

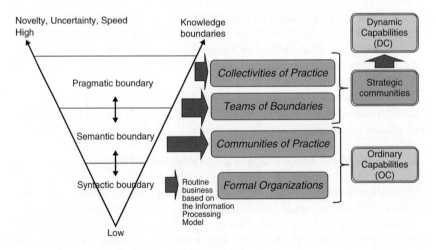

Note: This figure was generated based on Kodama (2007a).

Figure 2.1 Levels of informal organizational forms and boundaries

to sectionalism among business people in corporations separated by organizational boundaries, but also due to differences in personal values, backgrounds and skills. The reasons for these conflicts are the dominating path dependencies and personal mental models that business people gain through their different backgrounds and experience, which results in them expressing uneasiness or resistance when faced with new or unfamiliar knowledge at their organizational boundaries.

Temporary or informal project organizations consisting of people from a range of different specializations formed to deal with issues characterized by high levels of uncertainty and novelty (and sometimes including high-speed environments) have the characteristics of these pragmatic boundaries, because they contain large knowledge boundaries that cause friction and conflict. In contrast to the CoP in the semantic boundaries mentioned earlier, these types of project organizations that bring together personnel with knowledge in diverse specialist fields are called collectivities of practice[3] (Col.oP), a term coined by European scholars of Business Studies. These are not the same as CoP with their collective and organization knowledge and infrastructure based on knowledge common among the members in those organizations, because Col.oP are organizations of loosely bound personal knowledge that do not retain the knowledge shared in project organizations.[4]

This is a good place to introduce examples illustrating the difference between a project organization and a CoP.

Having research and business centers in 21 countries, Buckman Laboratories International is a company that contracts R&D from its main paper manufacturing business and has a network-based forum for the sharing and creation of knowledge that it calls "Techforum." Staff in any of these countries can access Techforum and rapidly search for advice from people with specialist knowledge from anywhere around the globe. Not only does this transcend the boundaries of international borders, but also crosses over the boundaries that lie between different areas of knowledge and organizations, and when many of the participants in the forum are in agreement with each other, autonomous project organizations form. Staff bring their own knowledge into the various projects born on the network, and exchange discussions with each other while proceeding with their R&D tasks. Including specialized paper manufacturing technologies, there are several tens of new technologies born every year through this project system.

CEO Buckman calls the Techforum an "issue-driven community" and says it has different characteristics to a CoP (Buckman, 2003). The point about this "issue-driven community" is that it forms informal and dynamic teams consisting of members in different areas of specialization to rapidly respond to issues. The speedy nature of this context and the variety of specializations involved is characteristic of Col.oP – dynamic human networking and collaboration that brings about new and novel knowledge (or close to ToB discussed next).

Because of frequent trade-offs and logical compromises however, there are cases of project organizations on pragmatic boundaries that don't always achieve genuine innovation. This is because idea creation and execution processes end up dominated by logic and rational dialogue among participants. In contrast, merging the characteristics of shared value in CoP as semantic boundaries with the collection of (or simultaneously use of) different kinds of specialized knowledge in Col.oP as pragmatic boundaries does not only promote rational decision-making, but also raises the potential for a shift to more productive innovation through creative dialogue among members.

The teams of business people with diverse knowledge formed along boundaries created from the merging and combining of these two semantic and pragmatic boundary characteristics, are referred to as ToB in this book (see Figure 2.1). ToB are organizational bodies that merge and combine the characteristics of both semantic and pragmatic boundaries and bring about the "creative collaboration" (discussed later) that promotes creative abrasion and productive friction among team members.

SC are formed from these ToB and Col.oP – two distinct organizational systems in which humans interact. SC can be dynamically adjusted between these two types of systems to meet changing business circumstances (novelty or uncertainty, or the level of knowledge boundaries and so forth).

In ToB and Col.oP, a range of arguments and battles arise because they often included contexts that negate the existing mental models or experience of business people. Furthermore, ToB and Col.oP that include certain customers present a range of customer demands, issues and problems, although to achieve innovation, especially in ToB, creative abrasion and productive action must be induced through creative dialogue among participants. Moreover, simple ToB and Col.oP are not enough for innovation in all cases, and a number of them may be merged within companies (between departments, businesses, management levels, and so on) and between companies (partners and customers) to form boundary networks. The more complicated a business model proposal, the greater the pressure on participants to form ToB and Col.oP and network these together. The author believes that the new knowledge born through boundary networks formed from ToB and Col.oP both in and out of companies is also a source of "organization capabilities" (described in detail in Chapter 3).

Formulating SC such as ToB and Col.oP that have pragmatic boundary characteristics raise the level of capabilities needed to drive strategic non-routine activities. Engaging in these sorts of processes is an example of DC, which are radically different to the OC of formal organizations on syntactic boundaries or the CoP on semantic boundaries used for routine (or higher-order routine) activities. Hence, as discussed by Helfat and Winter (2011), it can be also said that a clear distinction exists between the two capabilities (DC and OC) due to the differences in informal organizations on these boundaries, in that one capability is simply used dynamically or ordinarily.

Especially, the thinking and action of business people who merge new assets born of SC formed in and out of companies that include partners (in other words, merge SC that exist in and out the company) is a source of innovation that also ties in with the organization capabilities needed for sustained competitiveness. These boundary networks that link together and merge various SC in and outside of companies are a source of "asset orchestration" (see Figure 2.2).

Practitioners form SC and boundary networks (networked SC, and external and internal capabilities networks) across the boundaries within and outside companies including their customers and demonstrate DC to achieve radical innovations and high-speed incremental innovation in Domains I, II and III with their high degrees of uncertainty, and/or in businesses where markets are changing rapidly and competition is stiff. Thus, DC enable asset orchestration to integrate intangible assets in the wide-ranging SC. For this reason, to demonstrate DC, the formulation of informal SC and networked SC (boundary network) organizations and the characteristic of strategic non-routine activity is an important factor.

Chapter 3, section 3.4.2 discusses cases (of action research by the author) of new product and service development enabled by dynamic asset orchestration processes through the formulation of these kinds of informal organizations (SC and networked SC).

2.2.4   ToB Characteristics – The Four "Mean Points" of Creative Dialogue

ToB encourage creative dialogue, and the fundaments of creative dialogue lie in dialectical thinking. Dialectics are characteristically good at enabling people to find solutions to problems, because they incorporate both the intuitive and the analytical. In general terms, the process of problem solving can be understood as the "thesis" (positive), the "antithesis" (negative) and "synthesis" (negating the negative).

In dialectical thinking truth is dynamic, and the processes of "thesis," "antithesis" and "synthesis" help to develop creative dialogue. Productive

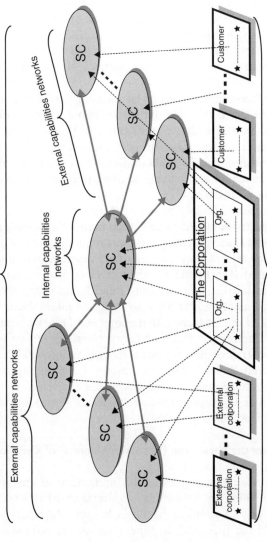

Figure 2.2   Dynamism of dynamic capabilities-generating strategic communities and boundary networks

34

dialectical thinking starts with "conflict and coexistence," "reconciliation and unification," and "negating the negative." However, in practicing this process of "thesis," "antithesis" and "synthesis" in real-life business situations, rather than engage in the western Hegel school of "hard dialectics" that aims to eliminate contradiction, it's better to embrace inconsistencies as natural and dynamic phenomena, allow ambiguity, and practice the "soft dialectic"[5] of the eastern approach to achieve balance. In the "soft dialect" approach, instead of interpreting things as elemental and abstract "absolute truths," they should be understood in terms of the whole context and their relationship to it, to dynamically create a "mean point" beyond compromise. Accordingly, team members must investigate new meanings and processes that pose the question "how can this be produced?" rather than engage in the formularized logic of syllogisms that ask whether something exists as a truth or not. To practice this kind of "contradictory productivity," business people need an open way of thinking that accepts contradiction as they get into the details (meanings) of the matters at hand. Business people need both self-assertiveness and humility to personally develop to a higher dimension and become a conduit for contradictions and confrontation with others, and need be aware that they themselves are not infallible (e.g., Kodama, 2007a).

The concept of "the mean point" of "soft dialectics" is clearly reflected in the characteristics of ToB. These characteristics can be defined as: (1) "the mean of knowledge;" (2) "the mean of relationships;" (3) "the mean of boundaries;" and (4) "the mean of thought worlds."

ToB encourage the dialectical elements of four middle-path Col.oP and CoP characteristics – harmonized knowledge, creative collaboration, boundary penetration and shared thought worlds. As quoted from Panasonic director Ohtsubo (Ohtsubo, 2006), "There is always some degree of overlap formed between different business functions, which greatly empowers the whole company. Most Japanese corporations have this culture of collecting and combining wisdom across their design, manufacture and resource sectors," hence, former Panasonic president Ohtsubo's comment reflects the harmonized knowledge and shared thought worlds of ToB. Similarly, as former NEC president Yano says:

> Adjacent organizations that are continually aware that they are working together can open up any number of new possibilities. Actually, we have advanced our cooperative relationships across organizational barriers quite substantially. ... So, I think now as much as ever, to break through the 'growth barrier,' it's important to continue to team up and cooperate with each other. (Yano, 2006)

This comment reflects the creative collaboration and boundary penetration in ToB, and as previously stated, this feature of ToB is not limited to

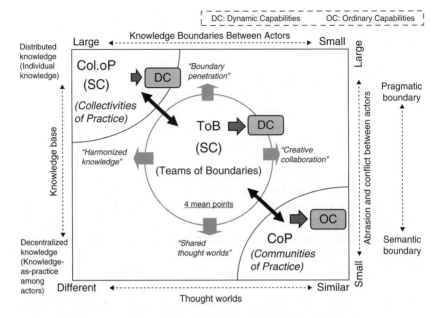

Note: This figure was generated based on Kodama (2007c).

Figure 2.3   Characteristics of three informal organizational systems

Japanese corporations, but is a project culture common throughout the leading high-tech companies of the world such as Apple.

Figure 2.3 illustrates the concepts and positioning of ToB, CoP and Col.oP organizational systems. The ToB is an organizational system that lies midway between the CoP and Col.oP and includes some of the features of both,[6] while SC are these two organizational systems dynamically adjusted to respond to changing business circumstances.

2.3   DRIVING DYNAMIC AND ORDINARY CAPABILITIES BY DYNAMIC ORGANIZATIONAL FORMS: ANALYSIS FROM THE FRAMEWORK OF "CAPABILITIES LIFECYCLES"

This section considers and analyzes the shift of capabilities through each Domain in response to changes in environments surrounding companies (speed, risk and uncertainty) and the dynamics of dynamic organizational forms, from the framework of the "Capabilities Lifecycles" of Helfat and Peteraf (2003). The capability lifecycle articulates general patterns and paths in the evolution of organizational capabilities over time. Thus, the capability lifecycle provides a foundational framework for the dynamic resource-based view of companies. There are three initial stages of a capability lifecycle – founding, development and maturity – which are followed by possible branching into six additional stages.

Once the capability reaches the maturity stage, or even before then, a variety of events may influence the future evolution of the capability. The capability then may branch into one of at least six additional stages of the capability lifecycle – retirement (death), retrenchment, renewal, replication, redeployment, and recombination. These six stages may follow one another in a variety of patterns over time. Some of these branching stages might also take place simultaneously. Importantly, in each branch of the capability lifecycle, historical antecedents in the form of capability evolution prior to branching influence the subsequent evolution of the capability.

These capability lifecycles go through the stages of founding, development and maturity in each of the domains. Hence, in these six additional stages, as a system of evolving new capabilities, renewal, replication, redeployment, and recombination can be interpreted as shifts to subsequent domains. These capabilities lifecycles offer new knowledge on the "dynamic view of capabilities" that describes the evolutionary processes of diverse capabilities in domains and shifting between domains in companies. Following, from the framework of capabilities lifestyles, this section describes capabilities in each domain, and the dynamic informal organizations that demonstrate these capabilities.

Figure 2.4 describes the organizational forms for demonstrating DC and OC in each domain. In positioning in the domains, in Domain I, which is where radical innovation is triggered, as discussed previously, the character of the informal organizations is close to Col.oP and ToB. In particular, in new fundamental or practical technological R&D, there are many cases where extremely few specialists with knowledge and skills in particular high-level fields of expertise who belong to certain formal organizations carry out R&D. Organizational characteristics (pragmatic boundaries) in which knowledge of different specialties intersects and that give rise to occasional friction and conflict can raise the probability of innovation being born (Kodama, 2007c, 2007d). Thus, SC – Col.oP and ToB – can also be called informal organizations characterized by pragmatic boundaries, in which DC can be easily demonstrated.

Nevertheless, since the members of Col.oP are specialists, it is not as if these organizations are devoid of a history of capabilities or start out with a blank slate. Obviously, each of the individuals in the founding team has human capital (context-specific knowledge, special skills, and experience), social capital (social ties within and outside of the team), and cognition (Helfat and Peteraf, 2003). Moreover, in teams with similar characteristics to ToB, in a group these individuals may have team-specific human capital if they have worked together previously in another setting.

Thus, Col.oP and ToB demonstrate the DC of Sensing → Seizing → Transforming to seek out and detect latent new markets, and to select and develop new technologies and processes to produce consistent R&D results. According to the capabilities lifecycles framework of Helfat and Peteraf (2003), capabilities in Col.oP or ToB go through the three stages of founding, development and maturity in Domain I. Figure 2.5 illustrates capabilities lifecycles on the Capabilities Map. However, there is a good chance of R&D failure in Domain I where risks and uncertainties are high, the results of which (failures) lead to the "retrenchment or retirement" described by Helfat and Peteraf (2003).

Here, it must be noted that regarding capabilities lifecycles, Helfat and Peteraf (2003, p.1004) assert that:

> It is important to bear in mind, however, that capability building and change do not require dynamic capabilities, either in the initial lifecycle or in subsequent branching. In the preceding analysis of a new capability in a new-to-the-world organization, dynamic capabilities do not enter as a factor determining the evolutionary path. Indeed, they cannot, since a new organization has no dynamic capabilities. In the founding and development stages of the capability lifecycle, a capability (including a dynamic one) evolves and changes over time without the action of any dynamic capabilities upon it.

However, if starting out a venture with just a few people (including people who have never met before) and its business operations are focusing on making rules, regulations and manuals, managing finances, and building operational processes, OC are sufficient, and DC are not required. However, Domain I mainly targets R&D departments in large corporations. Accordingly, in Domain I, it is assumed that Col.oP and ToB take realistic actions to uncover new R&D achievements in environments where managerial routines with OC are already established in companies (and in departments). For this reason, demonstrating DC in Domain I is critical, rather than OC.

Thus, according to capabilities lifecycles, the R&D achievements from Domain I shift as "selection events" to the commercial development of Domain II for the processes of renewal, replication, redeployment or recombination through enactment of new DC. Helfat and Peteraf (2003) describe this shift from Domain I to Domain II as being triggered by "capability opportunities" (see Figure 2.5). For example, there are cases of replication/redeployment in new areas (new products in new business territories) that the company has never handled in the past stemming from consistent successes in Domain I as core technologies. Or, through dramatic improvements in those R&D technologies through technical innovation, "renewal" could be enabled through radical innovation of final products (depending on the degree). As well as that, "recombination" of core technologies with those acquired through M&A can enable new commercial product developments in Domain I.

Hence, in Domain II, radical innovation measures are taken to match market and technological innovations to develop new products, services and business using new technologies and processes. Thus, similar to Domain I, there are many cases where informal organizations such as Col. oP and ToB are formed as organizational environments in which DC are demonstrated. In investigations of a large corporation in Japan, the author has seen many cases in which the members of Col.oP and ToB involved in business in Domain I shift to Domain II and take with them their R&D achievements for the development of practical applications. Then, to succeed with commercialization in Domain II, more resources are invested, and formal organizations are created. Multi-layered Col.oP and ToB are then formed between formal organizations in companies (and outside of companies). Here, as illustrated by Figure 2.2, asset orchestration is sped up by the formation of internal capabilities and external capabilities networks in which DC are enacted, that is, boundary networks (networked SC).

However, as discussed in Chapter 1, it's in this domain that the "valley of death" exists, raising the likelihood of failure of commercial developments. There are even cases that lead to failure where there are withdrawals in the prototype assessments or trial service stages or chances are taken to attempt commercialization despite high risk and uncertainty (there are many cases of DC having negative effects in Domain II, discussed in Chapter 7). Such failures lead to "retrenchment or retirement" of those commercial developments.

In contrast, according to capabilities lifecycles, the achievements of commercial development in Domain II shift as selection events to the establishment of new product value chains in Domain III for renewal, replication, redeployment, or recombination enabled by the enactment of new DC (see Figure 2.5). This shift from Domain II to Domain III is also triggered by "capability opportunities." In Domain III, further improvements or upgrades of new products accelerate renewal processes and bring about potentials for commercial development application, transfer or duplication in other business territories with "replication/redeployment." As well as that, the possibilities for new products and services brought about by "recombination" of one's company's products or services and those of another through strategic alliances or M&A also increase.

Hence, measures are required to evolve technologies sustainably for detecting rapid market changes and establish value chains in Domain III. Informal organizations enacting DC in Domain III are often ToB. As described later, the reason for this is the rapid incremental innovation of upgrading products and services that is unique to this domain. In other words, being closer boundary-wise to formal organizations and CoP, ToB offer the efficiency and effectiveness to raise the level of integration of DC and OC in Domain III (see Figure 2.1). Thus, this is the issue of combining efficiency with creativity. ToB pursue novelty with new product versions, while CoP are organizations that pursue product manufacture and sales efficiency, hence "co-specialization" can arise between these two types of organization (this will be discussed in detail in the "Organization Capabilities" section in Chapter 3).

Also, to successfully establish and sustainably expand sales of product in Domain III, further resources are invested and formal organizations are created. Then, multi-layered ToB are formed between formal organizations in companies (and outside of companies). Here, to upgrade products and services, asset orchestration is sped up by the formation of internal capabilities and external capabilities networks in which DC are enacted, that is, boundary networks (networked SC) as illustrated by Figure 2.2.

In contrast in Domain III, rapid incremental innovation by demonstrating strong DC is required to unceasingly upgrade and improve products and services, put newly developed products and services into orbit, and win out over the competition, as discussed earlier. At the same time, supervisors and staff in departments downstream in the routine value chain must use strong OC to thoroughly manage and reinforce their operations (sales, technology administration, procurement, manufacture and after support, and so on). Therefore, since best practices through strong OC must be pursued, the key is the formation of CoP that span the formal organizations within the company (including outsourcing as required). In Domain III then, to strengthen the value chain from upstream to downstream, strong interactive linkages are indispensable between ToB demonstrating strong DC and CoP demonstrating strong OC (see Figure 2.4).

Characteristically in many cases, formal organizations in Domain III adopt the form of an "integrated organization" (e.g., Kodama, 2003, 2004) as organization strategy to bring about strong DC and OC. This could mean for example, merging project-based organizations with functional organizations since they easily bring about ToB and CoP respectively. These details are discussed in cases of NTT DOCOMO in Chapter 3 (Box 3.2) and those in Chapter 7, but the key factor of forming these integrated organizations are the leader teams (LT) that bring about leadership capabilities in companies (and sometimes outside companies as well) (details in Chapter 3).

In contrast, Domain IV contains the products and services that have shifted from Domain III, and may include flagship products. In general in Domain IV, there is a low level of uncertainty, the pace of environmental change is soft, and product lineups feature various models. There are plenty of necessities in the B2B and B2C fields. These include a variety of completed products, various parts of completed products, livingware, food and so forth. As products that won out in Domain III to survive through to Domain IV, these also include traditional and classic products. In Domain IV, detection of gentle changes in existing markets and gradual incremental innovation through improvements of existing technologies and routines are repeated. Thus, in Domain IV, strong OC in CoP and formal organizations in value chains execute best practices and produce a product lineup. The shift from Domain III to Domain IV is also triggered by capability opportunities (however, in Domain III, some product are withdrawn due to stiff competition, which leads to them being retrenched or retired). In Domain IV, processes of product renewal through continuous and gentle incremental innovation are mainly performed, but in some cases, they might be replication or redeployment in other regional markets or business territories if market changes are sluggish (and the company has sufficient resources). Moreover, in slow-moving markets where there is not much uncertainty, there is also potential to bring about synergies by creating new products (or services) through recombination of company products or services with those of other companies through M&A or strategic alliances, by demonstrating strong OC in normal routines (see Figure 2.4).

However, product and service lineups in Domain IV gradually become more susceptible to influence from changes in customer tastes or technical innovations, and so on. For instance, there are good examples of analog products having been pushed out by digital products over long periods, or telephone services shifting to become Internet services. None of these have happened abruptly. In spite of that fact, there are plenty of cases of lagging behind such developments. In other words, strong OC begin to become a hindrance, and as environmental changes loom, product lineups that lag behind go down the path to retrenchment or retirement (see Figure 2.4).

For example, as discussed in detail in Chapter 6, Kodak was a company that took the path of retrenchment and retirement from Domain IV due to the effects of digitalization, whereas a Japanese company Fujifilm successfully and strategically shifted from Domain IV to Domain I with redeployment/recombination. Kodak felt the threats from the market changes accompanying digitalization early on, but persisted in sticking to its existing strong OC to seek to maximize its profits and shareholder value. Kodak consistently engaged in rigid strategies such as stock measures using its own substantial capital to buy its own shares. Furthermore at the time, Kodak's top management had no idea about orchestrating the company's high-level intangible assets to respond to the changing environment of digitalization.

In contrast, Fujifilm used the high-grade photographic film technologies it already had to develop protective film for LCD screens which the company successfully commercialized (applying its film technologies for LCD TVs – redeployment), and in another example of redeployment/ recombination of existing technology, Fujifilm used its collagen technologies that it had used to prevent photographic film from drying out to develop a cosmetic product that is now a hit. Hence, this company has successfully moved into the cosmetics business, a different field. As well as that, Fujifilm is also involved in medical product developments that are gaining attention in the fight against the Ebola virus. Differing from Kodak, Fujifilm didn't set out to maximize profits and shareholder value, but avoided zero profits to survive, and by orchestrating (with strong DC) the existing high-level intangible assets that the company had accumulated, it succeeded with radical innovation by shifting from Domain IV, onto Domain I → Domain II → Domain III (where shifting from Domains I to Domain II is the radical innovation, and Domain III is the incremental innovation) (Shift A in Figure 2.5).

In the case of Shift A in Figure 2.5, as the threats encroached, the company engaged in higher-order learning as it was well aware of the dangers, and engaged in strategic collaboration by forming informal networks with different areas of business (in other words, engaged in high-quality strategic non-routine activities) to demonstrate strong DC to raise the potential for a shift to Domain I. According to Helfat and Peteraf (2003), this is a good example of strategy transformation responding to capability threats. In addition, as Winter (2000) describes, organizations faced with threats are likely to be motivated to raise the level of their capabilities. When capabilities are renewed, new methods are explored and developed, and a stage of new progression comes about. In some cases, companies also redeploy their capabilities in markets for different products. Redeployment is not the same as replication of the same products and services in a different regional market, but rather involves targeting markets for different products and services with a strong association. Furthermore, when companies transfer capabilities to different businesses, but ones that have strong linkages to their current business, there are often cases that involve recombining of capabilities with other capabilities instead of replication and redeployment (Helfat and Peteraf, 2003). The success of Fujifilm can also be thought of as the result of the processes of renewal, redeployment or recombination successfully functioning through strong DC.

This can also be seen as the shift from Domain III → Domain I (Shift B in Figure 2.5). This is the concept of new radical innovation by discovering capability opportunities in rapidly changing environments and serious competition with rival companies. There are many cases of this, the most remarkable in the world being the case of strategy transformation through strong DC with Apple's radical innovation in its business shift from the PC to the music distribution business. Apple succeeded in new business by moving from its Mac development techniques (developed in-house) to orchestration of the best intangible assets both inside and outside of the company (co-specialized assets, discussed in detail in Chapter 3). This was the result of strong DC enabling processes of renewal, redeployment, or recombination to successfully function. The new Nintendo Wii and DS game concepts were also a radical innovation of gaming machines through redeployment to target customers in a completely different customer

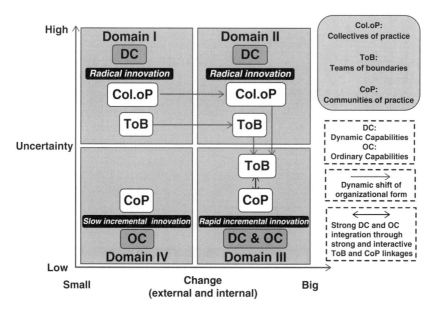

*Figure 2.4   Driving dynamic capabilities by dynamic informal
organizational forms*

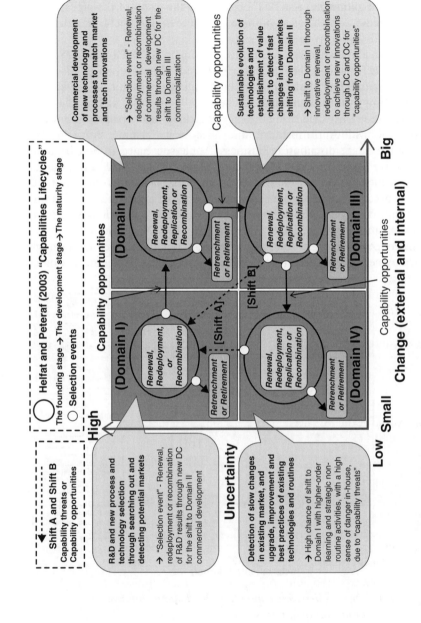

Figure 2.5   Capabilities lifecycles on the Capabilities Map

44

segment to the Sony PlayStation, a hugely popular product at the time (customers such as the elderly or housewives who had no previous interest in computerized games). Shift B in Figure 2.5 is also the strategy of aiming for yet-to-be-pioneered markets or technologies, common with the so-called "blue ocean strategies" (Kim and Mauborgne, 2005).

The above has considered the positioning and relationship of the four Domains in the Capabilities Map from "Capabilities Lifecycles" framework of Helfat and Peteraf (2003), in the perspective of the "dynamic view of capabilities." The capabilities that companies and organizations require change dynamically with the shift between each of these domains to respond to environmental changes (uncertainty and speed). Also, spiral feedback loops form through each selection event at the macro level in the shifts between the domains in Figure 2.5. In observing selection events in detail at the micro level (the micro strategy perspective), feedback mechanisms enabled by synergies (interactions) between each domain can also be seen. Viewed in the perspective of existing research on product development, the dynamic view in the Capabilities Map in Figure 2.5 encompasses the chain-linked model of Kline (1985), who discussed product development processes, which can also be said to be a further expanded model of individual product development processes at the business level.

In large corporations globally involved in R&D through to business development and product commercialization, there are always multiple Capabilities Maps and domains in which different capabilities exist (in amount and quality). Furthermore, to grow sustainably, leading companies can also be said to achieve strategic innovation by implementing spiraling strategic actions through these four domains through the synergies with dynamically changing environments as they constantly work to uncover new capability opportunities or on occasion face encroaching capability threats. Following, the author would like to discuss a detailed framework for the SIC needed to achieve this kind of strategic innovation sustainably.

2.4 THE STRATEGIC INNOVATION LOOPS AND STRATEGIC INNOVATION CAPABILITIES

When considered from the viewpoints of corporate exploration and exploitation processes based on the framework of capabilities lifecycles in Figure 2.5, radical and incremental innovation, and the time axis of business contexts, the four domains form a continuous domain loop (see Figure 2.6). The strategic emergence and selection domains, which are exploratory processes through DC (asset orchestration), are the core processes for radical innovation. "Strategic concentration" is the acceleration phase indicated by O'Connor and DeMartino (2006). This phase rapidly sets up new markets for products, services, and business models through the exploratory processes of strategic emergence and selection, and shifts domains from exploration to exploitation. Strategic concentration becomes the origin of newly generated strategic innovation that differs from existing business in the strategic efficiency domain.

In this strategic concentration domain, newly generated business initially always undergoes major internal or external changes. At this stage, internal elements aimed at building optimal value and supply chains in response to external change are transformed (discussed in detail in Chapter 3 as external and internal congruence in capabilities). In this strategic concentration domain, as discussed, strong integration of DC demonstrated by ToB informal organizations and OC demonstrated by CoP centered on formal organizations is required.

From among these strategic concentration businesses, which are subject to major change, businesses that succeed in establishing themselves in the market and achieving stability as their mainstream operations shift to the slow-moving (or small) "strategic efficiency" domain while promoting still greater operational and business process efficiency measures, either become part of the existing mainstream lineup or undergo business integration (which promotes still greater business process efficiency through strong OC).

However, businesses subject to major external change of markets and technologies following mainstream growth, and major internal changes in areas such as strategy, organization, technology, operations and leadership (discussed in detail in Chapter 3 as the necessity for dynamic congruence between these five internal factors) (for example, ICT industries involving broadband and smartphones, online businesses, and digital consumer electronics), always become positioned in this strategic concentration domain. Put another way, businesses growing in a mainstream direction become deployed in one or both of the strategic concentration and efficiency domains. Although new business in the strategic concentration domain is the "mainstream reserve," this does not mean that all business can grow in a mainstream environment subject to major changes, and some businesses have to withdraw (that is, retrenchment and retirement in capabilities lifecycles). This is especially true of the ICT industry. In this way, the flow of strategic innovation for major corporations shifts from Domain I to Domain II, then Domain III (where some businesses undergoing major changes maintain their position), and finally to Domain IV (see Figure 2.6).

In Domain IV, most of the businesses (products and services), including businesses that have survived the tough competition of Domain III and have shifted to Domain IV, are businesses that have been transformed from old to new over long periods of time (Markides, 2001). Put differently, business already in the strategic efficiency domain (Domain IV), may be targeted for transformation of old to new as new business in the strategic concentration of Domain III, through the shift along a new path (Domain I → Domain II → Domain III) due to strategic innovation. Markides' (2001) discussion of simultaneously managing existing and new strategic positions means the combination of Domains IV and III respectively, while the shift from the old position to the new implies that (all) existing business in Domain IV shifts to accelerate and grow as new business in Domain III.

Realistically however, although major corporations promote various strategically innovative projects, only some of them survive to become success stories after the natural selection process involved in the shift from Domains I to III. Amabile and Khaire (2008) note a number of cases where outstanding ideas and business models born in Domain I have been diluted and ended in failure after a major corporation employs a different managing organization to realize (commercialize) them. This is one issue surrounding strategic innovation in a major corporation. As discussed, in observing the selection events in Figure 2.5 at the micro level in the above domain shifts, feedback can be found in the synergies (interactions) between each Domain, which at the macro level are observed as spiral feedback loops (discussed later) that can also be described by the chain-linked model of Kline (1985).

The most important inter-domain shift is that from III and/or IV to I. This is the path that creates new strategic innovation (see Figure 2.6). In "Capabilities Lifecycles" (Helfat and Peteraf, 2003) in Figure 2.5 discussed above, companies running business in Domain III or IV uncover new capabilities opportunities, and sometimes undertake new corporate strategic actions when faced with Capability threats. It corresponds to the process that accelerates environmental and internal interaction and creates new ideas and new technological inventions and discoveries based on high-quality tacit knowledge (Nonaka and Takeuchi, 1995). This knowledge is cultivated by researchers, engineers, marketers, and strategy specialists in shifting from Domains I through IV (accumulating and integrating new practice through existing business and strategic innovation), via the "transformational experience" (King and Tucci, 2002; Amburgey et al., 1993) of previously existing business routines and strategic innovation (e.g., Kodama, 2007a). King and Tucci (2002) suggested that this transformational experience involved in the continual (Katz and Allen, 1982) and large-scale (Tushman and Romanelli, 1985; Amburgey et al., 1993) organizational innovation of product development teams leads to continuous new product innovation and overcomes rigid organizational inertia. Put another way, it enhances potential for embedding new capabilities in organization members for creating new DC-based non-routines to transform organizations and realize strategic innovation.

Although excessive adherence to existing knowledge to create new knowledge integration (knowledge convergence) (e.g., Kodama, 2014) becomes a hindrance, the absorption of knowledge from different sectors and industries from a scientific, technological, and marketing viewpoint and the knowledge integration process can trigger new strategic innovations. Various innovation theories including the importance of shedding the "mental model" (e.g., Spender, 1990), the focus on "peripheral vision" (Day and Schoemaker, 2005), "boundary vision" (Kodama, 2011), the challenge of achieving "cross innovation" (Johansson, 2004) and "destructive innovation" (Christensen, 1997) confer precious insights regarding innovators, but more detailed theories have not yet been developed. The author considers, as a proposition, that the evolution and diversification of high-level non-routines through the formation of SC (Col.oP and ToB) in Domains III and IV fundamentally promotes DC (asset orchestration) while inducing a shift from Domains III and/or IV back to Domain I arising from incremental innovating and integrating new knowledge (assets) inside and outside the company (Kodama, 2014), which raises the probability of achieving new knowledge integration as strategic innovation.

The author would like to explain the following three new insights obtained from this framework, and use them as a basis for explaining SIC. First, outstanding companies with the dynamic view of the capabilities deliberately (including some emergent elements) drive loops consisting of continuous shifts among domains ("strategic innovation loops," see Figure 2.6), from Domain I → Domain II → Domain III → Domain IV → Domain I and/or Domain III → Domain I. The dynamic view of capabilities establishes the different modes of the exploratory and exploitative processes and secures long-term corporate growth (e.g., March, 1996; Benner and Tushman, 2003; Tushman and O'Reilly, 1997). These two processes (March, 1991; Holland, 1975) do not entail opposing strategic activities; rather, companies must implement strategy while skillfully balancing their strategic activities in a mutually complementary way (He and Wong, 2004).

Zollo and Winter (2002) propose a knowledge evolution process based on adjusted evolutionary theory. Continuous routine activity well-considered within this process can trigger a shift from the exploitation to the exploration process, while experiential knowledge accumulated from learning activities can also be a factor in creating new DC (corresponding to a shift from Domain IV and/or Domain III to Domain I). These authors explain how the recursive processes and co-evolution of these different modes simultaneously promote corporate challenges and processes routines.

However, to demonstrate DC, accumulation of learning through existing routines or routines that other companies can copy through learning as mentioned are not required. Rather, strategic non-routine activities to bring about new routines (new business processes, operations and signature processes), which by nature are not best practices acquired through the formation of formal organization as the fundamental organizations or CoP, are required. Hence, as mentioned, the formation of SC such as Col. oP and ToB with pragmatic boundaries that drive strategic non-routine activities is required.

Second, observing large corporations at selected times indicates the presence of Domains I to IV with their different business contexts. In large corporations, there are multiple projects for strategic innovation that are layered as strategic innovation loops on different time axes. Therefore, top and middle management must manage appropriately within and between these domains. Management to smoothly implement the domain shift through the strategic innovation loop is also key, because different strategies, organizational structures, technologies, operations, and leadership are required within each of the domains.

However, so far from this discussion, an especially important question is what skills and expertise create strategic emergence in the new discovery and invention domain from accumulated experiential knowledge (arising from diverse high-level strategic non-routines through DC via the continuous strategic innovation loop), and how is new knowledge outside the company absorbed and integrated by the asset orchestration process.

Regardless, learning through higher-order routines (Amburgey et al., 1993; Nelson and Winter, 1982; Winter, 2000) alone does not make it easy to shift from Domain III and/or Domain IV to Domain I. In other words, to drive absorption and integration of new knowledge (assets) and capabilities, that is, asset orchestration through DC, the formation of SC such as Col.oP and ToB with pragmatic boundaries that drive strategic non-routine activities is required.

Moreover, O'Connor and DeMartino (2006) indicate the importance of the relationship between organizational structure and radical innovation capability with regard to the radical innovation development framework of major corporations moving from discovery, to cultivation, and then to acceleration (corresponding to Domains I to III respectively), and note that a new research area is opening into this topic.

Third, analysis of the case studies in this book suggests that the exploration and exploitation processes are especially interdependent. It has been argued that organizations within major corporations undertaking radical innovation should either be isolated both physically and organizationally from the mainstream organization, or else operate as independent venture companies (e.g., Hill and Rothaermel, 2003; Benner and Tushman, 2003; Burgelman and Sayles, 1988; Kanter, 1985). However, an appropriate interface with existing organizations is also potentially significant for accelerating strategic innovation from the viewpoint of strategy and resource integration (e.g., Heller, 1999; Kodama, 2003). Questions of organizational design are arguably more important in achieving strategic innovation (How much should a new business integrate with, or be separate from existing businesses? Is it better to have complete separation, complete integration, or something in between?) (e.g., Christensen, 1997; Goold and Campbell, 2002; Tushman and O'Reilly, 1997).

Much of the previous research discussed division of management processes and organization, such as two distinct archetypes – the exploitative and exploratory, or the incremental and radical (e.g., Greenwood and Hinings, 1993; Tushman and O'Reilly, 1997) and the ambidextrous organization (e.g., O'Reilly and Tushman, 2004). However, there has been little detailed of the interfaces and interactions among management elements such as strategy, organizational structure, technology, operation and leadership, each of which differ for each of these two archetypes (e.g., Kodama, 2003, 2007a). Nevertheless, the co-establishment and coexistence of these two archetypes within the same large corporation and the skillful management of strategic contradiction (Smith and Tushman, 2005), creative abrasion (Leonard-Barton, 1995) and productive friction (Hagel III and Brown, 2005) to create synergies are also important elements of successful strategic innovation. The coexistence of contradictions highlights the important roles not just of the top management (Smith and Tushman, 2005; Tushman and O'Reilly, 1997), but also of middle management and staff (Govindarajan and Trimble, 2005). The author calls this "dialectical management" (Kodama, 2004, 2007a).

Based on the three insights above, SIC is a concept that embraces the capabilities to integrate DC and OC throughout the company; the capabilities to implement spiral strategic innovation loops; capabilities within and between domains including shifts, and capabilities to achieve coexistence between the two archetypes through dialectic management (see Figure 2.6). SIC embraces the existing dynamic and MI dynamic capability (or Breakthrough Innovation Capability) concepts illustrated in Figure 1.1 and aims to expand DC and OC for individual product

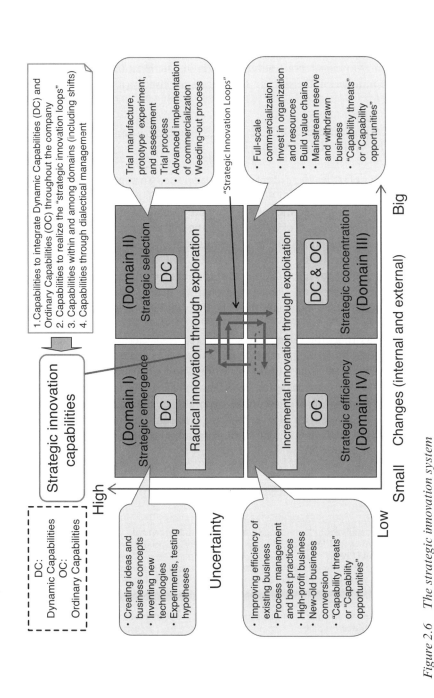

1. Capabilities to integrate Dynamic Capabilities (DC) and Ordinary Capabilities (OC) throughout the company
2. Capabilities to realize the "strategic innovation loops"
3. Capabilities within and among domains (including shifts)
4. Capabilities through dialectical management

DC: Dynamic Capabilities
OC: Ordinary Capabilities

Strategic innovation capabilities

High

Uncertainty

Low

(Domain I)
Strategic emergence

DC

(Domain II)
Strategic selection

DC

Radical innovation through exploration

"Strategic Innovation Loops"

Incremental innovation through exploitation

(Domain IV)
Strategic efficiency

OC

DC & OC

Strategic concentration
(Domain III)

Small   Changes (internal and external)   Big

· Creating ideas and business concepts
· Inventing new technologies
· Experiments, testing hypotheses

· Trial manufacture, prototype experiment, and assessment
· Trial process
· Advanced implementation of commercialization
· Weeding-out process

· Improving efficiency of existing business
· Process management and best practices
· High-profit business
· New-old business conversion
· "Capability threats" or "Capability opportunities"

· Full-scale commercialization
· Invest in organization and resources
· Build value chains
· Mainstream reserve and withdrawn business
· "Capability threats" or "Capability opportunities"

Figure 2.6   The strategic innovation system

51

development projects at large corporations and venture companies to innovate in corporate or management systems. This book calls the kind of management system that uses SIC to activate the spiral strategic innovation loop and continuously co-establish existing business with strategic innovation business the "strategic innovation system" (see Figure 2.6).

2.5   CHAPTER SUMMARY

This chapter clarifies the differences between the two types of capabilities required by companies – "DC" and "OC" – by focusing on the dynamically changing characteristics of the boundaries of informal organizations. In addition, regarding the dynamics of the shifting within and between each domain responding to the environmental changes surrounding corporations (uncertainties, risks and speed) and dynamic organizational forms responding to the environmental changes surrounding corporations (uncertainties, risks and speed), the chapter has presented the process of developing diverse capabilities in the framework of "Capabilities Lifecycles."

As well as that, the chapter has extracted four factors of capabilities (SIC) required for dynamic innovation processes to achieve strategic innovation (incremental and radical innovation), and hence corporate sustainable growth. Also, the chapter describes how leading companies entail the dynamic spiral of the two distinct types of capabilities – the DC and OC – on the Capabilities Map, which are skillfully combined and applied over time to achieve incremental innovation for exploitation and radical innovation for exploration.

NOTES

1. For more details about "knowledge boundaries," "thought worlds" and "mental models," refer to Brown and Duguid (2001), Dougherty (1992), Spender (1990) and Grinyer and McKiernan (1994).
2. Much of the existing research to date regarding cross-functional boundaries behind successful new product development (e.g., Allen, 1977; Tushman, 1977; Tushman and Nadler, 1978) suggests the need for smooth communications, or the need for the so-called "boundary spanner" (Brown and Eisenhardt, 1995).
3. The CoP theory has limitations and cannot be applied to all business contexts. For more details, see Roberts (2006).
4. Lindkvist (2005, p.1190) described project organizations as Col.oP.
5. Nisbett (2003) describes dialectical thinking by contrasting the analytical skills of western thinking with the broader understanding of eastern thinking as analogous to eastern

thinking looking across the whole forest, whereas western thinking stares at a single large tree.
6. The author proposed the concept of SC through my fieldwork to date. An SC can mean either type of ToB and Col.oP system. See Kodama (2007c) and Kodama and Shibata (2014b).

3. The concept of capabilities congruence: theoretical framework from three insights

This chapter presents the concept of "capabilities congruence," which is a business factor in large corporations that brings about sustainable growth over the long term by achieving strategic innovation as the corporation enacts dynamic capabilities and strategic innovation capabilities. The chapter also clarifies three important insights about capabilities congruence (Insight-1: dynamic congruence with the corporate capabilities (corporate systems) with environments; Insight-2: congruence between different capabilities within corporations (in corporate systems); Insight-3: congruence by orchestrating different co-specialized assets both in and out of corporations).

As new perspectives, the chapter describes how leaders and managers in large corporations achieve congruence across diverse internal and external boundaries by perception and cognition of the changing boundaries between environments and corporate systems and between various capabilities in corporate systems, in regards to the process of changing capabilities between their own companies, the environment and other companies. In rapidly changing environments, factors for executing capabilities congruence dynamically are of great importance for a corporation to achieve strategic innovation.

Moreover, regarding capabilities between Capabilities Maps and between the domains in those Capabilities Maps that are often born in large companies, this chapter discusses how negative interactions can seriously inhibit capabilities congruence.

3.1 CAPABILITIES CONGRUENCE IN AND OUT OF COMPANIES

This chapter presents a framework for a dynamic strategic management theory to achieve sustainable growth through the strategic innovation described in Chapter 2. The core theoretical concept lies in the framework of capabilities congruence, and is an attempt to make a new contribution to the framework of dynamic capabilities (DC). Including classic contingency theories (e.g., Burns and Stalker, 1961; Lawrence and Lorsch, 1967), much of the management and organization literature has discussed the importance of the internal fit between the strategy and the structure of firms (e.g., Chandler, 1962; Learned et al., 1965) and the external fit between the structure and the environment of firms (e.g., Lawrence and Lorsch, 1967; Pennings, 1987).

Moreover, in the field of strategic human resource management, it has been identified that high performance human resource systems entail companies (organizations) fitting personnel, technologies, duties and information to external environmental factors such as customer requests, environmental demands and opportunities (e.g., Nadler et al., 1992). Congruence is required when external environments and internal corporate factors dynamically change. If there are no changes inside or outside a company, and congruence is incorporated into the corporate system at the design stage, congruence could be maintained indefinitely. However, if there is a misfit in the initial design stage of a corporate system, congruence can be achieved by making suitable corrections to the design at a later stage. Regarding this context of fit inside and outside of corporations, Siggelkow (2001) asserted that for a firm that occupies a peak, environmental change can affect both external and internal fit, and presented a corporate change framework consisting of four patterns.

Congruence only appears in temporal states (or processes) in corporate systems, and finding one-time congruence (fit) is not the ultimate goal of corporate activity (Miles and Snow, 1994). In other words, after getting congruence, corporations must apply it whenever there are changes in the external environment or in internal corporate factors. Notably, Siggelkow (2001) identifies "Fit-conserving change," although internal fit has not been affected, external fit has decreased. In other words, the environmental change has left the internal logic of the firm's system of choices intact while decreasing the appropriateness of the system as a whole, in which the patterns present major issues for organizational sustainable growth to traditional large corporations that are bound by organizational inertia and mental models. Siggelkow (2001, p.853) also says that "Managers will have a particularly difficult time reacting to fit-conserving change because the internal logic of the existing system of choices remains intact."

In addition, existing research in the strategic management field asserts that strategic fit (or strategic congruence) is necessary for a corporation to grow sustainably (e.g., Miles and Snow, 1994; Tushman and O'Reilly, 1997; Collis and Montgomery, 1998; Teece, 2007; Kodama, 2010, 2015). Miles and Snow (1994) argue that the success of an organization depends on a process of external (the environment) and internal (strategy, structure, processes and ideology) fit, and assert that firms that match their situation to the environment can improve their performance, while those that do not run the risk of failure.

Viewed in the perspective of capabilities, corporations that achieve sustainable growth do not only need congruence for dynamically changing environments, but also must enable congruence between multiple different capabilities through coordination, alignment and realignment between different capabilities in companies. Thus, as discussed in Chapter 2, large companies simultaneously engage in incremental and radical innovation by demonstrating DC and strategic innovation capabilities by forming dynamic informal organizations to bring about DC. Thus, over the long term, the most important managerial factor in achieving sustainable growth is the new concept of capabilities congruence. Here, capabilities congruence is a requisite for a corporation to continuously bring about DC (and strategic innovation capabilities) to systematically engage in both incremental and radical innovation. Put differently, for sustainable growth in a large corporation, capabilities congruence entails optimizing capabilities both within a company and broadly across business ecosystems configured to include all stakeholders to achieve strategic innovation.

This capabilities congruence can be achieved through asset orchestration, a core function of DC. As the functions of asset orchestration, Teece (2014, p.333) presented the organizational processes of (1) coordination/ integration, (2) learning, and (3) reconfiguration. In this book, the author would like to add the processes of capabilities congruence as the fourth of these functions.

3.2 CAPABILITIES CONGRUENCE THROUGH DYNAMIC CAPABILITIES IN AND OUT OF COMPANIES: THE FRAMEWORK FOR DYNAMIC STRATEGIC MANAGEMENT

In the view of strategic management as a dynamic process, corporate systems (capabilities in a company such as strategies, organizations, technologies, operations and leadership, discussed later) must change dynamically to adapt to dynamically changing environments surrounding corporations (for example markets, technologies, competition and cooperation, structures) (Kodama, 2010). The borders or corporate boundaries between environments and corporate systems define the relationships with environments and company business models (Kodama, 2009b). Changes in environments bring about changes in corporate boundaries and simultaneously affect individual capabilities in corporate systems. Conversely, changes to the individual capabilities in corporate systems (either passive of active) bring about changes to the corporate boundaries of a company, and in turn also affect the environment.

Helfat et al. (2007) argue that in the activities of coordination and resource allocations by business persons, markets (or environments, ecosystems) form corporations, while in the same manner corporations form markets (or environments, ecosystems). In other words, companies and markets are in co-evolution relationships (see Figure 3.1). Thus, good asset orchestration of business persons who have technical fitness (that is, DC) enables a company to create favorable external environments, which as a result tie in with raising "evolutionary fitness" (Helfat et al., 2007).

Also, Teece (2007) states that in a multinational enterprise, one of the core functions of management is to develop and implement the company's unique strategies, which means they must "fit" assets, structures and processes globally (and their individual internal elements), while the company management team must also decide or uncover what technological opportunities and customer needs the company addresses while securing the resources and assets needed to execute strategy. Hence, the capabilities to proactively adapt, redeploy, and reconfigure in an entrepreneurial fashion gives meaning to "orchestration," and thus gives meaning also to "DC."

In a different interpretation, there is a necessity for practitioners to intentionally change business factors related to capabilities such as strategy, organizations, technologies, operations and leadership in corporate systems to bring congruence to the boundaries between capabilities so that corporations can adapt to changing environments (or ecosystems), or actively create new environments (the formulation and implementation of environment creation strategy discussed in Chapter 9). This means not only are the capabilities congruence between corporate systems and markets (ecosystems) (dynamic external congruence) (Insight-1), but capabilities congruence between capabilities in corporate systems (dynamic internal congruence (congruence between subsystems)) (Insight-2) are both required. The function that achieves capabilities congruence both in and outside of companies is asset orchestration through DC (see Figure 3.1).

Nevertheless, diverse management capabilities such as good organizational capabilities (capabilities in corporate systems) are formed, and as such, even if they are maintained, if they are routines dominated by stable patterns or ordinary capabilities (OC), companies must take into

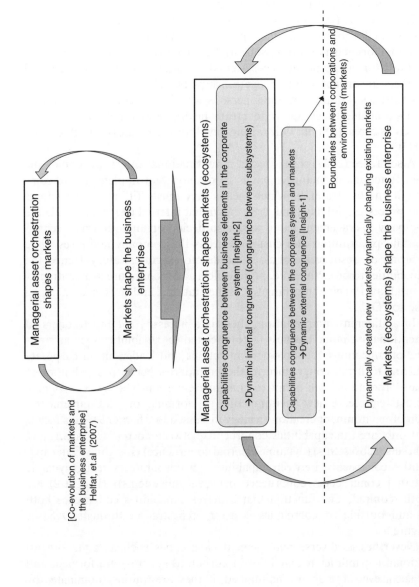

Figure 3.1 Capabilities congruence inside and outside of a company

account the possibility that their advantage may be lost when the environment changes. In other words, as discussed in Chapter 2, companies have to unceasingly renew their resource bases by integration, alignment and realignment of their diverse resources (capabilities) to change and reconfigure the capabilities in a corporate system ((1) strategy capabilities, (2) organizational capabilities, (3) technology capabilities, (4) operational capabilities, (5) leadership capabilities, described in detail in the next section) through the demonstration of DC (sensing → seizing → transforming), in step with changes in the environment.

Actually, on the forefront of business where DC must be demonstrated (the front line of business where strategic non-routine activities are executed through DC rather than the routine work involving OC) lie the questions "what are the product strategies that match the latent needs of users?," "what form should organizations and operations take to achieve strategic objectives?," "what is required for technical elements to achieve target products or business models?," "what kind of leadership do company leaders and managers need to enact to achieve new strategies?," "in what way does the awareness of staff need to be reformed?" and "how do in-house processes need to be reformed?" These are some of the practical issues that many practitioners face.

However, business factors such as strategy, organizations, technologies, operations and leadership exist in different contexts, while practitioners have dissimilar thought worlds (e.g., Dougherty, 1992) and individual mental models (e.g., Markides, 1999) based on their own different contexts and empirical knowledge. Also, different practitioners have different perspectives on the individual capabilities in environments and corporate systems. Accordingly, "knowledge boundaries," which are constraints between practitioners, naturally occur as barriers to congruence between these capabilities. However, practitioners driving innovations and business transformation have to see knowledge boundaries not as limitations, but triggers to bring about new capabilities (in his own experience when he was a practitioner, the author has found that effective practitioners tend to see knowledge boundaries as opportunities).

Regarding the process of changing environment and corporate systems, the important perspectives in dynamic strategic management are how practitioners use their DC to sense congruence on boundaries between environments and corporate systems (Insight-1), congruence on the boundaries between individual capabilities in corporate systems (Insight-2), and changes in these boundaries, and engage in sensing and transforming boundaries congruence with DC. In rapidly changing environments, practitioners need to engage in corporate management to execute processes to change strategic management and achieve the aforementioned environment adaption and environment creation strategies. Hence, by demonstrating DC (sensing → seizing → transforming), practitioners have to engage in the dynamic practice of bringing congruence to the boundaries between environment and corporate systems (Insight-1) and bring congruence to the boundaries between the individual capabilities within corporate systems (Insight-2).

For a company to develop and grow sustainably, practitioners must execute the processes of changing strategic management over time (that is, DC congruence processes, which are either gradual or rapid) through DC that are difficult for other companies to copy, so that they can create new products, services and business models that have the competitive edge. Here, the execution of this through the concept of capabilities congruence by asset orchestration mentioned earlier is crucial (see Figure 3.2).

Teece (2014, p.334) states that "Dynamic capabilities do not operate alone. They must be coupled with effective strategizing to bring about competitive advantage." Teece emphasizes evolution of DC interlocking with business environments and strategies, and presents three strategy kernels (Rumelt, 2011) as this "effective strategy." However, effective strategizing function by deeply interconnecting with four capabilities other than the new strategy capability proposed in this book (organizational capabilities, technology capabilities, operational capabilities, leadership capabilities). Hence, in Figure 3.2, the author adds these four capabilities in addition to the element of "strategizing," in other words strategy capabilities (strategy processes), and interprets that the corporate system in which congruence between the individual capability elements is achieved functions DC appropriately.

As mentioned later, these five capabilities can also be interpreted as "signature processes" (Gratton and Ghoshal, 2005). Signature processes are company's own intangible assets that are difficult for other companies to copy, and are rooted in company history and the individual thinking and actions of staff members, which also satisfy the VRIN standards of Barney (1991) (Teece, 2014, p.333) (see Figure 3.2).

Also, Teece (2014, p.334) asserts that "In short, the joint presence of strong dynamic capabilities, VRIN resources, and good strategy is necessary and sufficient for long-run enterprise financial success." Teece (2014, pp.340–341) also argues:

> In short, VRIN resources, in and of themselves, are inherently valuable by definition, but they do not generate long-term enterprise value (or military prowess) on their own. For long-term growth and survival of the enterprise, they must be cleverly managed, or orchestrated, by a dynamically capable management team pursuing a good strategy. This also means that the resource-based view of the

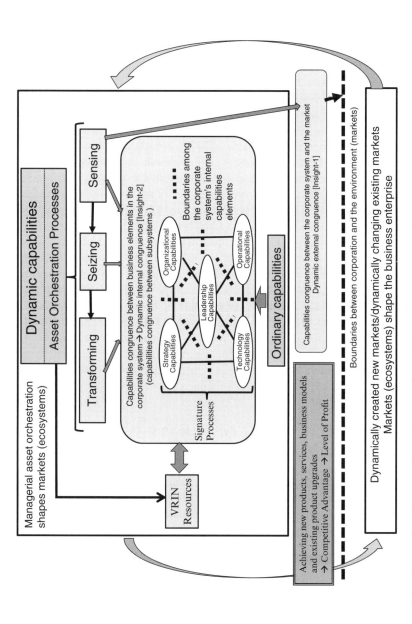

Figure 3.2   Internal and external consistency of capabilities congruence: a dynamic strategic management framework

firm needs dynamic capabilities to explain how assets get deployed and how rent streams get extended and renewed.

Meaning DC and VRIN resources can be interpreted as being in a mutually complementary relationship, hence the capabilities congruence framework in this book can also clearly position the role of VRIN resources (see Figure 3.2).

Also, in Figure 3.2, OC are described as the foundation of five capabilities. On this point, Teece (2014, p.334) says "Strong ordinary capabilities (operations, administration, governance) must be accessed by the enterprise, but they need not necessarily be owned. Managing a plethora of ordinary capabilities can undermine dynamic capabilities. In other words, ordinary capabilities are not sufficient for long-term financial success; they may not even be necessary." OC are required for the fast and slow incremental innovation in Domains III and IV respectively in the Capabilities Map discussed in Chapters 1 and 2. Moreover, strong integration of DC and OC in Domain III is an indispensable factor in winning out over other competitor companies in fast changing environments. OC are the basic functions of business persons in large corporations, and advance routines to achieve company-unique best practices through higher-order learning (Winter, 2003) (even upper managers in venture companies must focus on appropriate OC for company growth, because the volume of formulaic routine work increases as companies get bigger). Therefore, OC are fundamental to all of the five capabilities, and as such are tangible and intangible assets that cannot be ignored.

3.3   CAPABILITIES IN CORPORATE SYSTEMS HANDLING DYNAMIC CAPABILITIES

The author would like to further consider the "dynamic internal congruence" (congruence between subsystems) (Insight-2) – congruence between the various capabilities in a corporate system mentioned earlier. First, it's necessary to define the individual subsystem capabilities in a corporate system (subsystem elements required for capabilities congruence). In this research, the author extracts and analyzes factors of certain capabilities required for sustainable growth, from published secondary materials and massive amounts of interview data from large corporations (in Asia and the west, and so on) that have achieved (or failed at) sustainable growth through the practice of DC.

As empirical observations, the author first extracted first-order concepts related to various capability factors. Then, the author defined and categorized business factors related to various core capabilities required for capabilities congruence in corporate systems from the first-order concepts, and extracted second-order themes from theoretical observations. As a result of considering and analyzing these second-order themes, the author uncovered strong interactions between the various capabilities the author defined and categorized, as well as relationships of fitness and reinforcement.

As a core framework, these second-order themes lead to the main aggregate theoretical concepts ((1) strategy capabilities, (2) organizational capabilities, (3) technology capabilities, (4) operational capabilities, (5) leadership capabilities) of the five capabilities in corporate systems (see Figure 3.3).

These five capabilities in corporate systems are also subsystem elements observed in entire systems as the DC of corporate systems (that is, the entire company). Processes are one factor of DC, however, since the performance of DC is also the processes used to apply DC (Eisenhardt and Martin, 2000), these five capabilities can also be viewed as processes. In other words, they can be called "strategy processes," "organizational processes," "technological (creating) processes," "operational processes," and "leadership (demonstration) processes." These processes are thus similar to the aforementioned signature processes unique to a company.

Here, the author would like to briefly describe why leadership capabilities (leadership processes) are related to processes. Leadership is not a matter of a unique "style," but is something that should be perceived as a constantly changing process – in changing environments, leaders engage in different leadership behaviors moment-by-moment. Leadership as a process means particular leadership in situations that are always changing, which means unceasingly changing with each and every event or episode that occurs in innovation activities. As a process then, leadership constantly changes as the intangible assets of human empirical knowledge are constantly renewed through the actual experience of humans moving from the past, through the present, and into the future.

Thus, the resources that bring about new intangible assets are the dynamic generation and nature of actual events and episodes made up of the interactions between individuals in a range of changing contexts and backgrounds (actual entity) (Griffin and Sherburne, 1929/1978), and are by no means at all static. A fundamental analytical framework for perceiving dynamic corporate activity (for example, the knowledge integration (convergence) process (Kodama, 2011, 2014)) lies in the dynamic processes of the innovations activities of individual, association and organizations both inside and outside of companies, thus, for sustainable corporate growth, it is important to perceive these unceasing changes in the past, the present and the future, as "processes." Therefore, the leadership of leaders with good intangible assets dynamically change and strengthen as environments change, while strategic collaboration with other leaders brings about leadership synergies (in other words, co-specialization of intangible assets related to the quality of leadership). As discussed later, "leader teams" (LT) formed from excellent leaders are co-specialized. Accordingly, the leadership of individual leaders are valuable co-specialized assets of organizations.

Also, the "operational capabilities" (operation processes) discussed in this book do not mean exactly the same thing as an element of the OC (daily routines) in corporate activities discussed in Chapter 2. Teece (2007, p.1346) says:

> Yet it is perhaps an overstatement to say that "operations management" tools and procedures cannot be the basis of competitive advantage, or work against it. If there is a significant, tacit, non-inimitable component of an enterprise's superior operational competence, it has the potential for a time to support superior performance (it will, in fact, generate Ricardian rents). Nevertheless, superior operational efficiency, while valuable, is not a dynamic capability.

Teece (2014, p.333) also gives the example of "fast food industry dynamic capabilities figuring out new products to put on the menu, new operating hours (e.g., late night), and new locations (central versus suburban)," and "operations strategy as developing resources and configuring processes so that there is good strategic fit with the business environment (Van Mieghem, 2008)," thereby identifying DC in "operations."

Certainly, like Porter (1996), "operational management" tools and procedures cannot be identified as a source of competitiveness, although taking up the challenge of constantly innovating manufacturing (for example, developing new technologies for production automation), like the Japanese Fanuc and Canon have done, can bring about operational and supply chain management mechanisms that are difficult for other companies to copy. The operational capabilities to bring about operational strategies that fit strategy and technology in this way are thus factors of DC.

Teece (2007, p.1338) also says "Capturing co-specialization benefits may require integrated operations (Teece, 1980)." In other words, new operational capabilities can be interpreted as unique corporate operational capabilities that are difficult for another company to copy, brought about with co-specialization occurring with technological capabilities resulting from technological innovation of production systems by operational

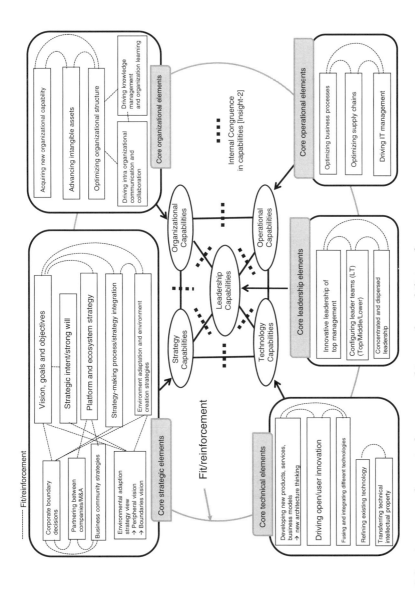

Figure 3.3   Aggregate theoretical concepts of internal capabilities elements

65

management. Accordingly, the author would like to emphasis that operational capabilities discussed in this book are not the OC discussed by Teece (2014), but are intangible assets that bring about co-specialization with other capabilities (e.g., technical and organizational capabilities). Therefore, the author will call capabilities that give rise to operational processes that are difficult for other companies to copy "operational capabilities."

As signature processes also, these five individual process capabilities are unique to companies, and bring about specific DC that are difficult to copy by other companies through "Fit" (or alignment, consistency, congruence), by co-specialization between these many process (Helfat et al., 2007). Thus, this (dynamic) internal congruence appears when consistency is generated between the five capabilities (process capabilities) elements. The even stronger form of internal congruence in capabilities thus refers to a state in which not only has consistency between the five capabilities been achieved, but the co-specialization is reinforced (complemented) (discussed later) to optimize the corporate system.

In existing research, Miles and Snow (1994) refer to the necessity for a "tight fit" between strategy, structure and process. Moreover, the five capabilities in a corporate system are consistent with the theoretical models of existing research – "Organization Architecture" (Tushman and O'Reilly, 1997) and the "Corporate Strategy Triangle" (Collis and Montgomery, 1998). Thus, as a company drives the asset orchestration process through DC (sensing → seizing → transforming), it also brings internal congruence between the five capabilities in the corporate system (see Figure 3.4).

Following, the author discusses the relationship between co-specialized asset orchestration and capabilities congruence.

3.4   CO-SPECIALIZED ASSET ORCHESTRATION AND CAPABILITIES CONGRUENCE

The asset orchestration process through DC (sensing → seizing → transforming) is required to achieve internal congruence between the five capabilities in corporate systems and external congruence between the corporate system and the environment. Teece (2007, p.1337) identifies the importance of "strategic fit" to strengthen corporate strategic management, and emphasizes co-specialization as an important aspect related to this "fit." In other words, orchestration of intangible assets such as co-specialized assets and complementary assets are important for achieving this kind of strategic fit (Teece, 2007; Helfat et al., 2007). This is because in systemic innovation, in bringing about innovations, co-specialization

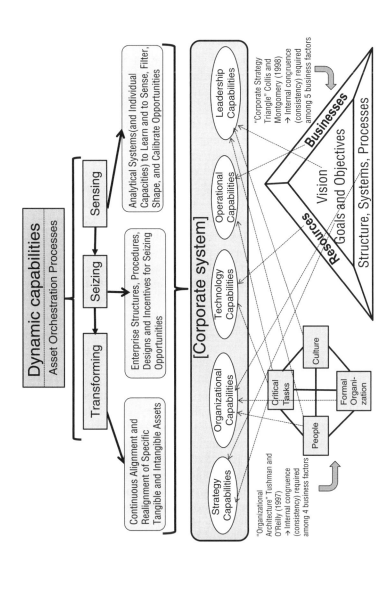

Source: Teece (2007).

Figure 3.4 Business elements of dynamic capabilities in corporate systems

67

between the subsystem elements that make up a system is crucial (Teece, 1986). For example, focusing on technical aspects one can see that high-tech products are often systems that are made up of mutually interacting structural elements supported by platforms – the importance of this co-specialization has been increasing in recent years.

Co-specialization involves complementary systems, for example, to meet customer demands for performance, co-specialization could describe part of a system in which technologies or other assets are closely integrated. Accordingly, with systems and networks, it is especially important to integrate not only company know-how (intangible assets), but also integrate know-how from external sources for business to succeed. This proposition is also closely related to congruence through orchestration of co-specialized assets inside and outside of companies, as described by Insight-3.

Co-specialization can also be thought of as co-specialization between assets (for example, technologies and capabilities), co-specialization between strategies and organizations, co-specialization between strategies and processes (for example, operations), co-specialization between technologies, and co-specialization between technologies and other parts of the value chain. Co-specialized assets are a particular class of complementary assets where the value of an asset is a function of its use in conjunction with other particular assets. With co-specialization, joint use is value enhancing (Teece, 2007, p.1338).

Regarding these co-specialized assets, Table 3.1 describes specific cases of the five capabilities in the corporate system.

3.4.1 Strategy Capabilities

Strategy capabilities bring about win–win synergies of strategies through platform-building capabilities with strategic partners (co-specialized/complementary). Teece (2007, pp.1332–1333) identifies the importance of "managing complements and platforms" to build co-specialized assets. Against the background of the advance of ICT business in recent years, from the perspective of business models and corporate strategies, platform strategies are becoming increasingly important (Kodama, 2009b, 2012). Since platforms are the foundations of products and services, configuring complementary services and products on platforms is considered as a way to provide even more value to customers. Microsoft in the software industry with its Windows operating system and Intel in the hardware industry with its MPU semiconductors have created a situation in which both companies are platform leaders (Gawer and Cusmano, 2004). Thus, with both companies maintaining strong competitiveness with their Windows and MPUs, positive feedback through network effects function as partners, the

Table 3.1 Capabilities by integration of co-specialized assets

Elements of Capabilities	Capabilities through integration of co-specialized assets (examples) (Strong dynamic capabilities bring mutual co-specialization and congruence to the 5 capabilities)
Strategy Capabilities	– Platform-building capabilities with strategic partners (co-specialized/complementary) → Win–win strategic synergies – Vertical integration capabilities for developing value chains → Strategic synergies accompanying strategic expansion upstream and downstream – Horizontal integration capabilities across domains → Strategic synergies with expansion geographically and globally, and into adjacent industries – Integrative capabilities with group company strategies → Strategic synergies that accompany group company partnering – Strategic synergies through integrative strategies with M&A, joint ventures and the company – Strategic synergies with integration of the dissimilar business models (e.g., fabless and foundry, IT and education, medical services)
Organizational Capabilities	– Ambidextrous organization configuring capabilities → Combining old and new enterprises – Dynamic, organic organization configuring capabilities → Management selecting and integrating Col.oP, ToB, CoP in the Capabilities Map – Network integrative capabilities between companies → Knowledge integration between different companies and organizations etc.
Technology Capabilities	– Integration and fusion of different (co-specialized) technologies in and out of companies → New products, services and business models – Integration and fusion of co-specialized technologies through open and hybrid innovation – Architecture innovation through integration of hardware and software → New products (e.g., iPhone) etc.
Operational Capabilities	– Integrative capabilities with IT and business processes (e.g., concurrent engineering with IT) – Integrative capabilities with automated production systems and business processes (e.g., automated manufacturing at Fanuc, Canon etc.) – Vertical integration capabilities with IT that include partners and customers
Leadership Capabilities	– Leader team formation capabilities (top/middle/lower) inside and outside (if required) companies → Knowledge sharing an integration through layered LT – Achieving all management capabilities (collective wisdom capabilities) etc.

69

complementary parties, provide applications and software to run on the systems.

The win–win relationships built between these platform leaders and complementary parties go on to create "business ecosystems." Other classic platform strategies (products) in the ICT business include the iPhone iOS application platform and the Google Android OS for smartphones on which a range of authentication, finance and transaction functions, diverse applications and software are provided.

For companies that aim to become platform leaders, it's important to decide upon a platform architecture that will encourage autonomous growth on the platform of various complementary commercial technologies, products and services. Then, at the same time as selecting and building a platform in product development, an important issue is to set down suitable vertical boundaries with external partners that are complementing company to develop an attractive platform on which the platform leader can encourage autonomous growth with those external partners.

While skillfully deriving and coordinating the co-specialized assets of partner companies (or customers or competitors) in relationships with one's own company, the core capabilities that drive the overall system on the company ICT platform (co-specialized assets), the system being made up of technologies, product and services developed independently by individual partners, become strategic capabilities. Companies such as Microsoft, Google, Intel, Qualcomm, NVIDIA, Apple, Sony Computer Entertainment (SCE) (see Box 3.1), Nintendo, are typical examples of these platform companies. Platform companies build open (or hybrid or half-open) platforms as modular systems while maintaining power over their own business, which enables them to grow long term. If these platform strategies can be skillfully deployed, businesses can be opened up that would be difficult to embark on with only a single company's resources and there is greater potential to bring about a business ecosystem involving "co-creation and co-evolution" among the company, its partners, its customers and even its competitors.

Moreover, strategy capabilities entail contexts in which there are synergies between diverse strategies. In particular, multinational enterprises have to orchestrate co-specialized assets on a global scale. Helfat et al. identify (2007, p.168) "replication capabilities" that bring about two types of strategic values (the ability to support geographic expansion, and the ability to support production line expansion) as another element of DC. The replication, redeployment and reconfiguration (or recombination) of these intangible assets can also be thought of as bringing about co-specialization, as synergies of global strategies enabled by strategic capabilities (here, this means the processes of "redeployment," "replication" and "recombination" as described by the "Capabilities Lifecycles" in Figure 2.5 in Chapter 2).

For example, these could be strategic synergies accompanying strategic expansion upstream and/or downstream in a value chain through vertical integration, global geographical expansion through a horizontal integration across domains, strategic synergies accompanying expansion of successful business models into adjacent industries, strategic synergies accompanying group company partnering through integration of group company strategies, or strategic synergies through integration of a company itself through joint ventures or M&A. Moreover, strategic synergies can be brought about through strategic capabilities by integrating different business models (for example, fabless and foundry, IT and education/healthcare services). These cases of integrating different capabilities, such as capability recombination (or knowledge integration) (Kogut and Zander, 1992; Helfat and Peteraf, 2003; Kodama, 2011, 2014) are cases where orchestration of co-specialized assets is required.

3.4.2 Organizational Capabilities

Following, the author discusses organizational capabilities. According to existing research, the ability to configure ambidextrous organizations (that is, organizational capabilities) through DC enables the combination of both old and new business (O'Reilly and Tushman, 2008). As discussed in Chapter 2, the ability to configure informal, dynamic organic organizations through collectivities of practice (Col.oP), teams of boundaries (ToB) or strategic communities (SC), brings about the organizational capabilities to demonstrate DC. As specific cases of organizational capabilities through networks between companies, the author presents the results of action research through his own experience. Hence, as discussed in Chapter 2, the author verified details of cases in which non-routine actions enabled by the configuration of SC and networked SC (boundary networks) have played an important role in bringing about the organizational capabilities and DC presented in this section.

Between 2000 and 2003 the author served as a product planning development project leader at NTT DOCOMO of Japan (DOCOMO hereinafter). This project took on the challenge to develop a new video communications service using third generation mobile telephone services, which was, at that time, planned for commencement in two years. The "mobile video-conferencing multipoint platform" which resulted from the new product and service development project was later presented with a 2003 R&D 100 Award (*R&D Magazine*) "as one of the 100 most technologically significant products introduced into the marketplace over the past year."[1] This commercial development process also entailed orchestration of various co-specialized assets (diverse organizational systems and organizational skills and know-how, and so on) through strategic alliances with strategic partners both within and outside of the company, including customers.

At the time the DOCOMO project team (service planning project) of which the author was serving as a leader had to surmount a number of hurdles to develop the new platform. The project involved many of the company's related departments which faced practical problems and challenging issues. The need to set up a system within the company for the new product and service development, and acquiring developmental resources within DOCOMO were particularly large issues. For this reason, the service planning project needed to clear a number of in-house decisions and get consensus from related in-house departments (for example, sales, development, facilities, maintenance, materials, planning, and so on). While the service planning project had to handle various conflicts and frictions within the company, eventually we were able to get the go-ahead for development and commercialization through a number of political negotiations and coordination within the company (the starting line for R&D in Domain I of the Capabilities Map).

SC-a in Figure 3.5 (SC, characteristic of the so-called cross-functional teams (CFT) – similar to Col.oP or ToB described in Chapter 2) was characterized by pragmatic boundaries that involved many related departments (Carlile, 2004). A vertically integrated, "structured informal organizational model" (Kodama, 2007d) was configured within SC-a, with many CFT, to progress with detailed studies on configuring specific details of business models and systems for the new product and service development within DOCOMO.

In February 2001, DOCOMO agreed to form a strategic partnership with Mitsubishi Electronic (Mitsubishi hereinafter), which had core capabilities in the multimedia technology of videoconferencing. The partnership's purpose was the joint development of a mobile videoconferencing multipoint system. For DOCOMO, the objective of the SC-b with Mitsubishi was to ignite the Japanese mobile videoconferencing market in a single stroke, and at the same time, launch the new wireless videoconferencing service to promote in the 3G mobile market. Through this strategic alliance, the joint development SC-b formed part of the horizontally integrated organizational network structure between DOCOMO and Mitsubishi. Thus, SC-b between DOCOMO and Mitsubishi continued with joint development to materialize the new products and services. SC-b did not just include Mitsubishi's development center, but also included middle managers and staff from the company's basic research labs and IT headquarters, and featured many debates about product specifications required to achieve the product architecture, business model and services.

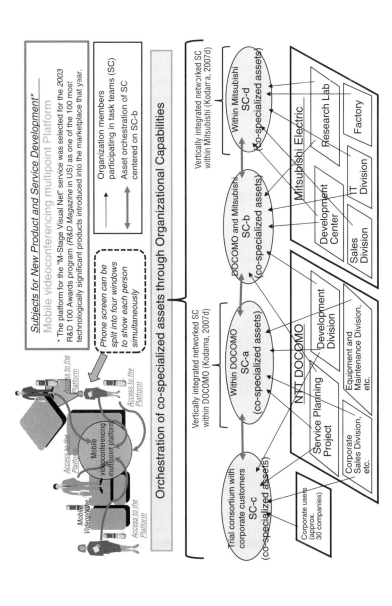

Figure 3.5 "Organizational Capabilities" of network integration through the orchestration of co-specialized assets (customers – DOCOMO – Mitsubishi)

The strategic alliance with DOCOMO was accepted within Mitsubishi, and a company-wide developmental system was put in place. Then, SC-d was newly formed from the pragmatic boundaries surrounding the various related departments in Mitsubishi. Because it was sometimes necessary to integrate technologies from different areas of expertise such as video, mobile communications, semiconductor, software, computer and human interface technologies in the target development, SC-d featured a vertically integrated structured informal organizational model formed within Mitsubishi as cross-functional task teams made up of specialists in a range of divisions (including personnel deployment) such as research laboratories in three of the company's departments, its development center, the software technology-related IT headquarters, production engineering headquarters and its manufacturing plants (Kodama, 2007d).

Additionally, as the first step toward commercialization of this DOCOMO service planning project, SC-c was formed with members of potential corporate customers, and a consortium was brought together to test product prototypes with the aim of developing the new products and services to satisfy the latent needs of corporate customers. The main aims of the consortium were to: (1) verify the experimental platform for multi-point videoconferencing, (2) use empirical tests to evaluate marketability, and (3) work toward the development of service-oriented applications. As a result of negotiations with corporate customers, the testing consortium was formed with the cooperation of about 30 companies. Thus, an important process for DOCOMO was to get certain customers to actually use the experimental service in business scenes, and then get the customers corporation with opinions and surveys on a range of issues such as usability, complaints and desires regarding the service.

At the time, using prototypes in this way and experimenting with the involvement of users was a first for DOCOMO (a novel situation with high uncertainty and so forth – an example of Domain II in the Capabilities Map). Also, SC-c had to engage in close collaboration with the development department, the service planning project, and the corporate sales department who were closely liaising with customers (to directly get complaints and demands from customers). SC-c was formed by combining SC-a in DOCOMO to form a horizontally integrated network organization between customer companies and DOCOMO. Meanwhile, SC-b, which had joint developmental functions between DOCOMO and Mitsubishi, bridged SC-a in DOCOMO and SC-d in Mitsubishi to form a horizontally integrated network organization between customer companies, DOCOMO and Mitsubishi, as shown in Figure 3.6 (in other words, integration of multiple SC between the different companies of DOCOMO, Mitsubishi, and customers). This horizontally integrated network organization (networked SC) interlocked customer needs and market opinions, which contributed to the creation of knowledge as a news service concept. Thus, DOCOMO, by orchestrating co-specialized assets in SC-a through to SC-d in DOCOMO and Mitsubishi including customers, was able to bring about organizational capabilities for new horizontal integration for this development. In contrast to the vertically integrated integration capabilities in DOCOMO and Mitsubishi discussed earlier, this situation was enabled by horizontally integrated external integration capability between customers, DOCOMO and Mitsubishi.

From the above case, it can be seen that through the demonstration of both vertically and horizontally integrated organizational capabilities at DOCOMO and Mitsubishi the dynamic combination of internal and external integration capabilities gave rise to DC needed to achieve this new product and service development. DC refer to the ability of leaders in corporations to create innovative responses to a changing business environment. Teece et al. (1997) identify three key elements for the creation of DC:

- The coordination and integration of both internal and external activities.
- Learning, seen as "social and collective," is defined as the "repetition and, experimentation which enable tasks to be performed better and quicker."
- Reconfiguration and transformation, which is based on surveillance of market and technological environments and "the more frequently practiced, the more easily accomplished."

Accordingly, using DC to flexibly orchestrate assets both inside and outside of the company to respond to changing environments (markets), and simultaneously create environments (markets) to sustainably bring about competitiveness is also an important practical perspective. By configuring SC and network SC through rapid strategic non-routine activities both inside and outside of a company in response to changing markets, the company was able to drive the construction of business model concepts, prototyping and experimentation and so forth, which finally enabled the achievement of this target development.

These SC (SC – ToB or Col.oP) are informal networks (or intentionally formed as formal networks in some companies), that have dispersed autonomous characteristics (Kodama, 2007c), and at the same time tie together multiple formal organizations within a company (and within other companies) in certain contexts and create new knowledge through these kinds of chains of strategic non-routine activities – most of the behaviors in these communities are strategic non-routine actions. As discussed in Chapter 2, SC, as ToB and Col.oP, can be formal, project-based organizations (Kodama, 2007c), or informal organizations that span different organizations such as CFT. Moreover, SC themselves have strong dispersed autonomy, and tie together various activities which require the coordination of complex business within and between companies as in this case, and play the role of bringing about achievements through new asset orchestration. This then, is nothing other than the functions of DC.

Teece (2007, p.1336) identifies the importance of "achieving decentralization near decomposability" as a factor of "transforming" microfoundations. Because large corporations are involved in many businesses, decentralization is required for multiple organizational groups with special missions, such as general business departments (or business headquarters), company systems or functional organizations. In contrast, from the perspective of driving company-wide integrative strategies for overall optimization, not only should autonomy and dispersion be promoted through segmenting efficient and effective business domains or divisions of labor, but also integration between these different formal organizations is required to properly combined functional roles (Lawrence and Lorsch, 1967; Carlile, 2004). Autonomous dispersion drives creativity, whereas integration drives efficiency. In other words, it's important for companies to find a balance between autonomy and integration, and the so-called "near decomposability" (Simon, 2002) function is also required. The organizational engine that brings about this balance between autonomy and integration is the ability to build SC and network SC (Kodama, 2004), and the organizational capabilities discussed here, which play the role of orchestrating the intangible assets (co-specialized assets) of multiple SC dispersed in and out of a company.

One of the requirements of innovative companies in the 21st century is orchestration of the characteristics of formal organizations and informal networks (organizations). By demonstrating strong DC, informal networks can maintain creativity and flexibility when corporate vision is externalized in specific non-routine strategic practice. In contrast, formal organizations maintain efficiency and precision in executing routine business through the demonstration of strong OC. Formal and informal organization must thus be used selectively to respond to situations to adapt to environmental uncertainty and the key here is to be able to flexibly change or improvise the structure of organizations (whether they be formal or informal) as required. In other words, in the Domains in the Capabilities Map in Figure 2.6 in Chapter 2, companies selectively use, combine and integrate

DC and OC to enable the demonstration of strategic innovation capabilities and strategic innovation loops.

One company that currently gains a lot of attention for its world-leading innovation business is undeniably Apple of the United States. Regarding its business systems that bring about innovations, the late Steve Jobs left us with the idea that "the mechanism has no mechanism" saying "there is no system. That doesn't mean we don't have process. Apple is a very disciplined company, and we have great processes. But that's not what it's about. Process makes you more efficient." and on bringing about innovation said:

> But innovation comes from people meeting up in the hallways or calling each other at 10:30 at night with a new idea, or because they realized something that shoots holes in how we've been thinking about a problem. It's ad hoc meetings of six people called by someone who thinks he has figured out the coolest new thing ever and who wants to know what other people think of his idea. (Burrows, 2004)

Jobs spoke of how innovations were born through these types of situations and discussions.

In addition, Teece (2012b, p.1399) had the following to say about Jobs' comments, suggesting that these non-routine strategizing and entrepreneurial activities are an important factor of DC:

> Jobs' description succinctly illustrates the theories advanced here. He seemed to say that, while Apple's ordinary capabilities are based in processes, its product development is several parts routine but at least one part "something else". The something else is non-routine strategizing and entrepreneurial activity, some of which might appear rather ad hoc. Apple's success appears to have stemmed in part from Jobs' prioritization of possibilities based on his deep understanding of the market and an uncompromising insistence on ease of use and appealing design. This approach can be routinized to some extent (the organization comes to know what Steve likes) but Apple and its customers unquestionably benefited from the touch of a creative and brilliant conceiver of new (categories of) electronics products that appeal to consumers around the world.

Once again, as discussed in Chapter 2, DC are mainly demonstrated in strategic non-routine activities in the informal organizations (networks) of SC.

Real innovation is achieved by striking a balance between efficiency and creativity. Decision-making rules, strict regulations and routines in formal organizations in companies bring efficiency to routines (the so-called OC factors). In contrast, as creativity, ideas for innovations are mainly brought about through non-routine interactions between human beings in informal human networks, in other words informal organizations (the so-called DC factors). Put differently, creativity emerges in dynamic and diverse non-routine practices between humans through non-continuous trial and error that has departed from efficient processes.

The cases of Sony (Box 3.1) and DOCOMO (Box 3.2) described later are cases of achieving innovations through the orchestration of co-specialized assets in the informal networks (ToB), through organizational capabilities to skillfully select formal or informal organizations (informal networks), and flexibly change or improvise organizational structures (between formal and informal).

3.4.3 Technology Capabilities

Technology capabilities is an important factor to achieve "systemic innovation" (Teece, 2000). New products, services and business models through integration and convergence of different technologies, or the Apple iPhone as architectural innovations that fuse hardware and software are good examples of orchestrating co-specialized assets through technological capabilities. With their developmental policy of unifying hardware and software (in other words, strengthening mutually dependent relationships and bundling, rather than modularizing individual technical elements), Apple has maintained a uniform identity since its foundation, while orchestrating its co-specialized assets with its technological capabilities that are difficult for other companies to imitate has enabled the company to bring about numerous new products.

Teece (2007, 2000) points out the importance of building, aligning and adapting co-specialized assets in platform products such as Apple iTMS or DRM, and wide-ranging digital products such as iPod, precision components, diesel-electric locomotives and aircraft. With iPod and so forth, Apple used its sensing functions to detect latent market needs, and used its technology capabilities to orchestrate unique designs of components comprising the best co-specialized assets around the world. Integrating co-specialized assets through technology capabilities is an extremely important factor in the high-tech field, which requires "capabilities congruence," in other words "fit" with the other elements of capabilities of (1) strategy capabilities, (2) organization capabilities, (3) operational capabilities, and (4) leadership capabilities to achieve co-specialization of intangible assets related to these kinds of technologies. In relation to this, the author discusses Sony (Box 3.1) and DOCOMO (Box 3.2) below.

3.4.4 Operational Capabilities

As discussed, operational capabilities do not have the same meaning as capabilities for regular routine activity (OC), and are capabilities that bring about (or create) new operational processes. For example automation of manufacturing processes including ICT developments promoted by Fanuc and Canon of Japan brought about intangible assets that are difficult to copy with automated production systems and business processes, which also in turn led to operational capabilities through orchestration of co-specialized assets at Fanuc and Canon.

As a brief discussion of the relationship of ICT with such operational capabilities, Dell sells PCs online, but relies on many external companies for the PC components manufacturer. Dell has to procure parts optimized to individual consumer needs and manufacturer PCs at low cost. However, Dell simultaneously pursues the advantages of efficiency through vertical disintegration with outsourcing in its business activities, and the advantages of close-knit coordination activities through vertical integration.

For efficient assembling of PCs to meet its individual customer orders at Dell, external companies produce the required parts at the required time and deliver them to the Dell assembly plant (there are five around the world) in a timely manner, which enables the company to reduce the amount of parts it has to hold in stock. Dell uses ICT to create inter-organization networks to promote close sharing of information about the company's consumer-oriented mass customization and corporate customer solution businesses, and also share information and knowledge in real-time with component manufacturers to reduce coordination costs and maintain supply chain efficiency.

In particular, the company configures close-knit ToB with component manufacturers and tight networks with certain corporate customers to collect information on customer needs in a timely manner and improve the quality of services, and hence promotes the sharing of information, contexts and knowledge. In general, close coordination is possible with vertical integration in manufacturing organizations to develop and manufacture parts or completed products, however Dell, in conjunction with its characteristic ICT use and strategic outsourcing partners, is able to reduce its governance costs as well as maintain quality in coordinating tasks by promoting the sharing of contexts and information between different companies. As in the Dell case, orchestration of the ICT development as co-specialized assets and co-specialized operational processes in the company to respond to changes bring about operational capabilities and create vertical boundaries as optimized value chains.

3.4.5 Leadership Capabilities

Toyota Motors is a good example of leadership capabilities. Toyota has multi-layered LT as ToB consisting of core staff members (leader class at all management levels) at all management levels (groups, sections, departments, divisions and the executive in administrative and headquarters sections) within the company. LT at group and section levels regularly engaged in finding solutions to chronic and technical problems, while LT at the section or department director level work to generate general solutions that can be universally applied, rather than only solutions to individual problems. LT at the executive level engage in activities related to initiatives for new global manufacturing systems, raising the level of linkages between departments, and the creation of advanced technologies. The company also has joint total task management teams that include its suppliers in Japan and around the world (keiretsu/non-keiretsu) and LT networks that engage in activities to ensure high reliability of products.

At Toyota, these LT are not only formed among the technical departments, but are total LT networks that span sales, development and design, manufacture and administration (13 departments in all) to enable the company to continually provide even better motor vehicles to its customers. Moreover, there are individual LT networks in layers between administration departments at HQ (technical management, production management, procurement management, sales management, information technology, quality assurance), and the company's back-office departments (general planning, total quality management (TQM) promotion, advertising and PR, safety, hygiene, environment, external affairs, finances, accounting, overseas businesses, personnel and general affairs) which the company combines for partial and total optimization by organically networking LT while invigorating resources and capabilities in the company (Amasaka, 2004). At Toyota, there are layered LT networks at various management levels that include external partners. These individual LT have unique co-specialized assets, and the LT networks are formulated to orchestrate these co-specialized assets. As mentioned, the formation of these LT is an important factor in bringing about organizational capabilities to drive the asset orchestration process through networked SC.

In Fanuc and Canon, companies that are highly selective about their technical developments, manufacturing is driven with unity between development and design, production technologies and manufacturing. There are multiple, multi-layered LT unified within the company as its product planning group, product development group, production technology group, and manufacturing group, and Fanuc and Canon pursue overall optimization of their businesses by layering these LT in their management hierarchy.

LT ensure creativity and flexibility when the company vision is externalized in particular business or when solutions to new problems need to be found. In addition, LT layering ensures efficiency, speed and quick decision with business to respond to changes in the environment. Particularly, by changing the corporate boundaries (vertical and horizontal boundaries) to respond to environmental uncertainties, LT layering can be selected for bureaucracy or network (networked LT), to bring about and maximize synergies between the characteristics of the two. Here, the key is executing strategy-making processes to change or improvise networked LT flexibly. Combining this creativity and efficiency is also enabled by orchestrating of the co-specialized assets of each LT, the core process of DC.

In networked LT, thorough understanding of problems and issues is promoted through creative dialogue among practitioners across different organizations and areas of specialization in which practitioners mutually understand each other's roles and value through mutual coordination and collaboration. As a result, practitioners are enabled to turn the various conflicts that emerge among themselves into constructive conflicts. Such positive behavior among practitioners is a factor in raising the potential for constructive and productive solutions as "capabilities abrasion and friction hindering capabilities congruence" discussed in section 3.7. In this process, practitioners require patterns of thinking and action that entail asking themselves the question "what actions should I take, with what strategies and tactics, and what will I contribute to the company innovation by doing so?" Creative dialogue combining self-assertiveness and humility is required. As well as that, the CEO, who is the final decision maker must at times demonstrate top-down leadership while simultaneously reinforcing linkages for close collaboration between company heads and management leaders by maximizing synergies of leadership coherence, which is the co-specialized assets of management leaders intentionally brought about by creative dialogue and discussions in LT.

As described above, for a company to grow sustainably, it must mobilize, align, and reconfigure intangible assets (including co-specialized and complementary assets) both inside and outside of the company to adapt to dynamic environments. Thus, by orchestrating this diversity of co-specialized assets a company can bring about intangible assets as the unique corporate signature processes of "(1) strategy capabilities, (2) organizational capabilities, (3) technology capabilities, (4) operational capabilities, (5) leadership capabilities," to realize congruence between these capabilities and external environments (ecosystems covering a wide range of customers, partners and so forth). Moreover, by driving co-specialization of these five capabilities with other capabilities, strong DC will function in the corporate system.

Teece (2014, pp.335–336) analyzed "strategic fit" in terms of existing strategy and organizational theories as follows:

> The potential transformation envisioned when an enterprise has strong dynamic capabilities goes beyond narrow notions of "strategic fit" seen as optimal in the "adaptation" school of organizational change research. That school sees the environment as exogenous. Teece (2007) and Sirmon, Hitt, and Ireland (2007) emphasized a "fit" that is far broader and embraces (1) the firm's internal processes, (2) partners, (3) customers, and (4) the business environment. Achieving tight "fit" with all four is likely to require strong dynamic capabilities.

Interpreting this perspective further, to achieve strong DC, not only is "strategic fit" over a narrow range required, but "fit" over a wide range beyond mutual co-specialization with five capabilities is required to bring about strong congruence (see Figure 3.6). By orchestrating co-specialized assets through strong DC, a company will achieve capabilities congruence (internal and external consistency in capabilities) (Insight-1 and Insight-2).

As is also described in the case study of Cisco (Chapter 5), strategic collaboration inside and outside of the company including its M&A strategy leading to a congruence model, also describes the internal congruence with these five capabilities (see Chapter 5).

3.5   CORPORATE BOUNDARIES, ASSET ORCHESTRATION, CAPABILITIES CONGRUENCE

As described, companies have to constantly strengthen their strategic positions by actively and dynamically changing their corporate governance structures and corporate boundaries in changing environments (or in environments that they themselves have created). Research to date on corporate boundaries describes corporate governance structures and corporate boundaries decision-making as dependent on various factors in various perspectives such as transaction costs, capabilities, competences and identities. Thus, in building value chains as strategic objectives, decision-making about what type of business activity should be carried out within a company, or what type of resources should be accessed externally through what type of agreements in the market are elements of corporate strategy that are important not only

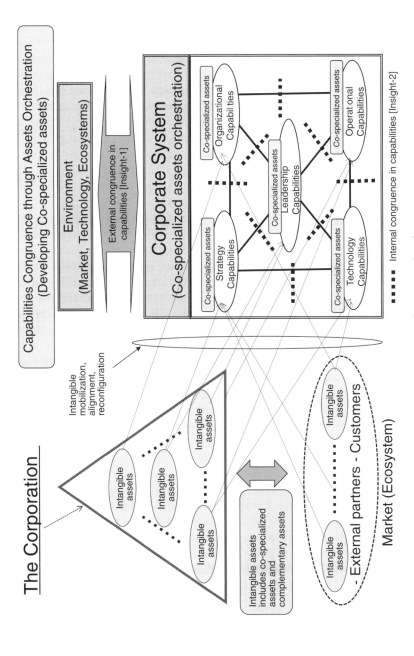

Figure 3.6   Capabilities congruence through orchestration of co-specialized assets

for large corporations but for ventures also (e.g., Pisano, 1991; Kodama, 2009a).

Santos and Eisenhardt (2005) described decisions about corporate boundaries as being characterized by four factors (efficiency, power, competence and identity). In corporate activities, these four factors, those of cost (efficiency), autonomy (power), growth (competence) and consistency (identity) are basic business issues that managers must question, and are serious issues that determine corporate boundaries. Particularly, in reducing costs in recent years, determining corporate boundaries by strategic outsourcing has become even more prevalent as a way of making corporate activity more efficient. Also, the keiretsu networks typical of the auto industry and rooted in long-term trust with contractor companies promote influence through power in corporate activities as well as autonomy for subcontractor companies.

In addition, the following can be said from research implications regarding competence identified by Santos and Eisenhardt (2005). Decisions about these corporate boundaries, boundaries conception through the creativity views centered on corporate leaders (Kodama, 2009a), drive self-creation for the creation of new business and expansion of business territory, competitiveness (creative abilities) through orchestration of co-specialized assets, which ties in with the achievements of strategies for corporate creativity over the long term. In deciding these corporate (organizational) boundaries, it's important in business to define the boundaries between the company (organization) and the environment to create, develop and grow new business ecosystems.

Furthermore in recent years, the smartphone, mobile phone application, content, game and semiconductor foundry business models have become characterized by the creation of new environments as business ecosystems through co-evolution processes with stakeholders, which has had massive impacts on the boundaries between many businesses and industries. For all of these industries and stakeholders, boundary conceptions with the "dialectic view" (Kodama, 2009a) centered on leader companies and main follower companies combine competition and cooperation (strategic synergies, or demonstration of strategy capabilities, described above), and through orchestration of co-specialized assets bring about innovations to expand markets. The five factors of boundary conceptions, efficiency, resources, value, creativity and the dialectic, are management drivers that determine corporate boundaries (vertical and horizontal) (Kodama, 2009a).

In considering congruence between the corporation and the environment in this way, from the perspective of how to dynamically change corporate boundaries and apply them to the environments of ecosystems that have already been created (or creating new environments as ecosystems, see Figure 3.2) these are important issues in executing corporate strategy. In other words, this is the importance of dynamic congruence between environments (ecosystems) and corporate systems. Accordingly, companies have to optimally design their vertical (value chains to achieve strategic objectives) and horizontal (diversification to expand business domains) boundaries to set down and achieve strategic objectives with sustainably competitive products, services and business models. To manage corporate boundaries with congruence with the environments of ecosystems (external congruence in capabilities) (Insight-1), management optimized through "capabilities congruence" (internal congruence in capabilities) (Insight-2) within a corporate system consisting of the capabilities factors of (1) strategy capabilities, (2) organizational capabilities, (3) technology capabilities, (4) operational capabilities, and (5) leadership capabilities is required (see Figure 3.7).

To achieve this, as mentioned, the most important factors are capabilities congruence (dynamic internal congruence, capabilities congruence within subsystems) between each capability in a corporate system and capabilities congruence (dynamic external congruence) between the corporate system and markets (ecosystems) achieved by orchestrating co-specialized assets through internal capabilities networks and external capabilities networks both in and out of the company. Hence, this refers to the importance of congruence both inside and outside of a company by orchestrating co-specialized assets, which is described by the new Insight-3 stated at the beginning of this book.

Repeating, to optimize a corporate system, partial and overall optimization (internal congruence in capabilities) between the individual capabilities of (1) strategy capabilities, (2) organizational capabilities, (3) technology capabilities, (4) operational capabilities and (5) leadership capabilities that make up the corporate system with the external environment of the ecosystem must be carried out. Optimization of a corporate system as an organic system in this way, or congruence with ecosystems and environments as "systems thinking" has a lot in common with the orchestration of co-specialized assets in the "dynamic capabilities framework" (Teece, 2007, 2014).

Next, the author describes specific cases of internal and external congruence in capabilities through orchestration of co-specialized assets both inside and outside of a company, they being the Sony PlayStation development (see Box 3.1) and strategy transformation at NTT DOCOMO (see Box 3.2).

The above two cases clarify how the function of orchestration realigning intangible assets (in particular, co-specialized assets) is an important

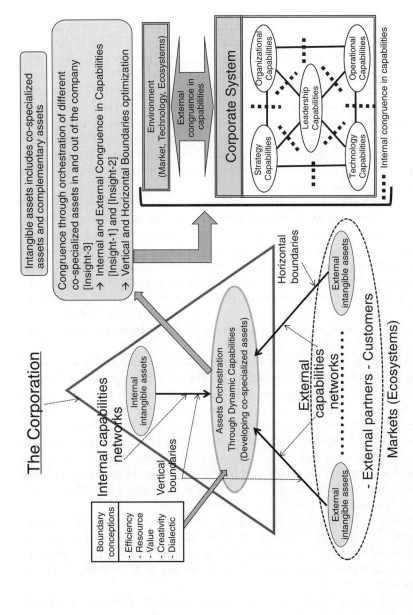

Figure 3.7 Corporate boundaries, assets orchestration, capabilities congruence

part of DC. Thus, in terms of planning and executing new products, services and business models, and selecting opportunities to invest in R&D, strategic alliances, strategic outsourcing and so forth, business persons in these two companies (including middle managers) were required to orchestrate new (and existing) intangible assets. Looking at this from the perspective of orchestrating co-specialized assets both inside and outside of a company, these two companies achieved, through the demonstration of DC, vertical and horizontal boundaries optimization while achieving internal and external congruence in capabilities (Insight-1 and Insight-2), and achieved congruence through orchestrating different co-specialized assets inside and outside of themselves (Insight-3) (see Figure 3.7).

The first of these new insights common to all three of these companies shows how each company mobilized the diverse intangible assets (capabilities) both inside and outside of the company, including those of customers, and achieved new strategic innovation and strategy transformation. This is an attempt to offer a new contribution to the knowledge of existing research, such as open innovation (Chesbrough, 2003, 2006), hybrid innovation (Kodama, 2012, 2014), and the theory of corporate and organization boundaries (e.g., Santos and Eisenhardt, 2005; Kodama, 2009a).

BOX 3.1   THE SONY PLAYSTATION DEVELOPMENT

Sony's strategy to conquer the game market is not only an example of successful product development, but is also a case of successful tight-knit linking between innovative marketing and technical strategies. From an organizational behavior perspective, innovative practitioners engaged in trial and error across knowledge boundaries between different industries and organizations, and between different areas of specialty, to uncover a new business concept for the game market and do a thorough job of making it a reality. Behind the SCE success lay the company's achievement of congruence between the corporate system and the environment (Insight-1), and congruence between individual capabilities within the corporate system (Insight-2) through congruence enabled by orchestration of co-specialized assets both inside and outside of the company (Insight-3) (see Figure 3.8).

Executing congruence between these capabilities – strategy, technology, operational and organizational capabilities – was enabled by the leadership of innovative practitioners centered on SCE, and the demonstration of their leadership capabilities centered on LT in the company brought about synergies among their mutual capabilities. The leadership of these leaders (top and middle management) successfully created win–win relationships among stakeholders by creating a new game market both inside and outside the company with the PlayStation, through orchestration of co-specialized assets.

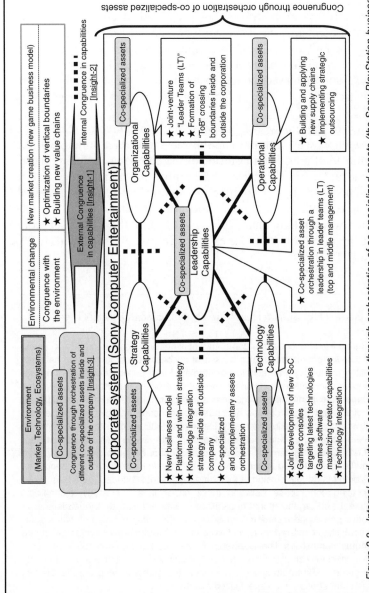

Congruence through orchestration of co-specialized assets

Environment (Market, Technology, Ecosystems)

Co-specialized assets

Congruence through orchestration of different co-specialized assets inside and outside of the company [Insight-3]

Environmental change	New market creation (new game business model)
Congruence with the environment	★ Optimization of vertical boundaries ★ Building new value chains

External Congruence in capabilities [Insight-1]

Internal Congruence in capabilities [Insight-2]

[Corporate system (Sony Computer Entertainment)]

Co-specialized assets — **Organizational Capabilities**

★ Joint-venture
★ "Leader Teams (LT)"
★ Formation of "ToB" crossing boundaries inside and outside the corporation

Co-specialized assets — **Operational Capabilities**

★ Building and applying new supply chains
★ Implementing strategic outsourcing

Co-specialized assets **Leadership Capabilities**

Co-specialized asset orchestration through a leadership in leader teams (LT) (top and middle management)

Co-specialized assets — **Strategy Capabilities**

★ New business model
★ Platform and win–win strategy
★ Knowledge integration strategy inside and outside company
★ Co-specialized and complementary assets orchestration

Co-specialized assets — **Technology Capabilities**

★ Joint development of new SoC
★ Games consoles targeting latest technologies
★ Games software maximizing creator capabilities
★ Technology integration

Figure 3.8 Internal and external congruence through orchestration of co-specialized assets (the Sony PlayStation business model development)

88

BOX 3.2   STRATEGY TRANSFORMATION AT NTT DOCOMO:
THE STRATEGIC SHIFT FROM TELEPHONE
SERVICES TO THE INTERNET

In this case, the author analyzes how a company achieves strategy transformation through capabilities congruence in the processes of evolving strategies. NTT DOCOMO (DOCOMO hereinafter) is the largest mobile communications carrier in Japan, and to strategically shift its telephone services to the Internet, the company achieved congruence between its corporate system and the environment (Insight-1) and congruence among individual capabilities in its corporate system (Insight-2) through congruence achieved by orchestrating co-specialized assets in and out of the company (Insight-3). In this strategy change, DOCOMO brought dynamic change to its renewed strategy processes (see Figure 3.9).

In the first period of this change, DOCOMO embarked on a new environment creation strategy both technically and marketwise in the Japanese mobile phone market, which at that time had almost no penetration, to create a value chain in the mobile telephone market and lead its competitor companies.

In the second period, the strategic transformation required a big shift by DOCOMO as the voice communications market had become dangerously saturated, and was the phase in which DOCOMO embarked on the creation, popularization and embedding of the new market for mobile phone Internet services (i-mode) (this strategy transformation corresponds to Shift B, or capabilities threats and capabilities opportunities moving from Domain III to Domain I in Figure 2.5) Differing from the first period, at this time DOCOMO required dynamic changes to strategy processes to bring congruence to different environments and the corporate system (Insight-1), and congruence between individual capabilities in the corporate system (Insight-2). For this, renewal of congruence through asset orchestration both inside and outside of the company was required (Insight-3).

Differing from the first period, DOCOMO redefined its vertical corporate boundaries, built a vertically integrated value chain to lead ahead of competitor companies through orchestrating the co-specialized assets of new stakeholders such as contents and applications providers (executing a platform strategy through strategy capabilities), optimized its vertical boundaries as corporate system, and dynamically brought congruence to changing environments.

In the second period, in bringing congruence between the capabilities of strategy, technology, operations and organizations, the leadership required by DOCOMO was not only the strong leadership demonstrated by DOCOMO's second CEO Tachikawa (succeeding Oboshi) but also the leadership forms centered on the in-house LT of middle managers demonstrating leadership capabilities following on from the corporate culture of DOCOMO in the first period. However at the same time, the orchestration of the co-specialized assets of external stakeholders by DOCOMO presenting its vision to many external partners upon configuring the new vertically integrated value chain to create a new market for i-mode was also a critical issue.

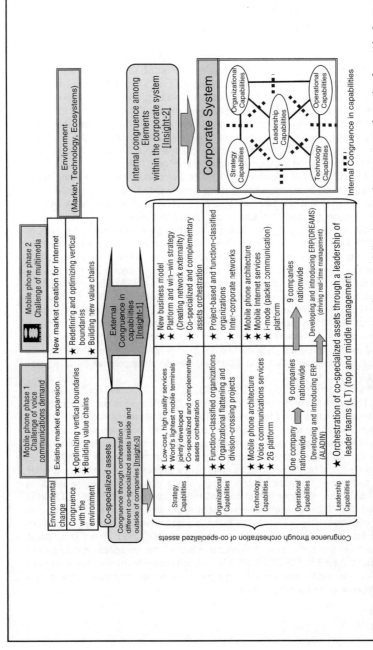

Figure 3.9 Internal and external congruence through orchestration of co-specialized assets (strategy transformation from telephones to Internet at NTT DOCOMO)

The orchestration of varied intangible assets (co-specialized assets and complementary assets) through the configuring of internal and external capabilities networks by large corporations across different businesses and industries, including markets, not only has the potential to create new markets as business ecosystems through exploration, but can also achieve thorough efficiency in management of existing business operations.

Insight-3 highlights congruence through orchestration of different capabilities in and out of the company (co-specialized assets), but also points to the requirements for generating new strategic innovation by driving congruence with corporate capabilities and environment (Insight-1), and capabilities congruence within companies (Insight-2). Moreover, dynamic organizational forms (for example, SC, ToB, networked ToB) that include potential partner companies and powerful corporate customers enable the creation of new capabilities to generate, develop and maintain business ecosystems. Going forward, there will come a greater need to explore congruence through orchestration between different capabilities (co-specialized assets) (Insight-3), both at the macro and micro levels in the value chains broadly spanning between companies and industries, and across entire business ecosystems.

The second new insight common to these two companies describes the existence of "entrepreneurial management" required to demonstrate DC. As described by Teece (2007, p.1346), "Entrepreneurship is about sensing and understanding opportunities, getting things started, and finding new and better ways of putting things together. It is about creatively coordinating the assembly of disparate and usually cospecialized elements, getting 'approvals' for non-routine activities, and sensing business opportunities." Thus, to create new markets, these two companies orchestrated co-specialized assets through entrepreneurial strategies and environment creation strategies enacted through informal networks (informal organizations – ToB and networked ToB) formed by teams of top managers (LT) and leading middle managers.

3.6 INTERNAL AND EXTERNAL CONGRUENCE IN CAPABILITIES IN THE CAPABILITIES MAP

Internal and external congruence in capabilities in the Capabilities Map is brought to each domain. Asset orchestration through DC is important in Domains I to III. As discussed in Chapter 2, the weight on the sensing, seizing and transforming functions is different in each domain (see Figure 3.10).

For example, the role of sensing in Domain I is particularly important.

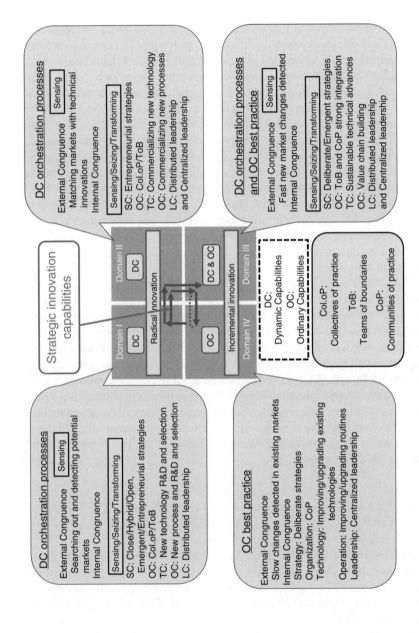

Figure 3.10   Internal and external congruence in the Capabilities Map

Sensing enables R&D organizations in large corporations to seek out and detect potential new markets, while the setting down of plans for R&D over the mid to long term in R&D organizations is enabled by sensing and transforming. Here, congruence is executed between the strategy capabilities, technology capabilities, organizational capabilities, operational capabilities, and leadership capabilities. As leadership capabilities, autonomous, distributed leadership (Kodama, 2004) for selection of new technologies and processes, and R&D, is mainly performed in organizations such as Col.oP or ToB, in which members bring congruence in capabilities in Domain I by pursuing either closed, hybrid or open innovation strategies through emergent and entrepreneurial strategies.

Furthermore, the role of seizing in departments involved with commercial developments on the business side in Domain II is particularly important. In departments involved in commercial development, sensing is performed to match markets and technical innovations, while seizing and transforming are performed to develop and commercialize new businesses, technologies and processes. Thus, Col.oP and ToB mainly pursue entrepreneurial strategies, and execute congruence in capabilities in Domain II. Here, the big difference with Domain I is, as leadership capabilities, not only the distributed leadership that mainly pursues emergence strategies in the development workplace, but also the execution of suitable decision-making processes for commercialization through organizationally integrated centralized leadership (Kodama, 2004) under basic policies of disciplined imagination and creativity (Kodama, 2007a), to bring congruence in capabilities in Domain II.

Also, the role of transforming at the business side is critical when environmental changes are rapid and competition is severe in Domain III. Particularly, departments involved in product planning and technical development at the business side have to use sensing to detect changes in new markets, and have to establish robust value chains by sustainably advancing technologies through seizing and transforming to upgrade and improve new businesses shifting from Domain II. As discussed in Chapter 2, in Domain III, strong integration of DC and OC is required through strong collaboration between ToB with responsibilities upstream in value chains and communities of practice (CoP) with responsibilities downstream in value chains. ToB, consisting of product planning departments and technical development departments pursue emergence strategies guided by close relationships with customers in the workplace, by demonstrating mainly strong DC to bring about upgrades to new products and businesses as rapid incremental innovation, whereas CoP consisting of departments involved with sales, production and support pursue deliberate strategies through operational management with strong OC to bring about congruence in capabilities in Domain III. Similar to Domain II, congruence in capabilities in Domain III is brought about by decision-making processes through leadership capabilities for distributed leadership pursuing emergence strategies mainly in the developmental workplace as well as centralized leadership driving deliberate strategies based on strict business planning and top-down management.

As discussed in Chapter 2, differing from the above three domains, the weight of DC in Domain IV is lower, and mainly best practices are demonstrated through OC. While simultaneously pursuing external congruence, strict, top-down centralized leadership in traditional existing organizations (business units and so forth) achieves internal congruence with strong OC by using path-dependent, planned and carefully considered deliberate strategies, organization structure consisting of formal organizations and CoP, existing technologies and operations, to gently innovate incrementally when existing market changes are detected to be soft.

As described above, dynamic internal and external congruence in capabilities is required in multiple Capabilities Maps in large corporations for the existence and development of a wide range of businesses. Here, the author would like to consider various interactions between multiple Capabilities Maps.

3.7   CAPABILITIES ABRASION AND FRICTION HINDERING CAPABILITIES CONGRUENCE

Large corporations simultaneously proceed with multiple businesses (products, services, and so on) that all have different characteristics, and these multiple businesses require different capabilities (in other words, different DC). In short, there are different and multi-layered Capabilities Maps that exist in large corporations, as described in Figure 3.10. Therefore, how do large corporations bring about diverse capabilities in these multiple Capabilities Maps, and how do large companies manage the diverse interactions between these multiple Capabilities Maps at the macro and micro levels?

First, there is a relationship between the Capabilities Map of the entire system of a large company and Capabilities Maps of its subsystems – those of its individual enterprises (business units). Specifically, how do these individual subsystem Capabilities Maps (DC and strategic innovation capabilities in individual domains) affect the Capabilities Map of the entire corporation (the whole system), and hence, its strategic innovation capabilities? Second, large companies have to appropriately and dynamically manage different DC in their various individual enterprises in their multiple Capabilities Maps, with all their different characteristics, to respond to changes in environments through time (uncertainties and speed). They must demonstrate strategic innovation capabilities to combine exploration and exploitation. Therefore what business elements do corporations need at their macro and micro levels to execute these?

In addition, in the DC suggested by Teece (2007), seizing that executes strategic decision-making consists of enterprise structures, procedures, designs and incentives. This seizing is particularly important in Domain II in Figure 3.10. In this domain, where environmental changes are particularly fast, and risks and uncertainties are large, there is a high probability of sustainable business performance being influenced by the selection of products, services and business models to solve customer issues. It's possible for new technologies and services to temporarily expand corporate performance, but for long-term sustainable growth, new business models must be selected that are in alignment with that aim. Furthermore, in selecting decision-making protocols, there is a tendency for large traditional corporations with bureaucratic organizational characteristics to fall into organizational rigidity. This is because organizational members have to accept beliefs and philosophies of management based on the entrepreneurship at the time of founding the business, which may make it difficult to bring about creative activities. Hence, selections that hinder innovation are not desirable for large corporations.

Despite that, there are plenty of cases where innovation has been hindered in large corporations. This is because, at a glance, the more different the characteristics of the multiple business enterprises that a corporation has to simultaneously run, the greater the shackle they are to strategy transformation or radical innovation. As identified by Teece (2007), specifically, often "batting and cannibalization" of businesses is observed in big corporations between their existing businesses (existing products and services) and new businesses (new products services and business models), or within the same business units or between different business units.

Teece (2007, p.1327) said the following:

> But innovation is often ill served by such structures, as the new and the radical will almost always appear threatening to some constituents. Strong leaders can frequently overcome such tendencies, but such leaders are not always present. One consequence is a "program persistence bias." Its corollary is various forms of "anti-innovation bias," including the "anticannibalization" bias discussed in a later section.

Also, often observed are mainstream capabilities in existing organizations that nip new potential organizational capabilities in the bud, and unproductive abrasion and friction between different capabilities that stifle potential for new innovation. This is mainly because there is often organizational superiority and pressure from in-house political power in a company originating in the negotiations regarding distribution of resources within or between business units or the advantages of its main businesses. As described by the case in Box 3.1, the Sony PlayStation development is a good example of success enabled by Sony configuring a new "breakout" structure (Teece, 2000). The i-mode commercialization by NTT DOCOMO (Box 3.2) is also an example of a similar new "breakout" structure (discussed later).

When a joint development agreement with Nintendo to develop the next generation gaming devices collapsed, Sony took an independent path with its game business development project. However, at the time, there was strong opposition to the gaming business within Sony (including its managers). Differing from audio and visual businesses, the game industry has a completely different culture, and since Sony was a number one brand in the audio and visual world, many questioned why it was necessary to purposely venture into the world of games, which after all were merely toys. The father of the PlayStation, Ken Kutaragi, had extraordinary technical talents and foresight, but felt that he couldn't act due to conflict and friction between the various departments within Sony regarding his assertions and opinions, which even for Sony, was a situation not unusual in large Japanese corporations. Taking into account Kutaragi's situation, the CEO at the time, Norio Oga, made a decision.

Oga felt that if Kutaragi were left in Sony, he would most certainly be crushed by the other people in the company. Thus, Oga made a snap decision to lend some office space to Kutaragi and his development team at Sony Music Entertainment (SME), a subsidiary of Sony, to provide him with an environment in which he could proceed with the development. Although dissatisfaction was expressed within Sony regarding Oga's decision, he went ahead with it anyway. Micro strategy processes, as discussed in Chapter 9, enabled the achievement of external and internal congruence in capabilities which led to the success of the PlayStation development, through the micro strategy elements of who, what, and when, as described in Box 3.1.

Helfat et al. (2007, p.63) said the following:

> Hence, it seems important to give greater prominence to the importance of context – both in terms of time and place. In this respect, we are very much in line with perhaps the most robust idea in all of organizational science – the concept of fit. Resources are valuable when they fit the requirements of customers in a particular place (country, market, industry) and a particular time (yesterday, today, tomorrow).

Strictly speaking, the meaning of the "concept of fit" is different from "capabilities congruence," but Finkelstein suggests its importance as a micro strategy process for success in business.

Thus, regarding capabilities, negative interactions often occur at the micro and macro level between different Capabilities Maps, or within Capabilities Maps between different domains, and are phenomena that can seriously hinder capabilities congruence (capabilities optimization). In this book, these negative interactions between different capabilities are called "capabilities abrasion and friction" (see Figure 3.11).

However in contrast, integrating or matching different capabilities can also raise the potential to bring about new capabilities (e.g., Kodama, 2007a). Thus, it seems clear that large companies that successfully grow sustainably promote creative capabilities abrasion and productive capabilities friction in the capabilities interactions between different domains within Capabilities Maps and between different Capabilities Maps. As a result, these factors of creative capabilities abrasion and production capabilities friction can raise the potential for the success of the combination of exploitation with exploration through strategic innovation capabilities by driving external and internal congruence in capabilities through asset orchestration with DC in large corporations. The world's first shift from mobile telephone to Internet services described by the NTT DOCOMO case in Box 3.2 is a good example of this.

At the time, to develop the i-mode mobile phones and servers, DOCOMO had to link up the functional organizations of its development, engineering and facilities departments. However, in the beginning, these organizations had negative opinions about the service, and conflicts arose due to differences in thinking and opinion regarding the service between the members of the new i-mode project and people in other departments. Nevertheless, product planning project leader Keiichi Enoki stood on the front line and found healthy and productive solutions to these various conflicts and contradictions between the new project and other organizations, through collaboration and tenacious dialectical dialogue (Kodama, 2007a) to coordinate between the different departments. Thus, the new project members' strong sense of purpose toward making the i-mode service succeed based on their professional pride, and Enoki's leadership to orchestrate the members provided the energy to move in-house organizations.

Enoki demonstrated strong leadership to achieve the i-mode service by getting the understanding and agreement of the leaders of functional organizations, and established the Mobile Gateway Service Implementation Promotion Coordinating Committee within DOCOMO. This committee consisted of leaders from all departments in DOCOMO including the president and Enoki, and enabled the sharing of information and knowledge to achieve the i-mode service among managers at the top level, and was a positioning of ToB as time and space for dialogue and decision-making to drive business.

As well as that, centered on Enoki, six working groups (WG) were established by the project leaders of the new project consisting of middle management in the new project and other functional organizations (network server WG, mobile phone WG, facilities construction WG, facilities maintenance WG, systems and sales WG, and contents/application WG). These WG were CFT that engaged in dialogue and discussion to extract specific individual problems and issues with achieving the i-mode service. As well as that, the "Gateway service specifications study group" met on Tuesdays every week as a task force specially brought together to develop i-mode mobile phones and the i-mode servers, and decide upon service and technical specifications to achieve the i-mode service. Also, to drive dialogue and collaboration within the new project organization itself, a regular meeting was held every Tuesday with participation from all members, to share information and knowledge among members of the new project, and hence enable sharing of values and awareness among all project members so that the i-mode service could be achieved.

At the core of the strategic capabilities that enabled the explosive growth of i-mode lay orchestration of co-specialized assets. The first of these co-specialized assets was the "portal strategy" and development of attractive new content that could be used with i-mode. The second of these co-specialized assets was the "terminal strategy" that enabled commercial development of new i-mode mobile phone terminals with new added functionality. The third of these co-specialized assets was the "platform strategy" that raised the level of convenience for both i-mode users and contents providers by providing authentication, billing, settlement and collection agency services. These three business strategies were mutually connected, and synergies were triggered by co-specialization.

In driving these business strategies, it was necessary to proactively promote strategic partnerships with external players to bring about specific results. As an organizational action that deserves attention, the new projects with individual partner corporations were born by DOCOMO presenting the new business strategies, and these external partners resonating with the strategies. In this way, DOCOMO purposefully engaged in strategic collaboration with its external partners. In this strategic collaboration, there was always engagement in creative dialogue (Kodama, 2007a) to spread and embed the mobile Internet culture, and bring about a new environment (markets and ecosystems). Thus, driving creative capabilities abrasion and productive capabilities friction enabled dialectical synthesis of various problems and issues which led to the generation of the new i-mode business concept. The DOCOMO case of strategy transformation shifting from telephone services to diversified Internet services was based on DC as the engine constantly driving creation, development and modification of the business model.

Thus the key to acquiring corporate value was sensing, seizing and transforming to select and execute the business model. In ICT companies like DOCOMO, it's important to form a platform of mutual dependence through which complementary partners can be managed, which requires the orchestration of co-specialized assets of those complementary partners. The management hierarchy at DOCOMO at the time, including the project leader, paid special attention to the ownership of the existing competitive resources (existing services such as the telephone service) and synergistic effects of decision-making biases. For this reason, DOCOMO had to skillfully coordinate the existing capabilities and management routines of its highly profitable businesses with these new capabilities (in other words combine exploitation and exploration), which required strong management leadership and leadership capabilities enabled by the formation of LT and networked LT between departments and across management hierarchies. Furthermore, for the success of DOCOMO's i-mode, the company had to execute the "three pronged strategy" described by Teece (2007, p.1329) (Chandler, 1990a, 1990b). In other words, DOCOMO engaged in (1) early and large-scale investments behind new technologies; (2) investment in product-specific marketing, distribution, and purchasing networks; and (3) recruiting and organizing the managers needed to supervise and coordinate functional activities, as important strategic activities that underpinned the success of the development.

As well as that, from the perspective of micro organizational structures, creative capabilities abrasion and productive capabilities friction as positive interactions in organizational forms (Col.oP, ToB and CoP) with different characteristics within and between domains promoted capabilities congruence (capabilities optimization) within and between domains, and hence reinforced the capabilities of the entire company. At the same time, with the shift between the domains, appropriate (optimum) change (switch) of these three types of dynamic organizational forms reinforced the congruence among the capabilities in DOCOMO (capabilities optimization), which has a positive effect on the creation of strategic innovation capabilities. Also, formal organizational structures brought about the success of DOCOMO i-mode,

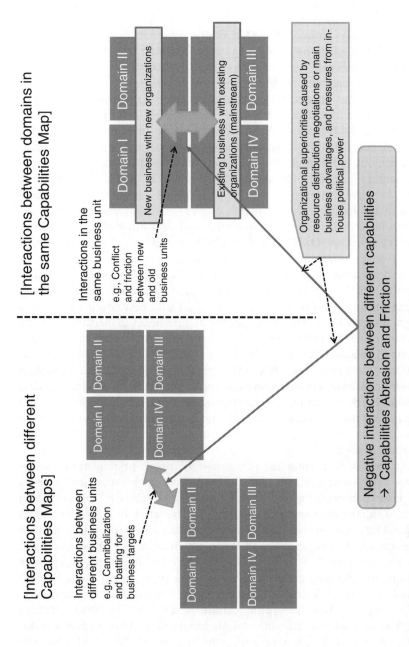

Figure 3.11   Capabilities abrasion and friction hindering capabilities congruence

characterized by the application of the "integrated organizations" (e.g., Kodama, 2003, 2004) discussed in Chapter 2. Integrated organizations, which are a combination of project-based organizations in which ToB are easily formed, and functional organizations in which CoP are easily formed bring about strong DC and OC through the strong interaction of ToB and CoP.

To advance research on micro strategy processes, the new insight into dynamically changing organizational forms that enable the interactions between different capabilities, the interactions between different organizations, and the creation of strategic innovation capabilities between different Capabilities Maps and between different domains within a Capabilities Map (described in detail in Chapter 9), must be further explored in future.

3.8 CHAPTER SUMMARY

This chapter has presented the concept of "capabilities congruence," which is a business factor in a large corporation that brings about sustainable growth over the long term by achieving strategic innovation as the corporation enacts DC and strategic innovation capabilities. From specific empirical data, the chapter has also clarified the importance of three insights about capabilities congruence (Insight-1: dynamic congruence between corporate capabilities (corporate systems) and environments; Insight-2: congruence between different capabilities within corporations (in corporate systems); Insight-3: congruence by orchestrating different co-specialized assets both in and out of corporations).

Moreover, the chapter has described how the more different the characteristics of the multiple business enterprises that a corporation has to simultaneously run, the greater the hindrance to strategy transformation or radical innovation, due to batting and cannibalization of business units. The chapter identified how the combination of exploitation and exploration is enabled through strategic innovation capabilities, by driving congruence of capabilities in large corporations through creative capabilities abrasion and productive capabilities friction in response to the negative interactions of abrasion and friction between different capabilities.

NOTE

1. The platform for the "M-Stage Visual Net" service has been selected on the 2003 R&D 100 Awards program (*R&D Magazine* in US) as one of the 100 most technologically

significant products introduced into the marketplace over the past year; see: https://www.rdmag.com/article/2010/08/2003-r-d-100-award-winners. The details of "M-Stage Visual Net" regarding the technologies and service are described in Kodama et al." (2002).

4. Apple versus Sony: strategy transformation by capabilities congruence through asset orchestration

Apple, a company that continuously brings about business innovations, achieved strategic innovation with its lineup of iPod, iPhone and iPad products and services enabled through convergence of diverse content and applications with a range of digital devices, based on the company's "Digital Hub" vision. Apple's redefining of its corporate boundaries to expand outwards from its Macintosh PC business into music distribution, smartphones and tablet PCs is also a good example of a corporate vision advancing for strategy transformation. In contrast, in spite of the fact that it had been way ahead of Apple with its successful commercialization of its "Walkman" portable music player, Sony lagged way behind in the music distribution business.

This chapter analyses the major differences in the strategic actions of Apple and Sony, and presents the capabilities congruence achieved through asset orchestration processes to mobilize the different capabilities both inside and outside of the company leading to the Apple success (with the iPod and iTunes music store, and later the iPhone and iPad). Also, as a micro organizational strategy at the company, behind the success of their new product developments, was the achievement of integration through asset orchestration processes enabled by the formation of strategic communities (SC) (and boundary networks) at Apple. In contrast, Sony lacked elements of capabilities congruence within its group companies, and failed to integrate its different capabilities. This chapter describes the five dynamic capabilities (DC) at Apple, and how Apple successfully achieved strategy transformation by bringing congruence between these capabilities.

4.1 APPLE STRATEGY CAPABILITIES AND TECHNOLOGY CAPABILITIES

Regarding the strategy transformation of Apple's shift to a music distribution company as described previously, this section describes the "strategy capabilities and technology capabilities" of the five basic elements of DC. The trigger of Apple's strategy transformation was Jobs' sensing, a core function of DC, which lead to the inspiration and discovery of new business. Jobs was warming to the idea of an online music store that brought together portable music players and content through iTunes that he had already developed. To this end, Jobs and his business team developed a music player with a unique and superior human interface that surpassed existing mobile music players, and thus satisfied his ambition to create a never-before-seen enterprise by seamlessly linking up this product with the already commercialized iTunes.

Right after announcing iTunes, the executives at Apple began studying the details of the music distribution business, and they began to get hints of a latent music distribution market. And what's more, they realized that they would be able to take advantage of the strengths of Apple to develop this market. In other words, this meant if they could deploy the product development capabilities of Apple to design a much easier to use interface, by dealing with all elements of product construction from hardware, OS, applications, software and design, the Apple executives including Jobs believe that they could develop a superior portable music player. These ideas and action were enabled by the sensing function of DC.

Leaders at Apple uncovered a new business model in the differing contexts and information relating to jukebox software, portable music players, musical content, Internet distribution, financial transactions and so on, and by seamlessly combining these co-specialized assets and engaging in asset orchestration to achieve a unique online music store (iTunes) that transcended the boundaries of different knowledge. From the perspective of strategy capabilities, as described in Table 3.1 in Chapter 3, Apple brought about a win–win synergy of strategies by creating the iTunes music store platform with its strategic (co-specialized/complementary) partners.

iPod and iTunes were achieved through the co-specialization of the product development and design capabilities of leaders in and out of Apple and technical capabilities spread around the globe. This was the music distribution business model that seamlessly linked the iPod hardware and software technologies with the iTunes software technologies. In the development of iPod and iTunes, Apple uncovered new co-specialization of its own intangible assets with those of other companies, while focusing on non-technical elements of marketing and design strategies to determine development themes, and executed the asset orchestration process to combine these co-specialized assets.

Specifically, for the iTunes development, this meant Apple purchasing the rights to the sound jam MP software developed by Jeffrey Robin et al. at Casady & Greene (the development team including Robin) on which iTunes was built, software that made it easier and simpler for users to read music from CDs, and encode, replay and manage their music. Furthermore, for its iPod development, Apple scouted for personnel with rich experience in planning and developing mobile music players. One of the key persons who later made a huge contribution to the iPod development was Anthony Fadell. It was his rich empirical knowledge in developing these technologies that contributed greatly to the creation of iPod – a revolutionary product. Hence, behind the success of iTunes and iPod was the significant influence of asset orchestration executed by leaders at Apple in bringing together excellent personnel. From the point of view of the congruent technology capabilities in Apple's strategy capabilities, Apple merged and integrated co-specialized technologies through the asset orchestration process with the aim of achieving new products, services and business models, by converging and integrating different technologies (co-specialized technologies) both inside and outside of the company.

Moreover, from the business ecosystem perspective, the iPod, and later the iPhone and iPad business developments entailed mobilizing the best external intangible assets of the knowledge ecosystems of a wide variety of different industries and customers including Apple's existing partner companies (EMS, parts developers, and so on), contents businesses (music, video, games, books, and so on) and the consumers that achieve a variety of application development as user innovations (and customers as innovators) (e.g., Von Hippel and Katz, 2002), through which the company brought about a new business model by orchestrating these external intangible assets with its own internal intangible assets, that is, its core knowledge (its product design capabilities, marketing capabilities, hardware and software development capabilities). Key to achieving this asset orchestration process was the forming of layered SC networks (networked SC, boundary networks) from the SC spanning the knowledge ecosystems centered on Apple. Taking diverse intangible assets from various dissimilar and dynamic contexts, Apple achieved a unique business model through the asset orchestration process between wide-ranging companies and industries, including customers, to accomplish its vision of absolute value (the digital hub concept) and its strategic objectives (to create customer value with new experiences) (see Figure 4.1).

Rather than only expand the vertical boundaries of its value chains

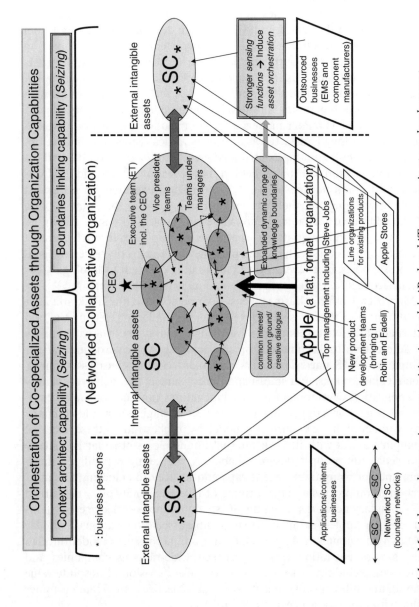

Figure 4.1   Multi-layered strategic communities in Apple's iPod and iTunes music store development

upstream and downstream (from product planning, developmental design to manufacture and sales), Apple achieved dynamic expansion of its horizontal boundaries into the unfamiliar domains of the music distribution and smartphone businesses. New product development at Apple entails team functioning, which not only involves SC of top management teams centered on Jobs or multi-layered collaboration SC between new product development teams (project organizations) (iPod/iPhone/iPad) with existing organizations (line organizations) within the company, but multi-layered networks involving these in-house SC, and SC involving the Apple Store – Apple's product sales and its marketing hub, and EMS companies focusing on manufacture and leading parts manufacturers, all of which make up the value chain of the Apple-centered business model. Apple also created SC with partners including content providers and application developers central to the creation of its new business domains to create value chains for its new businesses. The dynamic configuration of these multi-layered, vertically and horizontally spanned SC networks greatly contributed to the Apple asset orchestration process.

4.2   JOBS' DRIVING OF NEW PRODUCT CREATION STRATEGIES THROUGH NON-ROUTINE ENTREPRENEURIAL ACTIVITIES

This section discusses elements of DC through Jobs' non-routine strategic and entrepreneurial activities that drove the aforementioned strategy capabilities and technology capabilities.

Developing a new music distribution service, Jobs called upon Recording Industry Association of America CEO Hilary Rosen to meet in the role of consultant. After many corrections to draft proposals with Rosen and design engineers, the iTunes store was finally created. Jobs himself drove negotiations to persuade five major music labels to sell digitalized music. Jobs successfully secured contracts with five major music labels. Rosen believed there were two reasons why Jobs successfully persuaded the companies. As well as Jobs' strong will, there was a low perceived risk because of the small market share that Apple had.

So, why did Sony fail even though it had its hardware, software and content departments? (see Box 4.1). A system of independent profitability was adopted for each of Sony's departments. Hence, departments competed with each other without cooperating, which led to failure. In contrast, sections at Apple who did not cooperate in-house got fired. Another reason for Sony's failure was the fear that if a music player and service were created, it would impact on the sales of the record division, which could

BOX 4.1   SONY'S LACK OF DYNAMIC CAPABILITIES
           LEADING TO FAILURE IN THE MUSIC
           DISTRIBUTION BUSINESS

Sony has the so-called conglomerate archetype. Sony Corporation has formed group of businesses, and encompasses subsidiary businesses such as its original electronics business, entertainment (music, games and the arts), finance (banking and insurance) distribution and businesses in other fields. Linking all these different businesses together should produce synergistic effects which should demonstrate the unique strengths of the company, strengths that cannot be impersonated by competitive companies. However, in the music distribution business, these group companies did not partner well, and lagged behind as they slowed each other down. Adjusting the stakes of these group companies, in particular its consumer electronics division and music division (Sony Music Entertainment), was heavy going. This can be seen in the following comments made by Sony Computer Entertainment chief Ken Kutaragi, father of the PlayStation, on the occasion of his announcement of the downward revision of Sony's quarterly business results:

> For some years, staff at Sony, including me, have felt annoyed by the attitude of the management (excluding me) not to bring out a product like the Apple iPod. Their (Sony's) negative reasoning was due to concerns they held about the music and movie divisions protecting content copyrights. Due to these worries, the original entrepreneurial spirit of Sony as a producer of innovative technologies ended up becoming rarefied. (Kutaragi, 2005)

Behind Sony's failure of its music and movie divisions to develop a business like iPod + iTunes + iTunes music store was its fear of pirated versions in the MP3 format. There were more than a billion pirated music files (MP3 files) being swapped at no charge on the Internet every month. However, almost all of the portable music players including the iPod were capable of loading these MP3 files and replaying them. It was not possible to follow legal regulations and listen to all the files developed by different companies in the same industry such as the Apple AAC, the Microsoft WMA, and the Sony ATRAC3 formats, but it was possible to listen to the pirated music versions. Looking at this from the point of view of the music labels, this was an unacceptable reality.

In contrast, the portable digital music player manufacturers had to build devices that could replay MP3 files, because currently, most of the digital music that is out there in the world is in the MP3 format, hence users wouldn't buy devices that can't play MP3 files. That's because the free file sharing market was huge. Actually, at that time, even though iTunes music store had sold a billion songs, it was a tiny amount compared to that of the free file sharing market. Thus, a newcomer to the music business like Apple, without any ties, could commercialize and sell a digital player that could replay digital music industry standard MP3 files, pirated or otherwise, without any hesitation. In contrast, the consumer electronics division of the Sony Group, which had a major music label under its umbrella, could never produce a player for MP3s as the music label was the company's own flesh and blood. Behind Kutaragi's statements lay the above.

Thus, Sony's failure was triggered by the strong pull of the capabilities grown through habits and experiences built up over a long time in their existing businesses regarding environmental change (changing markets and technologies), for example the "competency trap" (e.g., Levitt and March, 1988; Martines and Kambil, 1999), "core rigidities" (Leonard-Barton, 1992, 1995) or the so-called "innovators dilemma" (Christensen, 1997). However, as discussed in Chapter 3, other reasons the company was unable to respond with potential new technologies and services such as the music distribution business were the various negative interactions of capabilities (abrasion and friction between capabilities) that caused the difficult adjustment of the stakes in the group, particularly between the music and commercial electronics divisions. The negative interactions between capabilities at Sony were the collision of the company's individual capabilities driving its consumer electronics and music businesses, and such negative abrasion and friction between capabilities is a hindrance to orchestrating different intangible assets. As a result, the Sony Group was unable to achieve co-specialization through the original DC that it'd had (supposedly).

Even though the Sony Group had a high level of technical fitness in its individual businesses, its DC were inclined in the negative direction, which meant that its "evolutionary fitness" was lacking, and the company could not demonstrate synergies as group strategies (Helfat et al., 2007). This also means that the Sony Group lacked the ability to set down and execute strategies with appropriate timing in the changing environment of the music industry. Appropriate strategies mean strategic investment and execution to achieve new products, services and business models that have congruence (fit) with the business environment (markets, and so on).

Thus, in this interpretation, the Sony Group failed to bring congruence between the corporate systems and the environment (Insight-1) and congruence between the individual capabilities in its corporate system (Insight-2) through the congruence by orchestrating co-specialized assets inside and outside of the company (Insight-3) through the demonstration of DC. In contrast, Jobs and his team of managers at Apple did not become entrenched in negative interactions, did not fear cannibalism, and engaged in the asset orchestration process through strategic non-routine activities transcending both the inside and outside of the company, based on the spirit of entrepreneurialism, which lead to the successful strategy transformation of the company through DC demonstrated through the execution of capabilities congruence (discussed later).

lead to it being cannibalized. Here again in contrast, Jobs made it a principle that cannibalizations should not be feared.

Thus, iTunes store was announced in San Francisco in 2003. Jobs had made a foray into a new field, had focused on user experience more than profit, had produced a product with a design over and above the product of other companies, and had achieved a fantastic business model, in which if iTunes sold, iPod would sell, and hence Macintosh would sell.

Leading companies must be careful with the impression that they give.

Jobs made plans based on the maxims of Mike Markkula, who said that the importance and value of a company must be conveyed through all aspects, from packaging through to marketing (Isaacson, 2011).

Jobs' vision of absolute value entailed a philosophy of thoroughly and completely controlling the entire product experience from design, through to manufacture and marketing, which meant that even the minutest of details of the Apple Store were considered. Many approaches have been taken in the stores such as portable terminals loaded with software for transacting to circumvent the need for cash registers, carefully selected materials and the "Genius Bar" for technical support. Apple Stores have also been set up in locations where there is a lot of pedestrian traffic, such as shopping malls and main streets. The first Apple Store opened in Virginia in 2001.

Even though Jobs expressed an essential entrepreneurial spirit with activities in which the leaders themselves became involved in the selection of, and were motivated by the details of, projects as described above – this is not a business element often introduced by the leaders of major corporations. Lashinsky (2012, pp.200–201) had the following to say:

> An unsung attribute of Steve Jobs that Apple also will miss is his role as a masterful networker and gatherer of information. Had times gotten really rough, Jobs would have made a fine journalist. He furiously worked the phones, calling up people he'd heard were worthy and requesting a meeting. No one turned down the chance to meet with Jobs, of course, and he used the opportunity to soak up information. His uncanny insight into trends in business and technology weren't a fluke. Jobs worked hard for his market intelligence.

Jobs' ability to gather and discern information going forward and his speed can be said to be part of his "sensing" ability, something that top managers should acquire.

Including Jobs, the individual and entrepreneurial roles played by the business persons in the Apple executive, that is, their strategic and entrepreneurial non-routine activities were one of the requirements for bringing about DC, as discussed in Chapter 2. DC operates in companies and their top management levels to enable predictions and estimation about latent consumer needs, business model diversification and technological development, and enables companies to achieve sustainable innovation by enabling verification of those predictions and estimates so that assets can be selected and integrated while engaging in trial and error so that new businesses can be proposed and executed.

DC, in part, reside with individual managers and the top management teams (Teece, 2014). When at the crossroads of deciding a future strategy for a company such as an innovative product development, the most remarkable characteristics of the DC the company has are the CEO and top managers' abilities to command the entire company by recognizing important developments and trends to devise ideas for future strategies and solutions to immediate problems (Adner and Helfat, 2003). As well as that, this means that DC do not just exist in high-level learning theory routines alone, but also entail combined relationships of high-level organizational routines as "signature processes," entrepreneurial leadership and the leadership of management teams (Augier and Teece, 2009; Teece, 2007, 2012b). Thus, in that character, the creative and strategic actions of business persons and entrepreneurs (in this case, the creation of new markets through the new product development and marketing strategies of the Apple executive including Jobs) are heavily weighted by strategic, entrepreneurial non-routine activities rather than routine ones. In reality in business, much of the strategic and entrepreneurial actions and reformations require non-routine activities that cannot be impersonated (Teece, 2012b).

As Teece (2014) also said, the existence of strategic, entrepreneurial and non-routine activities is crucial for the core DC framework, whereas strategic management theories that eliminate the possibilities of non-routine activities by top management teams are unnatural. In markets that change rapidly such as those of the digital industries, management teams must have the courage and motivation to stand up to high levels of risk and uncertainty, and hence, strategic processes that entail asset orchestration by interlocking sensing, seizing and transforming through the intuitive and improvisational responses of the CEO and the top management team are critical in such situations (see Domains I, II and III in Figure 2.6 in Chapter 2). The strategic and entrepreneurial non-routine activities of the CEO and the management team drive co-specialization of the company's intangible assets with those of other companies, and lead to DC for the company's sustainable growth, and strategic innovation capabilities, as mentioned in Chapter 2.

4.3   APPLE'S ORGANIZATIONAL CAPABILITIES

4.3.1   Getting the Best Personnel and a Simple Organizational Structure

Next, the author discusses the aforementioned organizational capabilities that are congruent with the Apple strategy and technology capabilities. Apple's organizational compositions are extremely simple, with only three layers of hierarchy. The company has done away with middle managers, which are normally found in large corporations, and created a flat type of organizational system in which teams report directly to the executive. In the case of Apple, the executive team (ET) that includes senior vice presidents and Jobs, and a 100-person vice president layer of business directors are the equivalent of the company's core members. This is so that the CEO can see over the entirety, and hence, most of the vice presidents are in the direct control of the management team. Due to the few hierarchical layers in the company, staff can also easily grasp the intentions of leaders, which makes decision-making and information flow speedy. Apple does not have a map of its organizational structure like an ordinary large corporation, but its employees know who the company's movers and shakers are. This is a corporate culture created by Jobs in the Next era, but was the archetype of the nascent Apple – the company's organizations are not hierarchical, there is full welfare at the company, and each and every person who works at Apple is not an "employee" but a "member."

Apple has organizational lines for each function. Apple did away with balance management so that the CFO could take charge over all. By doing this, it enabled executives in charge of other duties to focus on their respective strengths. Thus, Apple organizations are more like surfing than mountain climbing – organizations are suitably altered depending on other organizational changes to constantly optimize the company. Big projects are assigned to small groups. For example, the hard work of replacing Safari for iPad was left to only two engineers. Furthermore, industrial designers at Apple hold high positions and the design department is under the direct control of the CEO. When the design department starts up, all the remaining departments also begin to move, and it's the supply chain and engineering teams that hold responsibility for the product. This is how the Apple New Product Process (ANPP) begins. Often, development and manufacturing units degrade design, but at Apple, creativity is brought into the development method and manufacturing processes, so that the original design conception is maintained right up to product shipment. Jobs always had insights into the effects of collaboration, and in that vein, multiple teams are always working together at Apple.

In the current Apple management, there are nine senior vice presidents, the CEO Tim Cook, and eight executives. These senior vice presidents are all directly involved with products and their retail/online stores, Internet software and services, hardware and software engineering, design, high-end financial responsibilities, global marketing, general legal affairs and operations. This management team meets on Mondays every week to review Apple product planning and so forth (product study meetings).

One of the factors of Apple's success is its outstanding personnel. Jobs always preferred class A specialists versed in the area of a particular product, and hired them himself. Some of Jobs' work was to guarantee the best quality of the people the company worked with, something he was always thinking about. As well as that, he also focused on people that agreed with him on his vision for the future. The number of staff that Jobs personally decided to hire was in the thousands.

One particular great contributor to the success of Apple was the hardware designer Jonathan Ive. Ive proceeded with development buried in the locked-out design lab at Apple. Rubinstein, who was appointed by Jobs to head the iPod development, also played an important role in the development of products such as the iPod.

The concept of "responsibility" is important at Apple. Because the organizational structures are so simple, the scope of responsibilities for each of the divisions and individuals in the company is very clear. At Apple, the directly responsible individual (DRI) is the member of staff who will be rebuked when something does not go well with some task or other. For Jobs, the DRI was not just an abbreviation, but part of the Apple culture. This accountability was always from the lower layers to the top layers. Also, the discretionary scope of responsibilities allocated has the effect of bringing out the capabilities of staff, and under Apple's competitive structure encourages staff to perform at 100 percent of their abilities. In this way, Jobs brought together small numbers of talented people and let them work freely by doing away with common constraints.

By pursuing the "highest" as much as possible, Apple emitted its charm and summoned excellent personnel. Everyone understood that by joining Apple they would become involved in truly epochal projects, and that they would be able to engage in work with more enthusiasm than in any other company. The effect of the coolness of mood of the Apple effect was also intense on individuals, and the inflated egos of Apple staff were only commensurate with the extremely good work that they did. Apple's culture was never comfortable and far from relaxing, and was a culture of competition for the highest excellence.

In this way, Jobs also had a wonderful ability to nurture creativity. Jobs had an incredible ability to seek out talented people, employ and include them, and create environments in which magic could happen. This acquisition of excellent personnel and the simple organizational structure is one element of Apple's difficult-to-imitate organizational capabilities.

4.3.2 The Dynamic Range of Knowledge Boundaries: Strengthening Sensing Functions

Business persons have individual thought worlds and mental models. Not only do they have unique worldviews born from their personal social experiences, but also have empirical knowledge rooted in tacit knowledge deeply embedded within themselves both mentally and corporeally, born through various professional experiences and job functions. The higher the level of novelty and uncertainty of strategic details required to achieve a target, the easier it is for friction and conflict to occur between business persons due to the diversity and differences of their knowledge.

In particular, innovations such as new product or enterprise developments that are conceptually completely different to the conventional require business persons to transform their existing knowledge, although their deeply embedded existing knowledge can shackle them when it comes to taking on a challenge, as in the innovation dilemma (Christensen, 1997). As discussed in Chapter 2, to succeed with a new product or enterprise development by demonstrating DC, it's important to form SC (and boundary networks as SC and networked SC) to promote strategic non-routine activities (see Figure 4.1). Hence, first of all, business persons need mutual understanding so that they can engage in deep creative dialogue with each other to create new meaning.

Creative dialogue is an enabler for sharing and understanding meaning between business persons to meet new challenges. However, comments such as "we have general agreement, but there are problems with the details!" or "this lacks any concrete theory!" can be heard in discussions among practitioners in the business workplace. In other words, discussions such as "we know what needs to be done, but specifically who is going to do it and when, and how is it supposed to be done?" or "do we have the resources?" emerge. This kind of friction and discord between organizations is unavoidable. However, the friction and discord that arise in facing the challenge of new issues or current problems are also opportunities for innovation.

Business leaders in all management layers including top management have to take a serious and proactive approach through deep dialogue with others, regarding questions such as "where is the friction and discord?," "what are the problems, and what are the solutions?" It is no good to try reaching easy compromises in disputes with others including external partners either, because this will nip new business growth in the bud.

The journalist Lashinsky (2012, p.23) had the following to say in this regard:

> "High-performance teams should be at each other's throats" is how one person with multiple Apple executives summarized the culture. You don't get to the right trade-off without each person advocating aggressively for his position. Arguments at Apple are personal and confrontational. This began at the top, and it is part of the company's culture.

In this way, Jobs was never afraid of friction in the company, as it led to transformation.

To turn friction and discord into a growth driver for a corporation, business persons need to establish shared values and find common and mutual viewpoints that clarify specific actions (e.g., common interests between organizations) (Kodama, 2007c), motivate partners, and build win–win relationships with all stakeholders. This entails mutually shared perspectives among business people such as shared strategic objectives and clarified concrete business plans. In the internal context of a company, decision-making processes and rules about important items such as current and future priorities – what must be done now, and what investments need to be made – must also be clarified and disclosed fairly to all members of staff. If not, trust and unity through creative dialogue will not be engendered between business persons.

By forming boundary networks, common ground (Bechky, 2003) based on common interests and so forth can be established between business persons, and by converting frictions and conflicts into creative abrasion (Leonard-Barton, 1995) and productive friction (Hagel III and Brown, 2005), business persons can establish mutual trust and promote collaboration on dissimilar knowledge boundaries. Harvard Business School's Professor Rosabeth Moss Kanter (Kanter, 2001 p.231) perceives opposition as something that should be creatively encouraged. Hence, friction and conflict should not be thought of as things that lead to confusion or things to avoid.

Creative dialogue that builds common ground raises the capabilities of awareness of business persons of dissimilar contexts and knowledge, and simultaneously promotes creative collaboration between different areas or divisions of specialization. This raises the level of the recognition capabilities and common understanding of business persons about differing contexts and knowledge between business elements such as strategy, organizations, technology and operations, and promotes congruence between the elements of DC (strategy, technology, organizational, operational and leadership capabilities).

In other words, driving creative dialogue expands the dynamic range (referred to in this book as "the dynamic range of knowledge boundaries," see Figure 4.1) of business persons to alter the knowledge boundaries shuttling in formal organizations and boundary networks. As well as transcending the different contexts of different specialties and organizations, the knowledge boundaries of individual people are also broadened (or expanded), which leads to increased strategic non-routine work for people to bridge (or fill in) the gaps between these boundaries. It takes sensing with a discerning eye to bridge knowledge boundary gaps. By expanding the dynamic range of their thinking and actions through sensing, business persons raise their ability to recognize different kinds of knowledge, and give rise to effects that lead to the asset orchestration process. This expansion of the dynamic range of knowledge boundaries in turn ties in with strengthening of the sensing function in DC.

To succeed with innovations, demonstrating organizational capabilities by building new organizations to bring about asset orchestration by bringing congruence to strategy and technology capabilities is crucial. For one thing, this entails creating new organizational culture that does not exist in traditional organizations, and creating informal organizations as SC consisting of business persons with wide-ranging and dissimilar abilities, and business persons with backgrounds in different areas of expertise. Just as in the Apple case, it's also important to absorb the best people and their differing ideas from outside the company. These dissimilar teams or organizations blow new winds to existing traditional organizations, and stimulate and inspire practitioners as they work toward strategic objectives to achieve breakthroughs, transformation, creativity and innovation (and of course involve conflict and friction).

Jobs also made the following comment (Isaacson, 2011, pp.567–568):

> Edwin Land of Polaroid talked about the intersection of the humanities and science. I like that intersection. There's something magical about that place. There are a lot of people innovating, and that's not the main distinction of my career. The reason Apple resonates with people is that there's a deep current of humanity in our innovation. I think great artists and great engineers are similar, in that they both have a desire to express themselves. In fact some of the best people working on the original Mac were poets and musicians on the side. In the seventies computers became a way for people to express their creativity. Great artists like Leonardo da Vinci and Michelangelo were great at science. Michelangelo knew a lot about how to quarry some stone, not just how to be a sculptor.

Put differently, innovation occurs when business persons with differing cultures and areas of expertise intersect in the boundary networks of SC and networked SC (Kodama, 2009a). In boundary networks as intersections of ideas (Johansson, 2004), like the staff of Apple, business persons have to have the courage to conquer and transcend the knowledge boundaries between business people. Hence, the formation of boundary networks ties in with the forging of the sensing capabilities of business persons. And, the keys to this are, like Apple, the preparation of organizational environments that promote deep collaboration in SC through creative dialogue across teams and between organizations, the leadership of top management, and the ongoing commitment and support of top management (Apple obviously practices these).

4.3.3 Seizing Functions at Apple, as a Networked Collaborative Organization

The aforementioned dynamic range of knowledge boundaries refers to both the changing in width of contexts and knowledge as well as the width of business persons' ability to recognize wide-ranging values and diversity as their "sensing" function. At Apple, individual business people have a wide dynamic range of knowledge boundaries. The width of the dynamic range of knowledge boundaries in turn reinforces the sensing of business people regarding changing boundaries in the environment, and widens the dynamic range of their thinking and actions.

Moreover, creative dialogue widens the dynamic range of the thinking of business persons so that they can recognize diverse contexts and knowledge on boundary networks, and forms common meaning, common interests and common ground among members of organizations. Like Apple, this expansion of the dynamic range of knowledge boundaries enables business persons to share and resonate values, and build trust (Kodama, 2007b), and also fosters commitments and promotes creative collaboration.

Creative collaboration through creative dialogue in organic organizational forms that have boundary networks leads to the merging and integrating of diverse contexts and knowledge (the asset orchestration process). Thus, business persons bring congruence between the various business elements of DC (strategy, technology, organizational, operational and leadership capabilities) to solve urgent problems and issues in organizations, technologies and operations to achieve strategies for new challenges.

Through strategic innovation capabilities in Figure 2.6 in Chapter 2, it's important in innovating companies to set down and execute integrated strategies suitable for both incremental innovation for environmental changes (environment adaption strategy – exploitation) and radical innovation (environment creation strategy – exploration) to create new environments with new and never-before-seen businesses. For this reason, business persons must use their sensing functions to respond to changes on a diverse range of boundaries, and raise their level of awareness of wide-ranging contexts and knowledge. Hence, having organizational forms optimized and adapted for the thinking and actions of business persons is critical.

Companies like Apple that have business persons with high levels of recognition abilities regarding differing contexts and knowledge form networked collaborative organizations. A networked collaborative organization is a specific organizational form in which the dynamic asset orchestration process is performed by business persons to generate new knowledge and contexts by switching the relationships between people – the networks of people in response to the processes of generation and elimination of dynamically changing contexts.

The basic structural elements of a networked collaborative organization are formal organizations with flat organizational structures (functional organization in the case of Apple) and boundary networks created as distributed networks by the business persons of various formal organization (SC and networked SC, formal or informal) (see Figure 4.1). Boundary networks promote creative dialogue among business persons between knowledge boundaries, and are also organizational bodies that drive practical processes for new challenges, and generate new knowledge.

The specific work of business persons on boundary networks is centered on decision-making by the top management team (in the case of Apple, the ET of senior vice presidents, and including Jobs) about setting down important strategies (at Apple, this means strategic vision, new product concepts and designs, and so on), or integrating awareness in-house to set down and execute strategies, generating ideas, and proposing and executing solutions to problems at the practical level by the upper management team (at Apple, the 100-member vice president layer, the meaning of the vice president title varies from country to country, industry to industry, or job to job, but generally means upper levels of middle management). These approaches differ from every day routine-based activities, and are almost always strategic non-routine activities. Obviously, top and senior management involved in setting down and executing important strategies must have awareness integrated for, and be deeply coordinated with objective contexts and interests.[1] Moreover, task teams consisting of management layers and general staff (managers hereinafter) immerse themselves in discussion and dialogue about setting down and executing strategy, and more practical and concrete work in contexts related to specific issues to seek out and execute suitable solutions and move in the appropriate direction. As informal organizational platforms, boundary networks enlarge the dynamic range of knowledge boundaries of business persons, and raise the level of sensing, as recognition capability, of differing contexts and knowledge, and mutually and dynamically tie together different knowledge boundaries for problem solving and new challenges.

When talking about formal organizations in networked collaborative organizations, it does not mean old-fashioned hierarchical structured bureaucratic organizations. Networked collaborative organizations have formal organizations with flat organizational structures focused on delegation of authority (although Apple is top-down), personal responsibility and commitment, and quick decision-making. These flat organizations consist of multiple business units (in the case of Apple, functional organizations). In the specific tasks of business persons in formal organizations, it's important to thoroughly execute strategy within the territory of each business unit, to execute strategy decided upon by the practical processes on boundary networks.

Leading business persons who have DC expand their seizing functions and drive new asset orchestration through the formation of boundary networks and by interacting with customers and external partners when necessary. Knowledge is intrinsic to conditions, situations and spaces, in other words it's intrinsic to contexts. To create, acquire and share knowledge, business persons must share dynamically changing contexts among themselves. Moreover, to share specific contexts, business persons have to participate in specific SC from time to time and place to place. Then, knowledge is shared and integrated with the shared dynamic contexts as the medium. At this time, business persons voluntarily form SC as new knowledge boundaries, and draw business persons as their stakeholders into certain SC to tie together dissimilar contexts and bring about new context.

To draw business persons into knowledge boundaries, business persons use their context architect capability, and leading business persons form specific SC and bring certain business persons into them as required to bring about high-quality new knowledge. Moreover, business persons form or participate in various dissimilar SC voluntarily, and flow contexts and knowledge between dissimilar SC, and engage in actions to share and inspire these contexts and knowledge between business persons. This is the boundaries linking capability of business persons, which they use to network different SC (to form networked SC). These context architect and boundary linking capabilities bring about new ideas and solutions needed to set down and execute strategic objectives, and give rise to the dynamic practical processes of business persons shuttling between formal organizations and boundary networks. These context architect and boundaries linking capabilities are crucial aspects of the asset orchestration process, as the seizing functions in DC.

As described above, at Apple, not only are there top-down actions but also bottom-up factors are taken up because individual members of staff are expected to be empowered, and to contribute and respond to teams as leaders, pivoted on the formation of networked collaborative organizational structures and activities in SC and networked SC. Thus, as an element of Apple's organizational capabilities which have given rise to new product strategies to date, and which are congruent with the company's strategy and technology capabilities, the formation and management of dynamic networked collaborative organizations, SC and boundary networks based on the aforementioned employment of talented people is fundamental.

4.4   APPLE'S OPERATIONAL CAPABILITIES

Next, the author discusses elements of the operational capabilities that are congruent with the aforementioned Apple strategy, technology and organizational capabilities. As discussed in terms of organizational capabilities earlier, Apple carries out creative product development hinged on the formation of networked collaborative organizations and activities in SC and networked SC.

The Apple board of directors meets every quarter. The management team meets on Monday every week, and discusses various ideas without any formal agenda, and reviews product planning (a product study meeting). The company's marketing and advertising teams do the same thing on Wednesday afternoons. Project teams in the marketing team are small, and authority is given to capable members. Focus is on quality rather than quantity, and there are no formal meetings but progress is visualized in weekly increments. There are also regular one-to-one meetings between bosses and their subordinates. These are times that enable bosses and subordinates to talk privately without the involvement of others. There are also other meetings such as general meetings to inspire motivation in subordinates, meetings on forecasts for business performance, and regular study groups. The Mac study group used to meet once a week. Jobs believed in frequent meetings to keep abreast of the current state of product developments. Although discussions at Apple involve individuals coming head-to-head with each other, it's the aforementioned concept of creative dialogue that forms the basis of these discussions, begins with top management, and is part of the present-day culture at the company.

Jobs is often quoted as saying how Apple should be a company where anyone can casually approach the CEO with an idea. He was a leader who strongly encouraged open discussion. In an ordinary scene at Apple, two engineers meet in a hallway, one of them letting the other know of an idea he has been fomenting. And the engineer who is listening encourages him to get started on it. Then, the engineer with the idea gets back to his or her post, and quickly forms a team who spend some months developing the idea – it is not uncommon at Apple for new projects to start up from such conversations. Such non-routine activities are an element of Apple's DC.

Apple staff engage in discussions through deep collaboration, mutual interactions and concurrent engineering on a regular basis. In other words, the various processes of development are not performed independently in a sequential order, but proceed in parallel with each other, and are accompanied by discussions. All divisions involved in design, hardware and software, and so on are in unity as work proceeds, and designs are rethought many times along the way. The customer support team also prepares reports about complaints from customers and trends which it sends to other divisions, they also refine data, and are pleased because information can be useful in subsequent developments.

Meanwhile "the top 100" as they are known, the 100 persons around the world making the biggest contributions, meet once a year. In this conference, strategies for the coming year are established, and the outlook beyond that is discussed. At Jobs' discretion, low-ranking engineers could be included and vice presidents could be excluded. The purpose of these meetings were also to forge bonds among administrators at the level lower than the management team. Being in a silo organization, there would not have been any opportunity to interact were if not for this meeting.

Jobs was also a master of managing business through on-site intervention. Jobs' daily activities entailed regular meetings with various teams, refinement of ideas and finding solutions to the new problems that accompany new products. By that, participating in various meetings and checking up on the workplace, Jobs was able to produce goods that delighted consumers.

Jobs didn't like PowerPoint presentations and materials, and held conversations with people looking at them straight in the face. This is because Jobs believed that creativity came from non-routine thinking and actions such as spontaneous meetings and random conversations, a fundamental element of DC. Hence, Jobs encouraged informal meetings. Thus, whenever ideas or questions spring to mind, people at Apple often give a colleague a call to list up what needs to be done, no matter what time of day it is. Apple does not have an in-house video or telephone conferencing culture, but its staff don't hesitate to jump on a plane when something is up. Meetings are usually held in Cupertino, and all staff involved in management are in Cupertino, and meet each other face-to-face. Jobs took active advantage of email, but was always a hands-on person through and through.

As described above, to achieve the product strategies interlocked with Apple's firm vision of absolute value, the company drove creative and strategic non-routine activities among staff for regular deep collaboration, mutual interactions and concurrent engineering, and brought about new operational capabilities unique to Apple, as elements of DC congruent with strategy, technology and organizational capabilities.

4.5   APPLE'S LEADERSHIP CAPABILITIES

This section discusses the leadership capabilities congruent with the aforementioned four elements of strategy, technology, organizational and operational capabilities at Apple.

4.5.1   "Control and Distribution" and "Top-down, Bottom-up" Decision-making Processes

Jobs was a dictator who made all the important decisions at Apple. At Apple, it is no exaggeration to say that business orders are absolute, and if the boss says look right and the employee doesn't, they will be fired. When Jobs was in charge, it's possible that because he made all the decisions he kept Apple from becoming a large market-driven or bureaucratic organization. For example, Apple's brand team only needed the approval of the CEO.

Apple is a top-down company, but in fact is a company that absorbs the opinions of the management team upwards. That's because the in-house teams are always prepared to offer opinions to their boss who gives presentations in the management team meeting, or their boss's boss. By strictly adhering to a system of "communicate up/manage down," Apple is able to bring about speed and clarity to its decision-making. The speed of Apple's decision-making is also encouraged in narrowing down of information that is transferred out of the management team. In-house teams get prompt feedback, but only for what is seen as necessary (Lashinsky, 2012). Also, because the range of business and product lineups of Apple are extremely small, there is only a small number of things that need be considered in decision-making. As discussed earlier, it's Apple's aim for simplicity that gives its action agility. Jobs' belief that everything was important and that success was in the details brought about the unique leadership capabilities of the company – the entrepreneurial spirit, the DC elements of the top and management team. In other words, it's important that a top management team also pay attention to details when bringing down big decisions.

4.5.2   Centralized Leadership Creating Rules, and Distributed Leadership Bringing about Creativity

Jobs had mastered the behaviors of a leader. Jobs knew that when leaders are directly and proactively involved in a product, the willingness of subordinates naturally grows, and that this was the best way to inspire other people. For him, strategic objectives meant pouring his energies into people all throughout the organization and giving them the same level of enthusiasm that he had.

People around Jobs were limited to those who fit his style and thinking, and they happily accepted his leadership. Those who didn't like it, left. Apple's executive praised Jobs' charisma – it was not democracy that brought about great products, but a company led by a talented tyrant. Maccoby (2000) described Jobs as a "productive narcissist" who was also a charismatic leader with passionate beliefs and desires that wanted to change the world with his vision of absolute value. Hence, as an element of DC, it can also be said that charisma is an important part of the personality and instincts of a CEO.

Former product marketing manager Michael Haley reflected on the success of Apple, saying the reason for it was the leadership structures centered on Jobs. Apple had a leader with a vision of absolute value, and the leader had people working for him whom he trusted and had confidence in, to achieve that vision. Thus, through Jobs' intensely centralized leadership, he involved himself in all processes from beginning to end, and adjusted them to suit his vision. And he never failed to checked things, no matter how small. From these processes, firm regulations are created.

Jobs also took every available opportunity to stimulate the artistic charms and creativity of his engineers. In this way, Jobs was able to raise the motivations of subordinates, trigger creativity in individuals and knew the secret of stimulating their "distributed leadership" (Kodama, 2004).

As described above, Apple was able to bring about leadership capabilities on the principle axis of a leadership structure unique to the company that brought congruence to the company's strategy, technology, organizational and operational capabilities. Responding to the changes in customer needs, the leadership capabilities under the centralized leadership through the strong vision of absolute value that drive innovation through the distributed leadership of the teams of individual staff members are important intangible assets at Apple. Thus, as discussed below, the five capabilities (strategy, technology, organizational, operational and leadership capabilities) drive congruence between the internal and external capabilities at Apple.

4.6 INTERNAL AND EXTERNAL CONGRUENCE IN CAPABILITIES AT APPLE: A COMPANY EXPERT AT INTEGRATION THROUGH ASSET ORCHESTRATION

In the past, Apple's business strategy (new product and service strategies) was to achieve radical innovation (of new products, services and business models) by orchestrating the company's core intangible assets with new intangible assets acquired externally (skills, technologies, know-how, and so on). This is an example of congruence by orchestrating co-specialized assets both inside and outside of the company (Insight-3). Moreover, as discussed in Chapter 3, the asset orchestration process drives internal and external congruence in capabilities in a company (Insights 1 and 2). Behind the success of Apple lay the company's achievement of congruence between the corporate system and the environment (Insight-1) and congruence between individual capabilities within the corporate system (Insight-2) through congruence enabled by orchestration of co-specialized assets both inside and outside of the company (Insight-3) (see Figure 4.2).

Therefore, why does the asset orchestration process bring about capabilities congruence? Jobs himself, people involved with Apple and journalists familiar with the detail of the company made the interesting comments below. For example, in 2008 Jobs said the following in an interview with *Fortune Magazine* about Apple's approach to business (Lashinsky, 2012, pp.57–58): "You can't do what you can do at Apple anywhere else," he said:

> The engineering is long gone in most PC companies. In the consumer-electronics companies, they don't understand the software parts of it. And so you really can't make the products that you can make at Apple anywhere else right now. Apple's the only company that has everything under one roof. There's no other company that could make a MacBook Air and the reason is that not only do we control the hardware, but we control the operating system. And it is the intimate interaction between the operating system and the hardware that allows us to do that.

He also said the following about the company's approach to products (Isaacson, 2011, p.568):

> People pay us to integrate things for them, because they don't have the time to think about this stuff 24/7. If you have an extreme passion for producing great products, it pushes you to be integrated, to connect your hardware and your software and content management. You want to break new ground, so you have to do it yourself. If you want to allow your products to be open to other hardware or software, you have to give up some of your vision.

Also, Apple's former vice president Rob Schoeben said the following: "Everyone knows that seamless integration between the various parts is key to making the magic happen" (Lashinsky, 2012). As well as that, the journalist Isaacson (2011, p.362) said the following:

> Because he believed that Apple's great advantage was its integration of the whole widget – from design to hardware to software to content – he wanted all

departments at the company to work together in parallel. The phrases he used were "deep collaboration" and "concurrent engineering." Instead of a development process in which a product would be passed sequentially from engineering to design to manufacturing to marketing and distribution, these various departments collaborated simultaneously. "Our method was to develop integrated products, and that meant our process had to be integrated and collaborative." Jobs said.

Also, Tim Cook, a longtime executive at Apple and its current CEO, said in February 2013, with reference to the company's integration of hardware, software, and services: "Apple has the ability to innovate in all three of these spheres and create magic . . . This isn't something you can just write a check for. This is something you build over decades" (AFP, 2013).

In this way, Apple's strength is in its integration as its unique "signature processes," and the factor that enables this integration that is difficult for other companies to imitate is the "asset orchestration process." The asset orchestration process brings about congruence and synergies between the elements of the aforementioned DC (strategy, technology, organizational, operational and leadership capabilities) (Insight-2). The integration of Apple's signature processes, its unique intangible assets, bring about congruence between each of these capabilities, and congruence with the external environment (broad ecosystems including customers and partners). Moreover, as discussed in Chapter 3, Apple drives mutual co-specialization of these five capabilities to bring about strong DC as the corporate system. Apple's demonstration of strong DC achieves congruence between the corporate system and the environment (Insight-1) and congruence between individual capabilities within the corporate system (Insight-2) through congruence enabled by orchestration of co-specialized assets both inside and outside of the company (Insight-3).

Through Apple's vision of absolute value and its aim for simplicity focusing on design, the company seamlessly integrates the required hardware, software and services for its new product developments, and has continuously brought forth new radical innovations. Also, to maintain its market share by responding to competitors and the changing competitive environment, the company engages in rapid incremental innovation (an example of demonstrating strong DC in Domains I, II and III in Figure 2.6 in Chapter 2).

From the perspective of strategy capabilities also, Apple integrates EMS virtually to bring about new vertical integration systems that are different than those of other companies in the same industry. Apple's strategy capabilities generate vertically integrated value chains by orchestrating co-specialized assets from the end user, application and content partners,

Apple and suppliers (EMS and parts manufacturers). Apple optimizes its vertical boundaries through asset orchestration in its corporate system, and dynamically brings congruence with environments (Insight-1) as new market creation through its absolute value strategy.

Also, to bring about technology capabilities to support these strategy capabilities, Apple engages in its characteristic design-driven innovation (e.g., Verganti, 2009; Utterback et al., 2006) with its aim for simplicity in its radical innovation. From the perspective of technology capabilities, behind these technology processes, Apple engaged in asset orchestration of diverse valuable co-specialized technologies such as parts inside or outside of the company for integration to bring about new product development.

Also, one of the features of the organizational system at Apple – its organizational capabilities that bring congruence with its strategy and technology capabilities – is its simple organizational form and its excellent human resources. Second, the fundaments of networked collaborative organizational structures are the SC (and boundary networks) that are organizational infrastructure for core strategic non-routine activities. Here, not only top-down elements are taken up, but also bottom-up elements, and all persons contribute to the teams as leaders. The multiple teams as SC enabled by Apple's networked collaborative organizations bring about different capabilities to those of the ordinary operational management of routing activities. This is an example of the organizational capabilities, which are an element of Apple's DC for dealing with dynamic environments. Organizational capabilities born through the configuration of dynamic organizational forms like SC and networked SC (boundary networks) orchestrate co-specialized assets both in and out of companies and achieve platforms (strategies and technologies) to bring about new business models.

Moreover, to steadfastly execute strategy, technology and organizational capabilities, Apple engages in deep collaboration, mutual exchange and concurrent engineering to drive strategic and creative non-routine activities in its staff and bring about new operational capabilities unique to that company that are an element of DC bringing congruence to the company's strategy, technology and organizational capabilities to achieve new product strategies interlocked with its firm vision of absolute value.

And it's leadership capabilities that play the central role in executing congruence between strategy, technology, organizational and operational capabilities. This is the leadership of Jobs and his team of managers – of an innovative team of practitioners, who demonstrated their leadership capabilities in their ET in networked collaborative organizations, hence demonstrating synergies between their various abilities. Moreover, the

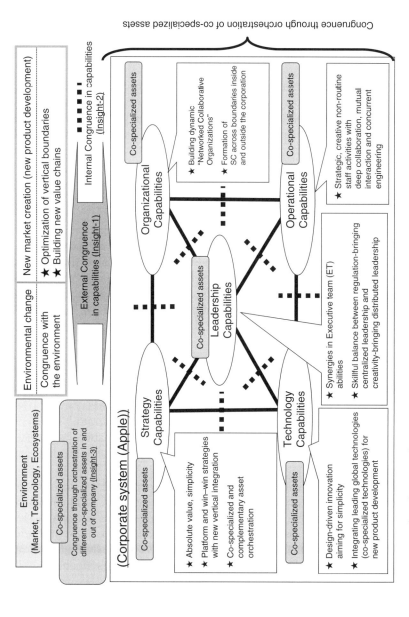

Figure 4.2   Internal and external congruence through orchestration of co-specialized assets (the Apple case)

127

leadership system at Apple with its balance between centralized leadership centered on Jobs and top management bringing about regulations and its distributed leadership bring about creativity among all staff drives integration through orchestration of the global co-specialized assets both inside and outside of the company to create new products, services and markets. Thus, Apple builds win–win relationships among its stakeholders (users and partners).

Apple, a master of integration through asset orchestration, achieves congruence between the corporate system and the environment (Insight-1), congruence between the individual capabilities in the corporate system (Insight-2) and congruence between co-specialized assets both inside and outside of the company (Insight-3).

4.7   CHAPTER SUMMARY

This chapter has considered and analyzed the five micro elements of Apple's DC and its capabilities congruence in and outside the company. Apple's success (iPod and iTunes music store, and later the iPhone, iPad) indicated capabilities congruence enabled by the asset orchestration process which mobilized various different capabilities both inside and outside of the company. Apple successfully demonstrated DC by integrating capabilities inside and outside of the company through capabilities congruence.

In contrast, Sony was plagued by various negative interactions of capabilities (abrasion and friction between capabilities) that caused the difficult coordination of its stakes between its music (Sony Music Entertainment) and its commercial electronics divisions. Such negative abrasion and friction between capabilities is also a hindrance to orchestrating different intangible assets. As a result, there was a lack of capabilities congruence in the Sony Group, and the Sony Group failed to integrate different capabilities.

On the other hand, it was the achievement of integration through the asset orchestration process enabled by the formation of SC (and boundary networks) at Apple that lay behind the company's successful new product developments. This asset orchestration process achieved internal and external congruence in capabilities at Apple, and was the driving force of ongoing strategic innovations for the company to grow sustainably.

NOTE

1. Deep integration and coordination of awareness between top and middle management teams is often carried out in leading Japanese corporations. Refer to Kodama (2007a).

5. Capabilities congruence through collaboration management at Cisco

This chapter considers and analyzes micromanagement elements of dynamic capabilities (DC) in a large corporation, through the example of the American Cisco Systems. Through the company's "collaboration management," practitioners in all management layers overcome various contradictions and take up the challenge of new innovation through strategic collaboration by forming company-wide networked collaborative organizations. Cisco enables the processes of creative dialogue, understanding and cooperation, and prompt decision-making and action by demonstrating DC that span different business units, and thus simultaneously executes radical innovation to create the new businesses of the future while regularly reinforcing incremental innovation for the company's main businesses.

Demonstrating DC through strategic collaboration centered on all staff including the middle managers and the executive in the company in this way enables the best ideas and opinions to be taken up by the organization quickly, and enables study and action on various problems as a team. This chapter considers and analyzes capabilities congruence between the five elements of DC needed to achieve sustainable growth through strategic innovation enabled by Cisco's collaborative management as it changes the actions of staff and its corporate culture.

5.1 SYNERGIES THROUGH M&A STRATEGIES: CISCO'S STRATEGY AND TECHNOLOGY CAPABILITIES

The "build, buy, partner" approach is central to Cisco's innovation culture, and gives impetus to the company's M&A strategies. Thus, this excellent M&A strategy, done with the aim of building new markets by expanding technologies and business models enabled Cisco to grow from a router manufacturer to an all-round ICT company.

As an all-round ICT company, Cisco covers all areas of products and services such as wide-ranging network products, Internet service provider

(ISP) infrastructure, collaboration tools, data centers and virtualization, and so on. Modern Cisco is no longer just a network vendor – as an all-round ICT company, Cisco covers every corner of the Internet and communications field through strategic collaboration with its diversity of partner companies. Using ICT, Cisco aims to achieve human networks that promote collaboration management and smooth communications between people, particularly in corporations.

Currently, Cisco's innovations that began with its routers are pushing the company toward becoming a world-leading ICT corporation providing never-before-seen familiar and high value network connection as the company positions itself for the era of "the Internet of everything," hailed as the next generation of the Internet. Cisco purposefully drives sustainable growth through these continuous innovations to not only provide resources for strengthening its in-house R&D systems and personnel training, but also in parallel, through M&A strategies, innovates by externally acquiring valuable intangible assets such as the best technologies and business models, and human resources.

Viewed from the perspective of the "strategy and technology capabilities" components of DC discussed in Chapter 3, Cisco's M&A strategies have brought about the individual synergies in strategies and technologies that have enabled the company to grow to become an all-round ITC corporation. These individual strategies and technologies are the individual product strategies required for network solutions (the diversity of routers, switches, storage, software, endpoints and services, and so on) and the technical strategies to support those. Moreover, these individual products and technologies are mutually positioned in the domains of adjacent (peripheral) products and technologies. Thinking about this from the viewpoint described by the strategy capabilities in Table 3.1 in Chapter 3, getting all products and technologies in hand from R&D through to sales and support is an example of a vertically integrated and evolved value chain at the product and technology levels. Also, from the viewpoint of technology capabilities, M&A strategies bring about total network solutions by integrating and converging different technologies (co-specialized technologies). At the same time, the individual products and technologies have become the co-specialized assets of the company's total network solutions.

The strategic synergies and technologies synergies provided by Cisco have an even greater meaning for its customers. This can also be described by the concept of co-specialized assets in terms of customer value creation (for example, refer to Chapter 7 of Kodama, 2007b). If customers (enterprises) order their network solutions that they purchase and build from Cisco in batches, it eliminates the need to use multi-vendor systems, lowers transaction costs incurred by customers (in-house coordination and negotiations with multiple vendors), solves problems of overall implementation costs, and technical problems of connectivity between various devices, and enables to maintain a consistent level of ongoing technical support after implementation. And, new value is also brought about for customers when the network systems they implement are interlocked with in-house management systems, which creates co-specialization with customers also. In this world of ICT solutions, the DC at the provision end of products and services have effects on customers (in particular corporate users), for example, customers can acquire new ICT capabilities (e.g., Kodama, 2012) to create new businesses. Searching for the concept of such chaining of DC between corporations may be an important future research topic.

5.2 DRIVING M&A STRATEGIES THROUGH CHAMBERS' STRATEGIC NON-ROUTINE ACTIVITIES

Chambers retired in June 2015. It was 20 years earlier, when the Internet was becoming popular, that Chambers took up the post as CEO of Cisco, and it was Cisco led by Chambers, which made a tremendous contribution to the spread of the Internet, as the giant network equipment vendor. Chambers was the CEO of one of the few companies that have changed the world with the Internet.

Like Chambers, the entrepreneurial role of managerial activities, in other words strategic non-routine activities performed by managers, are a requirement for bringing about DC as discussed in Chapter 2. When corporations and their top management demonstrate DC, they make inferences about consumer tastes, business problems and technical advances, and carefully consider those inferences and adjust them to execute actions by coordinating capital and activity to continually bring about innovation and change.

DC, in part, reside with individual managers and the top management teams (Teece, 2014). At decisive junctures such as M&A strategies, the abilities of the CEO and top managers to recognize important developments and trends, produce ideas about future strategies, problems on hand and response measures while driving the company forward are the most remarkable characteristics of the DC equipping their company (Adner and Helfat, 2003).

As well as that, and as discussed in Chapter 2, DC do not only exist in high-level routine activities, but are also related to the combinations of organizational routines as signature processes, entrepreneurial leadership and the leadership of management teams (Teece, 2007, 2012b; Augier and Teece, 2009). The creative actions of business persons and entrepreneurs (in this case, the creation of new markets through the M&A strategies of Cisco's management team including Chambers) are characteristically weighted more toward strategic, non-routine activities rather than routines. In the reality of business, much of the strategic actions and reformations require strategic non-routine activities that cannot be copied (Teece, 2012b).

As Teece (2014) states, competition theories that eliminate the potential for non-routine activities by top management teams are unnatural, and strategic non-routine activities are crucial for the core DC framework. While Eisenhardt and Martin (2000) assert that emotionally, it isn't possible for top management teams to face uncertainty in rapidly changing markets, the strategic processes of asset orchestration through sensing, seizing and transformation through the instinctive and responsive actions of the CEO and top management teams are important in these situations. Strategic non-routine activities by the CEO and top management team drive co-specialization of the company's intangible assets with the intangible assets of other companies, and bring about DC for the company's sustainable growth.

5.3   CISCO'S ORGANIZATIONAL CAPABILITIES

Next, the author discusses the organization capabilities that are congruent with the aforementioned strategy and technology capabilities of Cisco. In 2009, Chambers altered Cisco's top-down decision-making system by introducing a number of councils to make decisions. Cisco executives participated in each of these councils, which provided strategic advice, and assessed the progress of projects (Blodget, 2009). However, there were some cases of slow decision-making with this system, and cases it wasn't clear where responsibility lies, so in 2011, the organization was restructured so that the nine councils were reduced to three.

Collaborative management through networked collaborative organizations in the company centered on the councils, boards and working groups, brings about different capabilities to those of operations management through normal routine activities. This is an example of organizational capabilities, which are an element of Cisco's DC for dealing with dynamic environments. In this book the author calls Cisco's organizational systems "networked collaborative organizations."[1] As discussed in Chapter 2, the strategic non-routine activities enacted through these dynamic strategic communities (SC) structures are important elements that bring about organizational and DC.

The core driver of organizational capabilities is human resources, and Cisco also focuses on them. For this reason, the company summarizes the key competence of human resources as five keywords (collaboration, learn, execution, accelerate, disrupt) it calls "C-LEAD." The most important of these is collaboration, because collaboration is the most effective method of structuring an organization so that it can respond to rapidly changing markets.

Also, Cisco's culture is made up of 13 codes of conduct. These are innovation, fun, no technology religion, continuous improvement/ stretch goals, quality team, profit contribution (frugality), giving back/ trust/fairness/integrity, collaboration and teamwork, market transitions, inclusion, drive change, empowerment and open communication (Cisco, 2011). Even when buying a company, and integration of it takes place over a short time, Cisco is very careful about not rushing organizational integration of human resources and does not relieve anyone of their employment. Regarding the StrataCom buyout, Cisco did not recklessly execute organizational integration and so forth. This is because rushed or haphazard integration can conversely lead to negative DC (Helfat et al., 2007).

As described above, Cisco takes up bottom-up factors pivoting on collaboration activities, rather than top-down factors only, and individual staff members are empowered, and they are expected to contribute and respond to teams as leaders. Hence, as an organizational capability congruent with Cisco's strategy and technology capabilities it uses to achieve its M&A strategies, collaboration management enabled by the dynamic networked collaborative organizations and good quality human resources discussed earlier is fundamental to the company.

5.4   CISCO'S OPERATIONAL CAPABILITIES

In this section, the author discusses the operational capabilities that are congruent with the aforementioned Cisco's strategy, technology and organizational capabilities. As discussed in terms of organizational capabilities, Cisco believes that driving collaboration is an efficient method of bringing out the best of staff abilities and getting organizations to move swiftly for success. Collaboration does not mean "making something together," but rather means "co-creation" that in organizational operations, entails bringing together human resources to cooperate in creating new ideas. Collaboration is included in Cisco's code of conduct, its leadership competency, and all five areas of Cisco's focus, and for it to be enacted smoothly requires changes to culture, processes (exchanges between people) and technologies (Ricci and Wiese, 2011). By demonstrating organizational capabilities brought about from networked collaborative organizations across the different business units in the company, Cisco enables the operational capabilities processes of creative dialogue, understanding and cooperation and quick decision-making and action, which not only regularly strengthen incremental innovation in the company's main businesses, but also enable the company to step up to the challenge of radical innovation to create new businesses in the future.

Chambers emphasizes that collaboration enables people in organizations to effectively combine their abilities and release each other's talents to respond to new market opportunities with agility. Collaboration is used at Cisco not only for communications between the company's top, middle and lower layers but also for meetings and problem solving. The effectiveness of collaboration is demonstrated when all members of an organization come to understand the optimum ways to share ideas and opinions. Cisco defines four types of thinking (leader, starter, planner and influencer) (Ricci and Wiese, 2011). Since teams can collapse if communication styles are different, productive and creative thinking can be used to overcome mutual differences and contradictions if one changes one's style a little to adapt to the styles of others. Hence, by identifying other parties or groups for communication, Cisco is able to hold meetings smoothly and effectively through creative dialogue. This kind of creative dialogue drives understanding and cooperation between members of staff, and is a factor in achieving swift decision-making and action as a company.

Nevertheless, collaboration is not a simple thing. The form and quality of it has to change to suit changing environments and situations that staff are facing. Collaboration is not recyclable – it's irreversible and is the non-routine activities of staff. Strategic collaboration at Cisco can also be called strategic non-routine activity discussed in Chapter 2, and this kind of collaboration shows its power through the formation of effective SC between staff members. In other words, strategic collaboration is an important factor in bringing about DC. As many consultants opine, collaboration is one way to achieve best practices, but achieving strategic collaboration is easier said than done. In particular, strategic collaboration establishes the unique organizational culture of a company and raises the potential for "signature processes" – operational capabilities that cannot be easily copied by other companies.

At Cisco, VSEM has been established as common vocabulary for decision-making to enable teams to have a clear understanding of goals, and to avoid miscommunications. VSEM means "Vision, Strategy,

Execution and Metrics." All Team VSEM at Cisco are published on the company intranet, and are included in performance assessment systems (Ricci and Wiese, 2011).

Visions in VSEM are called "Vision Statements," which clarify common goals to all members of teams. Cisco's vision statement is "Changing the way we work, live, play and learn." The 'S' for "strategy" in VSEM briefly describes the methods to use to advance toward the vision, where the roles played by leaders entail the sensing and seizing functions of DC as they search out and define business resources and assets required by teams, and set down new strategic schemes.

The 'E' in VSEM is the specific "transforming" step of DC to support and achieve strategy in the short or long term. Leaders openly engage in dialogue with team members through collaboration when deciding on execution plans, by summarizing the actual tasks that teams will undertake in lists, and so on. Execution plans assign responsibilities to people to carry out certain tasks, while individual goals for staff performance assessments are linked to the team strategy. The 'M' in VSEM entails the use of Balanced Score Card (BSC), and responsibility is given to individuals and teams as standard. This enables managers to get an overall view of performance and progress (Ricci and Wiese, 2011).

VSEM shows each team which direction they are headed, while the separate "team charter" that contains basic rules for reaching goals enables teams to guarantee that their operations are correct. These enable smooth communications and are tried and tested ways to build relationships of trust, and contain specific expressions about team objectives, roles, goals and the scope of business. In this way, by clarifying common language (VSEM) and the team charter, Cisco has created an environment in which miscommunications in the teams are avoided, trust is built, and responses are swift as staff collaborate toward the company visions.

Toward the above solid visions and strategies (R&D, M&A and strategic alliances), the implementation of new work processes drives collaboration as strategic non-routine activities between staff, and brings about new operational capabilities, an element of Cisco's unique DC that is congruent with the strategy, technology, and organizational capabilities of the company.

5.5   CISCO'S LEADERSHIP CAPABILITIES THROUGH STRATEGIC COLLABORATION

In this section, the author discusses the leadership capabilities that are congruent with the four strategic, technological, organizational and operational capabilities discussed previously.

5.5.1   Centralized and Dispersed Decision-making Processes

As discussed in the operational capabilities section above, Cisco has deployed a collaboration system for better decision-making, for which common language is indispensable. This collaboration system enables clear decision-making in a short amount of time. However, in some instances, centralized leadership must be demonstrated (Kodama, 2004). In the initial stages of processes to propose, set down and execute optimized strategies across an entire organization, collaboration through the formation of SC is the most important element. As the stage of executing specific strategies approaches, the responsibilities must be clarified, and there must be mechanisms to provide remunerations in line with contributions. However, in situations where time is limited such as times of danger or when a response to an important market opportunity is required, there is more weight on centralized leadership for decision-making by top management and executives through strategic non-routine activities. Cisco knows when to apply the concept of collaboration, and when to return back to the centralized leadership approach – the company can proceed with a task with a 30-person group and bring down decisions quickly (Ricci and Wiese, 2011).

Furthermore, using common language enables the company to make decisions with a high degree of transparency. All staff understand the decision-making processes, those who make decisions, and the meaning of the results of those decisions, which enables them to accept them and proceed with their tasks. It's also clear who should participate in meetings, who has the authority to make decisions at certain points in time, and at what level debate should proceed. After creating common language vision and strategy, the authority to execute is given over to all staff, which, from these processes, enables them to acquire project ownership, the appropriate skills and a team spirit (Ricci and Wiese, 2011; Anderson, 2013).

At Cisco, ambiguity is the enemy of collaboration. Accordingly, at Cisco, there are five important processes the company requires that entail organizations being clearly defined, and entails thorough transparency with decision-making and sharing strategies and objectives among staff. These five processes are: (1) conveying who is making decisions to subordinates, (2) conveying how decisions are made to subordinates, (3) removing ambiguity from classifications, (4) deciding on common language, and spreading decisions widely, and (5) making sure that multiple teams simultaneously and instantly have the same ideas.

Cisco has at most two patterns of cases of teamwork not going so well. In group discussions, when certain members of staff do not state their opposition, and then later indirectly attack the decision with criticism, and so on, or the case where a staff member does not properly understand the intentions of the decision maker, and takes the decision to be something else (Ricci and Wiese, 2011). To prevent this, the best approach is to agree upon visions in meetings, have motivation and a sense of purpose, have everyone keep pace with each other, and set down strategies to achieve goals. Thus, this entails deciding on an overview, necessary procedures, and framework to measure results needed to execute strategies (in other words operations). Summarizing these decisions on one page, delegating persons in charge for each product and clearly defining where responsibility lies is key at Cisco. In reality, to make collaboration a success, the company is progressive with transferring authority for decision-making in the workplace, and decision-making is performed in each workplace.

In this way, if we were to use sports as an analogy, rather than a baseball team, Cisco is a dynamic network collaborative organization as discussed earlier (see Figure 5.1), or a soccer team-like organization in which each person can respond to changes as they come. Cisco takes on distributed leadership (Kodama, 2004) to respond to environmental changes as required, delegates authority to each workplace to make decisions to enable swift decision-making and autonomous actions. Hence, Cisco's leadership capabilities are characterized by the skillful balancing of centralized and distributed leadership.

5.5.2　Networked Collaborative Organizations Bring About Leadership Capabilities

Chambers saw through a managerial system that enables flexibility and agility to respond to change at any time, to proactively cause change, and the acceptance of change. Cisco transformed the old organizational forms in which the boss gave instructions to subordinates so they can act, and instead builds and promotes networked collaborative organizations that enable staff to collaborate autonomously. An networked collaborative organization is an organizational model designed to create more collaborative business ecosystems in companies (at times, with the inclusion of partners), and one that purposefully adopts distributed leadership systems. Although in the past, the executive was involved in all business activities, to trigger innovation, Cisco transitioned authority so that new businesses could be begun on multiple management levels, by eliminating the ultimate authority of top-down management structures and building networks of councils, stated in the organizational capabilities section. In this way, Cisco purposefully distributed its leadership and decision-making (London, 2011).

By building networked collaborative organizations, bottlenecks in organizational hierarchies were eliminated, and authority was given to council networks so that they could make important decisions themselves. As a result of configuring networked collaborative organizations, the company was able to optimize the value of its businesses associated with market changes (Cisco, 2011). As well as that, management at Cisco is an example of middle up/down management (Nonaka, 1988) functioning extremely well. Cisco continues with its distributed structures, where decisions are not made for subordinates, but are the result of direct three-dimensional integration of people with specialist knowledge, people with authority, and people who have information on execution of tasks. In other words, organizational authority is not hierarchical but horizontally structured so that individual contributors can make decisions and take actions without the approval of executives, depending on the situation (Cisco, 2011). This came about as a result of an old staff empowerment motto at Cisco of "Don't wait for approvals, ask for forgiveness later" (Young, 2001).

Cisco's leaders pay special attention to the following four points to drive collaboration: demonstrate true leadership, do not attack others; always try to make decisions with high degrees of transparency; use various resources as tools to take action; and clarify the relationship between authority, responsibility and remuneration (Ricci and Wiese, 2011). Collaboration accelerates the sharing of knowledge and skills, brings about innovation from the ideas of staff, and as a result enables an organization to reap even greater successes.

At Cisco, even remunerations are adjusted with organizational changes. By introducing distributed management, their remunerations system depends on the top, middle and lower management working together toward the same long-term goals. By using Web 2.0 technology, the company is able to strengthen communications between different layers and different divisions, and increase productivity (London, 2011). In this way, Cisco maintains a balance between the contribution of individuals, and the contribution of the group. Most remuneration of the top management layer depends on how well they collaborate, and is decided upon through the assessments made by the middle and lower layers (Ancora and Backman, 2010). The top layer states in detail the results that they expect the middle layer to produce, and middle management can understand what needs to be done as leaders, and how assessments should be made. Hence, if results are good, pay increases follow. As such, Cisco has introduced a system in which subsequent leaders are trained and given responsibility for new businesses (Hegar, 2011).

Also, as the organizational structure becomes flat, leading managers don't appoint or instruct micro and lower managers, but have to understand intellectually diverse personnel and organizational elements. These new style managers put more value on building and coaching teams than directing teams and sharing values about visions and strategic objectives, while at the same time stimulating staff. In addition, the role of middle management has changed as follows: With modern day ICT, it takes less time for middle management to convey top-down information and business data from top management to lower management. In other words, the value of middle management is in their networking and wide-ranging social relationship building skills, dynamic team building and rebuilding, collaboration among team leaders, adjustment and vertical and horizontal direction between teams, information sharing, and their ability to demonstrate initiative to achieve solutions to problems, and build new business by diagnosing problems. In other words, the capabilities sought in middle management are not conventional ordinary capabilities (OC) based on routines, but DC through strategic non-routine activities through the configuration of dynamic SC.

In short, not only must DC be demonstrated through the high-quality strategic non-routine activities of executives, but by middle managers also. In dynamic networked collaborative organizations, multi layers of leaders flexibly strike a balance between centralized and distributed leadership, appropriately demonstrate these leaderships, and generate synergies of leaderships between leaders to bring about leadership capabilities, an element of DC. In this way, Cisco generates new leadership capabilities pivoting on the company's unique collaboration management, which is congruent with its strategy, technology, organizational and operational capabilities. Leadership capabilities that promote collaboration in response to changing times and give authority to staff and teams to drive innovation are important intangible assets at Cisco. Thus, as discussed below, the five capabilities (strategy, technology, organizational, operational and leadership capabilities) drive internal and external congruence in capabilities at Cisco.

5.6   INTERNAL AND EXTERNAL CONGRUENCE IN CAPABILITIES AT CISCO (SEE FIGURE 5.1)

Cisco obtains new intangible assets from the outside with its M&A strategies (technologies, skills, know-how, and so on) and orchestrates them with its own core intangible assets, which at the same time heightens the potential for synergies with existing businesses to strengthen incremental innovations, and also achieves new radical innovation (product, service and business model innovations for a variety of network solutions). To succeed with new innovations spanning different fields of specialization (in particular radical innovation), existing research into knowledge management and strategic management emphasizes the importance of knowledge integration (e.g., Kline, 1985). The occurrence of new innovation is interpreted as the combination of dissimilar specialized knowledge in the convergence process (e.g., Hacklin et al., 2009; Rafols and Meyer, 2010), or in other words the knowledge integration process having been executed at a level spanning different areas of specialization (e.g., Kodama, 2009a, 2014). The integration of various knowledge which used to belong to different individual areas of specialization in the past, depending on its character, has been a prerequisite for technical convergence. Therefore, to make technical convergence occur, integration of knowledge from different areas of technical expertise is indispensable.

Thus, such knowledge integration process is an example of the asset orchestration process, a major element of DC. As discussed in Chapter 3, the asset orchestration process is an important factor in achieving sustainable growth through a corporation's strategic innovation (incremental and radical innovation). For this reason, the achievement of internal and external congruence in capabilities in corporations is crucial, as described below.

Cisco's execution of M&A strategies to date has its essence in this type of asset orchestration process. As an example of the company's M&A, in 2007 Cisco bought up WebEx, a leader in the B2B collaboration application market, and in 2010 bought up Tandberg, a company based in Oslo, Norway, and a leader in the market for high-end business user video conferencing systems. By purchasing these two companies, Cisco orchestrated the intangible Internet assets it had built up over many years with the video collaboration technologies of the two companies, and strategically created its new service innovation called "unified communications" that is expected to grow rapidly into the future. In B2B and B2C (including customers) businesses, collaboration strategies have become increasingly important in the workplace in recent years. As a result, to achieve business efficiency and transformation, many companies achieved "workplace innovations" to raise the productivity and creativity of all practitioners in all kinds of situations through the use of wide-ranging face-to-face and video collaboration.

Also, regarding its M&A (of companies Composite Software and Assemblage) to achieve the vision of Internet of Everything (IoE) also called the Internet of Things (IoT) linked to the company's cloud computing vision, as described above, Cisco is taking the strategic actions of orchestrating a range of different technologies (intangible assets) to bring about new service innovations. Behind the M&A strategies of Cisco lies the objective of achieving new innovation (incremental or radical) through the asset orchestration process. As also discussed in Chapter 3, the asset orchestration process drives the achievement of internal and external congruence in capabilities at Cisco.

Essentially, Cisco's M&A strategies are not only examples of successful product development, but are also cases of successful tight-knit linking between innovative marketing and technical strategies. Viewed from the perspective of organizational behavior, Cisco's CEO and innovative business persons representing its executive engage in, and properly execute, entrepreneurship and trial and error across the knowledge boundaries between different technical fields, to uncover and create new businesses (products and services) in the network market. Behind the Cisco successes lay the company's achievement of congruence between the corporate system and the environment (Insight-1), and congruence between individual capabilities within the corporate system (Insight-2) through congruence enabled by orchestration of co-specialized assets both inside and outside of the company (Insight-3).

Breaking into the router market, devices necessary for the Internet, Cisco merged its R&D and M&A strategies to successively bring about new radical innovation to produce network externalities in the network product market, in both aspects of marketing and technologies. Thus, Cisco leads the competition by offering "total network solutions" (providing a full line up by vertical integration of all types of network products), for enterprises and network and service providers. From the perspective of strategy capabilities, this is also vertical integration of value chain development at the product level.

Additionally, with Cisco's strategy capabilities, the company has created a vertically integrated value chain through orchestration of the co-specialized assets of the end users (enterprises and network and service providers), through to its technical and sales partners, and suppliers (EMS, and so on). As corporate systems, Cisco optimizes its vertical boundaries to dynamically bring about congruence with the expanding and changing network market through its M&A strategies. As well as that, Cisco engages in rapid incremental innovation to secure its market share in response to competitors and changing competitive environments.

Also, to bring about technology capabilities to support these strategy capabilities, the company engages in its characteristic technology strategies to achieve radical innovation, through M&A. From the perspective of technology capabilities, M&A strategies are examples of achieving network solutions through the merging and integration of different technologies (co-specialized technologies). Thus, the individual products and technologies that the company buys up are also co-specialized assets for the company's total network solutions.

Cisco's organizational systems, its organizational capabilities congruent with its strategy and technology capabilities, are characterized by incorporation of bottom-up elements based on collaboration, rather than top-down elements. Collaboration empowers individual members of staff, and enables them to respond and contribute to teams as leaders. Hence, the factors of Cisco's organizational systems that have brought about success in its M&A strategies are founded on the building of dynamic networked collaborative organizations, and collaboration management with the best available people.

Collaborative management through networked collaborative organizations in the company centered on the councils, boards and working groups brings about different capabilities to those of operations management through normal routine activities. This is an example of organizational capabilities, which are an element of Cisco's DC for dealing with dynamic environments.

While forming SC consisting of various groups of specialists based on flat organizations formed around products (businesses), these SC are organically linked in networks to bring together the diverse intangible assets spread around the globe. Organizational capabilities, enabled by the formation of these dynamic organizations, SC and networked SC, enable the orchestration of Cisco's co-specialized assets spread around the world, and achieve platforms (strategic and technological) to create new business models.

To properly demonstrate these strategy, technology, and organizational capabilities, Cisco implements new work processes in its operations using ICT and pivoting on collaboration at the global level, to achieve its strategies (R&D, M&A and strategic alliances), which are based on the company's solid visions. Collaboration, as strategic non-routine activities among staff, establishes the company's unique culture, and brings about operational capabilities as signature processes that are difficult for other companies to copy.

Hence, bringing congruence to all capabilities elements, those of strategy, technology, organization and operations, comes about through the leadership of the CEO, the executive and innovative business persons mainly in middle management, who demonstrate their leadership capabilities in councils, boards and working groups in networked collaborative organizations in the company, and demonstrate synergies between their mutual capabilities. Leadership at Cisco, through strategic collaboration between all staff, drives orchestration of co-specialized assets around the world, and both inside and outside of the company to create new markets with network technologies. Thus, Cisco builds win–win relationships among its stakeholders (users and partners).

To create value in the era of IoE (IoT), Cisco is advocating "fog computing" architecture that entails developing new networking, computing and storage from the cloud to the edge, and to achieve new market expansion,

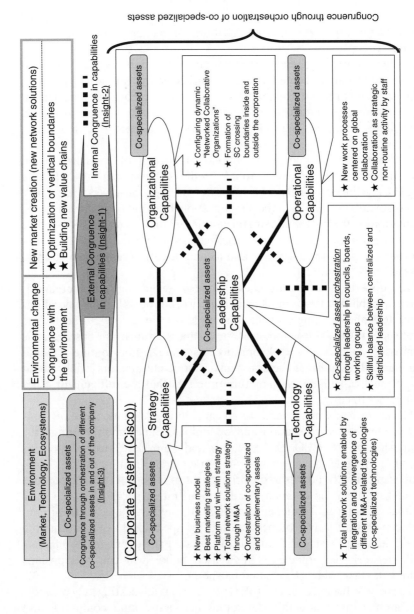

Congruence through orchestration of co-specialized assets

Environment (Market, Technology, Ecosystems)	Environmental change	New market creation (new network solutions)
	Congruence with the environment	★ Optimization of vertical boundaries ★ Building new value chains

Co-specialized assets

Congruence through orchestration of different co-specialized assets in and out of the company (Insight-3)

External Congruence in capabilities (Insight-1)

Internal Congruence in capabilities (Insight-2)

(Corporate system (Cisco))

Strategy Capabilities

Co-specialized assets

★ New business model
★ Best marketing strategies
★ Platform and win–win strategy
★ Total network solutions strategy through M&A
★ Orchestration of co-specialized and complementary assets

Organizational Capabilities

Co-specialized assets

★ Configuring dynamic "Networked Collaborative Organizations"
★ Formation of SC crossing boundaries inside and outside the corporation

Leadership Capabilities

Co-specialized assets

★ *Co-specialized asset orchestration* through leadership in councils, boards, working groups
★ Skilful balance between centralized and distributed leadership

Operational Capabilities

Co-specialized assets

★ New work processes centered on global collaboration
★ Collaboration as strategic non-routine activity by staff

Technology Capabilities

Co-specialized assets

★ Total network solutions enabled by integration and convergence of different M&A-related technologies (co-specialized technologies)

Figure 5.1 Internal and external congruence through orchestration of co-specialized assets (at Cisco)

144

the company is pushing for co-innovation strategies through strategic ecosystem partnerships in addition to its conventional M&A and capital expenditure strategies. Going forward, to achieve innovation as new business ecosystems through these IoE (IoT) strategies, Cisco will require DC to bring together all stakeholders including its staff, partners and customers, and leaders in diverse global industries, to use the different knowledge of all those involved to the fullest, and orchestrate the company's intangible assets with all of these different intangible assets. To achieve this, collaboration management both inside and outside of the company, including its customers, as was driven by Chambers and the company executive, will be the most important factor.

5.7   CHAPTER SUMMARY

This chapter has considered and analyzed the five micro elements of DC in a large corporation, Cisco, and capabilities congruence in and outside of the company. Behind the success of Cisco's M&A strategies lies the achievement of new innovation (incremental or radical, or strategic innovation is a combination of these) enabled by the asset orchestration process through the company's strategic collaboration management. This asset orchestration process achieved internal and external congruence in capabilities at Cisco, and has been the driving force of ongoing strategic innovations for the company to grow sustainably.

NOTE

1.   Regarding "networked collaborative organizations" see Figure 5.3 in the Cisco case study in Kodama (2017).

6. New product innovation through dynamic capabilities: the case of Fujifilm versus Kodak

Once total global demand for color film peaked in the year 2000, Fujifilm of Japan nosedived into debt by 2005 forcing the company to rapidly restructure. Nevertheless, Fujifilm had accumulated a wide range of technologies in the film business, and also had considerable brand power. Fujifilm had chemical, mechanical and software resources with which it had been taking on the global competition, which, in a sense, also enabled the company to come together and take up the challenge of structural reform. Around this time, Fujifilm took a huge turn toward massive strategy transformation in its "Second Foundation."

Moreover, in this second founding, Fujifilm's mid-term "Vision 75" business plan included top-down orders in the company to raise new cash cows. This resulted in the company producing hit products one after the other such as the Astalift cosmetics lineup, the similar case search system designed for lung cancer diagnosis support, and the polarizing tack film indispensable to LCD panels.

There were massive differences between the strategic reactions of Kodak and Fujifilm when the digital camera appeared on the global scene. In contrast to the structural reforms Fujifilm achieved in the face of attack on its capabilities, Kodak's strategy was to defend its capabilities. Kodak limited itself to protecting its existing patented capabilities, and was unable to structurally reform its capabilities by seeking out or creating new capabilities for transformation.

Using comparative research, this chapter discusses and analyzes differences in strategic approaches of Fujifilm and Kodak, from the perspective of corporate governance reform. The chapter also goes into detail about Fujifilm's demonstration of dynamic capabilities (DC) through asset orchestration by building of a triad model for strategic communities (SC) spanning both the insides and outsides of the company, which led to the company's successful strategy transformation. Finally, the chapter presents the concept of "SC-based firm" as a new governance system that brings about DC through the formation of SC.

6.1 FACTORS IN THE DECLINE OF KODAK: THE PERSPECTIVES OF ORDINARY CAPABILITIES, DYNAMIC CAPABILITIES, REFORM OF GOVERNANCE AND COMPARATIVE ANALYSIS WITH FUJIFILM

Kodak was founded by George Eastman in 1888. Eastman developed a photographic dry plate, which was instrumental in popularizing the camera with the general public. Later, in 1935, Kodak released its definitive camera film, "Kodachrome," securing the company a position in the world of photography. With this release, the world's first color film, Kodak went on to release a range of related film products to enable people to enjoy photography more simply and with greater convenience. Then in 1975, the company released the world's first digital camera, and developed an organic EL light emitting element. At its peak, the company's stock market capitalization exceeded JPY 4 trillion. However, the company's photographic business (silver halide film, development, silver halide printing), which constituted the majority of its profits, peaked in developed countries in 1993, and then began its decline. In 1975, Kodak successfully developed the world's first digital camera. However, with the encroaching popularity of the digital SLR camera developed by five companies in Japan, the PC (applications to process digital images and share images on the Internet), the mobile telephone with built-in camera and later the smartphone, Kodak retreated from the digital camera business in 2012, after it fell into the red.

It was well understood at the time that if Kodak did not make a sharp turn into the digital business away from its silver halide film business, for which demand had seriously slowed, then the company would go into decline. Many Kodak staff accurately predicted the threat of the digital camera. In particular, the executive at the time had a heightened sense of danger, and were prepared to take initiatives for full shift to digital business with an eye on the future, but many of the company's investors were not interested. These investors felt the destruction of the company's existing photographic film business would be in conflict with their interests, since the film business had been producing profits.

Shubei Nire, a US Kodak staffer at the time, said that the cause of the company's destruction was its over-established business model (revenues from the three-staged model of film, development and printing), which had been a highly profitable structure (Nire, 2013). Nire also said that Kodak had executed a strategy to cross the bridge from analog (silver halide) to digital, but ended up thinking that its printing business would be secured to some degree, because of the superior durability characteristics of the printed silver halide images (The author thinks that it was a reasonable decision by Kodak at the time). This is because Kodak had hypothesized because of the lack of peripheral equipment such as high-end printers capable of silver halide printing, and that users would want to print out and keep photographs even if they were captured with digital photography. However, later on, with the advent of technical means such as the mobile phone with built-in camera, and the ease with which it became possible to share and publish photographs through blogs and so forth on the Internet, the way users enjoyed photography changed, and the frequency at which they used silver halide prints fell suddenly and dramatically.

In addition, the executives at the company who had felt the future threat to the silver halide film had continued to diversify business not only by developing the instant photography business for which Kodak had lost out to Polaroid in the completion in the 1970s but also by buying companies to develop new business in the 1980s and 1990s. The company bought up Verbatim with the aim of moving into the battery and floppy disk market, and bought up Sterling Drug and L&F Products with the aim of moving into the pharmaceutical industry. However, focus on the tendency of investors to demand short-term profits meant that Kodak management at the time had to approach diversification with caution. The aforementioned Shubei Nire described how in America, the more consistently a company could boast high profits, it became increasingly difficult for it to take the challenge of large investments into new business. This is because the shareholders aren't interested in converting or diversifying businesses. To them, what is more important than the state of the company in 10 years, are this year's dividends – if there are no problems with business at present, and sufficient profit is being produced, then shareholders feel that instead of investing capital into new business that they don't understand, they should have those funds as increased dividends. Hence, first of all, pushing forward into the digitalization of photography meant the self-destruction of a highly profitable structure – from the outset, why would that be necessary? (Nire, 2013, p.19).

For these reasons, Kodak concentrated on its film business. However, in 1994, with Apple's release of the QuickTake 100, the world's first consumer digital camera, and with the advance of the digital camera business into the 2000s, Kodak was not able to perform well, and being unable to switch over to other businesses, its long-running chained business model of silver halide film, development and silver halide printing collapsed, and put the company in a state of crisis. Then in January of 2012, Kodak applied for application of the Federal bankruptcy law, Article 11.

Hence, Kodak's concentration of resources into its existing film business is clearly distinguishable from Fujifilm's business. Prior to Antonio Perez being appointed as CEO from HP, Kodak had focused on developing, manufacturing and marketing consumers, specialists and health, as well as other imaging products and services. In 1993, the time that George Fisher was called in from Motorola, Kodak was under attack from Xerox with its large-size digital copiers, and Canon and Ricoh's low-cost, high-quality products, which led Kodak to sell off its copier sales and after service department to Danka, and then in 1997 sold a manufacturing plant to leading German printer manufacturer Heidelberg. The funds raised from these sales ended up getting used to buy back its stocks.

However, with Perez at the helm in 2003, Kodak moved into the ink jet printer business, but switched over to mainly providing top-line products and services in the photograph, graphic communications and healthcare markets, concentrating its business on photographs and printing. But in 2007, Kodak then went on to sell off its healthcare interests to Canadian investment company Onex for JPY 200 billion. Kodak's retreat from healthcare was mirrored in its 1994 sale of its pharmaceutical business to Bayer in order to buy back its stocks. Then in 2010, it sold its organic EL materials business to LG of Korea, technology that was anticipated as a future replacement for liquid crystal materials.

In contrast, Fujifilm decreased its dependence on its imaging solutions business, and raised its level of dependence on its information solutions and document solutions businesses, which entailed the company buying a further 25 percent of the 50/50 Fuji Xerox joint venture with the US Xerox Corp in 2001 bringing its stake to 75 percent, taking leadership of the company and making it a consolidated subsidiary. This business is currently the major earner for Fujifilm Holdings. For LCD materials too, Fujifilm also began its 1958 Fujitac (tac film) technology and in 1996 introduced a wide viewing angle film. After that, the company expanded its production with factories at Yoshida and Kumamoto. These businesses compensated for the gradual decline in the profitability of the photographic business.

Fujifilm also recognized that it should strategically nurture its Fujitac, cosmetic and supplement products and so on to be offered in the market as products moving away from imaging solutions. Fujifilm also strategically developed life-related businesses. This entailed specifically Fujifilm buying up Toyama Chemical in 2008 and later SonoSite. With the acquisition of the American Cellular Dynamics International, an iPS regenerative medicine venture, the company aims to become a comprehensive regenerative medicine enterprise.

As described above, Kodak strategically concentrated on its photographic, graphics and commercial businesses, and selected and concentrated with software developments for mainly managing images and image editing. Kodak also concentrated its businesses by merging its health imaging business with other businesses. In this way, Kodak aimed to rejuvenate its existing imaging businesses, while Fujifilm aimed at ensuring new dynamism for growth, a major difference compared to Kodak. Put differently, Kodak concentrated on exploitation, while Fujifilm concentrated on exploration. Behind the different outcomes of the business development of both of these companies was the different governance of their executive, and the differences in awareness of their management teams, including their external directors.

Even though Kodak was quick to feel the threat from the changing market for film, the company was entrenched in its ordinary capabilities (OC), in other words its existing routines, because of the demands of the doctrine of short-term performance to maximize value for shareholders. OC have been described as achieving technical efficiency and "doing things right" in core capabilities of a business, that is, operations, administration, and governance (Teece, 2014). Kodak also consistently engaged in rigid strategies such as stock measures using its own substantial capital to buy a large amount of its own shares with the proceeds from sales of its enterprises. All of these actions were done through Kodak's OC. At Kodak, there wasn't any thought about responding to the changing environment by orchestrating assets with DC to merge the company's high-level existing knowledge assets and technologies with knowledge assets from outside the company. Kodak concentrated on demonstrating its OC to defend its existing explicit knowledge such as its existing film business and patents, and was unable to structurally reform its knowledge with DC to create and accumulate new knowledge assets. In stark contrast to this, Fujifilm demonstrated DC to orchestrate co-specialized assets and achieve structural knowledge reforms that enabled it to develop new businesses.

Looking at the causes of the decline of Kodak from the capabilities view, it can be surmised that the company was unable to reform its existing governance, one of its OC. Kodak's business philosophy (The Kodak Value) entails respect for human beings, uncompromised integrity, entrepreneurship, staff trust, and ongoing learning and improvement in the workplace, values that were maintained over the long years since George Eastman founded the company. However, consciously ignoring the business philosophy of George Eastman, the company tended toward becoming shareholder-centric, and in the 1970s in the preamble to its Corporate Responsibility Principles added that good relations with its shareholders were of utmost importance. In other words, the good relations built up with shareholders created the perspective that raising the shareholder value was top priority.

Former Fujifilm Senior Executive Vice President Tasuku Imai stated three reasons for the demise of Kodak: (1) the shareholder centrism, (2) members invited to the board were CEOs invited from other companies and outside independent directors, and (3) there was nobody on the board with familiarity with the existing business (Imai, 2015). In actual fact, in the past, board members had included CEOs (two with 16 years of service) from high-tech IT companies (Motorola and HP), but with the Corporate Responsibility Principles focused on shareholder centrism, the company used funds associated with industrial sales such as its failing copier business to buy back shares, which lead to excessive debt and weakened the company's business base. Moreover, as most of the board were executives from outside the company, hardly any of them had much understanding of Kodak's business. Notably in 2007, the board consisted of CEO Antoni Perez from HP and eight independent external directors; there was not one director from within the company, and there remain questions as to whether decisions about sales of existing healthcare and organic EL businesses and the ink jet printer new market entrant (which later made serious losses) were appropriate. More than that, it is highly questionable whether growth strategies for new Kodak businesses were sufficiently discussed and proper judgments made.

The spectacular decline of Kodak can be interpreted as due to a lack of DC to achieve sweeping reforms to the company's existing governance systems, an element of the OC of the company, and bring about strategic proposals and the abilities to execute those proposals based on the new governance concepts. Making no governance reforms and changes in investment patterns and routines is a sign of organizational sclerosis. In the DC framework, routines and business models cannot be viewed as completely fixed. While it is true that routines are bound in rules, customs and traditions, in most cases, routines can be changed, which particularly requires strong leadership like that of Fujifilm (Teece, 2014). Kodak acquiring strong DC would not only entail adjusting strategies and organizations to suit predicted changes in business environments such as market and technical changes, but also would importantly entail changes (reforms) to its OC and routines that form the base of the OC.

In contrast, in a dramatically changing business environment in 2006, Fujifilm renewed its corporate philosophy and code of conduct, and consciously reformed the entire company as well as its organizations to converge the knowledge of its technologies fostered through its past involvement in the photography business with new technologies to expand peripheral businesses through the asset orchestration process (see Box 6.1). Moreover, as a new growth strategy, the company reviewed its R&D systems with the establishment of Advanced Research Laboratories and

BOX 6.1   DYNAMIC CAPABILITIES THROUGH ASSET
ORCHESTRATION BY BUILDING OF A TRIAD
MODEL FOR STRATEGIC COMMUNITIES

Aiming to restructure the R&D organization to one with clearly stated functions and roles and to pursue development directly linked to business, Fujifilm introduced divisional labs and, as a new organizational concept, adopted a framework for implementing activities from R&D to commercialization as one continuous process. This kind of vertical integration of organizations from upstream to downstream, that is, from R&D to commercialization (with divisional labs directly linked to business divisions) was designed to efficiently pursue development directly linked to business and to create "exploitation SC" through collaboration between divisional labs to create synergies between business divisions (see Figure 6.1). Color film, which represents Fujifilm's core technology accumulated over decades, has a total film thickness of 20 micrometers and is carefully coated with 16 to 20 coats in such a way to ensure against interfacial mixing between layers. Inside the film is silver halide, which is surrounded by various organic materials that precisely adsorb the halide, and various nanodispersed organic materials are dispersed around these materials. Thoroughly exploiting this photo technology, Fujifilm developed a commercialization strategy for using this technology in various business areas, particularly in exploitation SC centered on the respective business divisions. This type of exploitation SC demonstrated dynamic capabilities through orchestration of diverse co-specialized assets, not only to upgrade and improve existing products, but also to develop new ones.

Moreover, Fujifilm strengthened collaboration among organizations to reinforce fundamental technologies and advanced research across different areas of specialization (directly linking corporate labs, technology centers, divisional labs and the R&D Management Headquarters) and organizations directly connected with business mentioned earlier (directly linking divisional labs and business divisions). Advanced research at Fujifilm includes the three Frontier Core-Technology Laboratories, Synthetic Organic Chemistry Laboratories, and Advanced Marking Research Laboratories (called "corporate laboratories" at Fujifilm), which pursue fundamental research in new fundamental technologies and new products and foster creative exploration SC. These Advanced Research Laboratories aim to create new value through "intellectual fusion and innovation." At Fujifilm, "intellectual fusion" refers to the convergence of knowledge and thinking approaches of engineers in different fields, while "innovation" refers to the creation of new disruptive innovation technology and new values. Exploration SC have an accurate understanding of the strengths and weaknesses of their technology infrastructure and core technologies the company has at present and make efforts to further build on its strengths in a creative manner through asset orchestration processes with a view to strengthening fundamental technology to thoroughly exploit photo-related technologies (see Figure 6.1). Exploration SC are critical organizational infrastructure for bringing about dynamic capabilities for asset orchestration.

Elemental technology labs previously located in various areas of Japan are now centralized in three large research departments in the Advanced Research Laboratories. These three research labs within the Advanced Research Laboratories are matrix-type organizations and have a system whereby researchers come together in particular laboratories according to individual research themes, where they deliberately form autonomous exploration SC. When required, external partner companies also participate in research projects. The slogan of the Advanced Research Laboratories is "Intellectual Fusion, Innovation and Value Creation," and their engineers, hailing from different cultures and different technologies, come together to create new innovation through the fusion of advanced technologies. Of critical importance in their efforts are the engineers' own promotion of paradigm transformations.

When there is a need for the integration of technologies, "feasibility teams" are formed to consider the possibilities, and when there is a strong likelihood that new elemental technology can be achieved through the integration of technologies, project teams are formed and proceed with investigation of development. This process will be discussed later. When the teams reach the stage of the actual product development and manufacturing technology, an exploitation SC that integrates relevant departments led by relevant divisional labs or business divisions is formed and proceeds with the actual product development. External partner companies will also participate in the product development as required.

The third SC that organically link exploration and exploitation SC are synthesis SC formed by corporate laboratories and divisional laboratories (which will be discussed later), and these three SC achieve the creation of new convergence knowledge through the demonstration of asset orchestration process based on dynamic capabilities. Synthesis SC consist mainly of feasibility teams and project teams formed by corporate laboratories (in some cases they include some divisional labs) (see Figure 6.1). Ideas and technologies generated in the Frontier Core-Technology Laboratories, the Synthetic Organic Chemistry Laboratories, and the Advanced Marking Research Laboratories are thoroughly discussed and researched through the establishment of feasibility teams that determine the potential of particular technologies and project teams for developing elemental technology. Moreover, to bring research to the new product stage, they are transferred to R&D, manufacturing and commercialization in the divisional labs and business divisions.

At the same time, the Technology Strategy Division of the R&D Management Headquarters oversees the company's R&D as a whole and contributes significantly as a coordinator in forming optimal teams (including feasibility and project teams) across organizational divisions to resolve various technological issues. The R&D Management Headquarters, as a cross-organizational synthesis SC, which includes the Intellectual Assets Division, holds an important position in the optimization of the company's R&D as a whole and in enhancing its productivity.

In such exploration SC, exploitation SC and synthesis SC, members selected from among researchers of the Fujifilm group make efforts to maximize results of activities through collaboration. In this way, the company creates various new businesses and products through "intellectual fusion and innovation."

There is a pervasive belief within the company that communication and collaboration based on shared R&D goals with specialists in different fields, who have dispensed of any adherence to their own particular fields as researchers or developers, will lead to success in development that capitalizes on synergy effects. Dispensing with adherence to specialist fields of technology is the first step in "intellectual fusion" and "innovation," and the strengthening of teamwork through

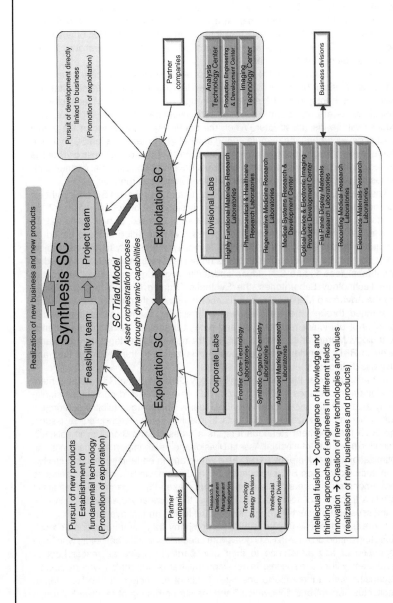

Figure 6.1 Realization of "intellectual fusion and innovation" through the formation of multi-layered strategic communities

the mutual utilization and application of knowledge and innovation among researchers and engineers in various different fields leads to the establishment of multi-layered SC as shown in Figure 6.1. Fujifilm's keywords – look through, think through, carry through and verify through – are also indicative of the company's perceived need for aggressive R&D, which sums up the essence of Fujifilm's approach to business. The SC also involve commitments at technology strategy meetings attended by top management. In specific terms, SC play a vital role as Ba (Nonaka and Takeuchi, 1995; Kodama, 2005) not only for reducing the distance between management and the front line of research and increasing the motivation of researchers but also for enabling management to gain an accurate understanding of the status of R&D and to give specific instructions based on timely decision-making. In addition, a further role of the SC is to ensure that certain execution of action plans decided on at technology strategy meetings leads to improvement in research efficiency and productivity.

In this way, exploration SC serve as organizational infrastructure for the smooth execution of the "research-driven cycle" from basic research to applied research, while exploitation SC serve as organizational infrastructure for the smooth execution of the "development-driven cycle" in bringing projects to the business and product stages. Synthesis SC also form a large number of teams linking the corporate labs focusing on research with divisional labs focusing on development to prevent the formation of boundaries between the respective labs. In other words, they have the function of smoothly bridging what a number of academics describe as the "valley of death" (Branscomb et al., 2001; Markham, 2002; Merrifield, 1995) between R&D (as well as the commercialization process).

Close examination of Fujifilm's organizational framework and strategy from the perspective of asset orchestration processes makes it clear that its SC triad model functions successfully. To be specific, the creation of new convergence knowledge is a key factor in exploration SC. Furthermore, to advance efforts in commercialization, the synthesis SC of the feasibility teams and project teams activate the exploitation SC for commercialization and enable the creation of new convergence knowledge to realize new business. The existence of this SC triad model as an SC multi-layered network is an important element in bringing about dynamic capabilities.

so forth, and through M&A in 2001, strengthened its copier business with a tie up with subsidiary Fuji Xerox, and in 2008 reinforced its healthcare business with its JPY 130 billion purchase of Toyama Chemical, moves that the company made to make new investments for future businesses, differing from Kodak. In contrast to Kodak, the Fujifilm board was not composed entirely of external directors, with only four additional external directors in the 17-member board. This executive was unified, and demonstrated the entrepreneurial spirit in its initiatives to consciously reform the entire company and strengthen the company's existing and peripheral businesses. The entrepreneurship of Fujifilm centered on its top management was a crucial element of its DC.

Ultimately for productive reforms to achieve corporate growth, what is required are the instincts and actions of sensing, seizing and transforming, which are core elements of the DC of CEO and top management in a rapidly changing environment like that of Fujifilm (Teece, 2007). Corporate sustainable growth requires new routines and entrepreneurial actions centered on top management to introduce new strategic actions taken concurrently with existing business areas. As exemplified by Kodak, in general, there are many cases of companies that have failed to create new strategic routines for sustainable growth, even though they may have the process management and best practices available as their OC routines for corporate downsizing. This is a tendency of many large corporations.

6.2 CORPORATE GOVERNANCE FOR DEMONSTRATING DYNAMIC CAPABILITIES BASED ON THE ENTREPRENEURIAL SPIRIT

The author describes the concepts of corporate governance at Fujifilm and Kodak. Although there are divergent interpretations from country to country, and company to company, in its basic concept the essence of corporate governance is the pursuit of management to dialectically synthesize opposing factors for all stakeholders. Corporations should place strategic importance on building win–win relationships with their customers, staff and partners, including shareholders. Thus, while simultaneously providing customers with new value, there should be emphasis on creating business models and profit structures that mutually give both a company and its partners competitiveness. Like Fujifilm, these sorts of concepts and actions also turn profits for shareholders. This is not the character of management like that of Kodak which prioritized the principle of short-term corporate performance to raise the shareholder value. While it might be possible to produce short-term performance by driving existing OC, this approach will not bring about sustainable competitiveness. Corporate management is not just all about strategic business from the financial perspective of shareholder value like that of Kodak – in contrast, top management must see its corporate organizations as organic structures composed of managers, staff, partners, shareholders and customers, and steer the company toward business that is based in human values.

What should management actually do to get the best results in terms of customer value creation? The more a company rationalizes and makes business more cost efficient to generate short-term profits, the more it tends toward cheapening customer value. Certainly it is possible to achieve short-term profits by cutting costs, restructuring and selling businesses, but in Kodak's case, not only its sales of or withdrawal from its copier, healthcare and organic EL businesses, but also its overemphasis on short-term profits by controlling investment through business concentration and selection seriously hindered the intrinsic motivation of its staff (Osterlof and Frey, 2000) and stifled any new innovations to develop new businesses through R&D activities before they even started (e.g., Vogel, 2006; Handy, 2002, Kennedy, 2000; Cappelli, 1999). Hence, rather than focusing only on short-term profits, taking the long-term perspective and tenaciously continuing with investments for customer satisfaction is the way for a company to create customer value and achieve sustainable competitiveness. The abilities a company must have to do this are "dynamic capabilities."

For customer value creation management (Kodama, 2007b), top management must demonstrate DC, and not only should they continually make investments to execute long-term R&D and human resource development strategies, but also engage in productive and creative dialogue with staff and partner companies to deeply share visions and missions, and share values to achieve new business. Promoting productive and creative dialogue within and between companies enables resonance of values (Kodama, 2007b) among staff and partner companies and the building of trust (e.g., Kodama, 2007a). This results in raising the level of commitment and motivation of staff and workers. Further building of trust and resonating of values promote the configuration of SC, factors that drive DC in and between companies, and they enable deep collaboration to develop among members (Kodama, 2007b, 2015). This concept simultaneously brings about short-term profits with a focus on shareholders and long-term profits by using DC to create new businesses (in other words, innovations), and is the driving force behind the sustainable competitiveness of a corporation. In short, the simultaneous pursuit of both exploitation and exploration enables business achievement.

For example, not only top management thinking in the typically American excellent companies (Peters and Waterman, 1982) and visionary companies (Collins and Porras, 1994) that have been successful in generating continual profits, but also that in western family businesses (American companies such as Walmart, Cargill, Estée Lauder, and Levi Strauss, and European companies such as Porsche, FIAT, Hermès, Salvatore Ferragamo, Michelin, Chopard) (e.g., Miller and Le Breton-Miller, 2005) does not put the pursuit of shareholder interests as the top priority, but rather prioritizes investment in R&D, staff training and staff motivation. Basically, companies that perform well are based in concepts that put the greatest emphasis on the value of their human resources (O'Reilly and Pfeffer, 2000).

So then how should corporate governance for building win–win relationships with customers, staff and partners, including the shareholders be? What form should corporate organizational and strategic management take to achieve innovation with DC? The message of this chapter is the achievement of "the SC-based firm" through the formation of DC to bring about DC both within and between companies.

6.3   THE STRATEGIC COMMUNITY-BASED FIRM BRINGING ABOUT DYNAMIC CAPABILITIES

As shown in Figure 6.2, SC, the organizational engine for generating DC, are configured within a company and across companies including executive teams, external partners and customers, and can also be networked together to become multi-layered SC (called networked SC). In this figure, the in-house SC (SC-A) is a multi-layered network that consists of multiple SC in management layers (SC-A-1, SC-A-2). Legal authority and responsibility for the direction and performance of corporate strategy is given to team members of the board of directors elected by shareholders at general meetings, and so on. It's important that board member appointments also include talented people from outside with diverse insights. In fact, in some countries and companies, there are cases in which the roles of board members and top management (CEO and senior management) are ambiguous. Nevertheless, for corporate governance, the mission of the executive team is important in terms of gaining insights from new perspectives, and clarifying and presenting direction.

In the deep tight SC (SC-D) of top management and executive teams, top and external executives must deeply and mutually share missions and visions through productive and creative dialogue, and repeatedly engage in discussions from various viewpoints for setting down corporate strategy and achieving objectives. Executive teams should not just adopt people who are bright specialists in the company's own area of business, but should also, as much as possible, bring in persons with wide-ranging expertise and track records in industries different from that of the company. In SC-D in Figure 6.2, the missions and ideas of executive and management teams, and even opinions from the market and shareholders collide, hence, discussions in SC-D must be constructive and productive. The purpose of SC-D is essentially aimed at building processes of good governance. In other words, in pursuit of the correct mission of corporate strategy, objectives and business to create customer value, it's important for top management and executive teams to vigorously discuss the details of strategies for both the long and the short term, and coordinate through productive and creative dialogue.

In particular, top management teams must drive non-routine strategic activity in SC-D. Non-routine strategic activities are especially important as the framework for DC (Teece, 2014). In addition, a board shouldn't just have a formal ceremonial function – instead it should be a place for pro-actively presenting and discussing opinions including competing opinions from new perspectives and insights on the corporate strategies described by top management teams. Looking back to the past, surely top management at Kodak should have engaged in constructive and productive debate and actions to set down and execute business revitalization and sustainable growth strategies. The company needed to formulate and execute basic strategies in light of, and unwavering from the basics of the original "Kodak Value" business philosophy of George Eastman, Kodak's founder, values which were handed down over many years (basic values such as human dignity, uncompromised integrity, entrepreneurship, staff trust and ongoing improvement and training in the workplace). The company should have done everything possible to eliminate the concept of first-priority shareholder centrism from its Corporate Responsibility Principles. In contrast, Fujifilm's successful corporate reforms can be said to be due to the company unifying itself with external director teams and properly debating and executing growth strategies and business reboots.

Generally, in improving the effects of corporate governance, there should be a clear separation between the roles and responsibilities of a board and the top management team, in other words, direction (and approval) of corporate strategy by the board, and its execution by top management enable quick managerial decision-making and business transparency. However, for even better quality corporate governance, dynamic processes of coordination through deep interaction between the processes of direction and execution enable better quality corporate strategy formulation and implementation.

A board meeting must not be a spot facade presenting as an event. This means there needs to be regular, deep and close interaction between the board team and the top management team. Hence, it's important to build, maintain and activate SC to generate DC. Rather than a formal board of directors, board member teams should set up informal meetings with top management teams frequently to promote productive and creative dialogue and non-routine strategic activities. In other words, executive teams should properly recognize that the direction process is a continual and dynamic strategic process rather than a temporary one. Thus, through performance in activated SC (SC-D), top management teams simultaneously pursue existing business for short-term profits and innovations for the long term by combining exploration and exploitation to execute corporate strategy.

In companies, while maintaining the SC (SC-D) formation with the executive team, the top management teams mutually form networked SC with the middle and lower management layers (SC-A-a and SC-A-2) to formulate and execute specific strategies. Hence, they promote not only daily operations with OC, but also non-routine strategic activities to solve problems and issues associated with the creation of new business. Members in SC (SC-A-a and SC-A-2) have to thoroughly understand each other's job positions and roles, and promote productive and creative dialogue, and collaboration. Moreover, company staff must not only proactively create in-house SC (SC-A), but also create SC with external partners and certain customers (SC-B, SC-C) to absorb new market information, contexts and knowledge by using their sensing functions of their DC. These kinds of companies form multi-layered networked SC across the chain of their shareholders from board members, to company staff, external partners and customers (including shareholders), and deeply share the values, missions and visions that the company should be aiming for with individual staff members, certain customers and partner corporations. As shown in Figure 6.1, a good example of this is realization of "intellectual fusion and innovation" through the formation of multi-layered SC brought about in Fujifilm, which was the result of the achievement of asset orchestration through the demonstration of DC.

Networked SC with external partners and certain customers generates new knowledge and innovation (Kodama, 2007b), and enables the creation of win–win relationships with partner companies and customers. The formation of networked SC with the company, external partners and customers enables the sharing of core knowledge as mutual strengths of one's own company and partner companies (including certain corporate customers), and enables matching of business models of one's own company with the objective business models of partners, by enabling the integration of core knowledge (in other words asset orchestration through DC). The purposeful configuring of multi-layered networked SC in a company to bring about the asset orchestration process enables the building of win–win relationships among all shareholders, including customers, who are the end users.

From the analysis of the Fujifilm case, the following new insights can be gained from the execution of asset orchestration through DC in multi-layered network SC formed both in and out of the company.

[Insight-1]   The asset orchestration process through DC promotes the building of new business models across differing industries to respond to the increasing diversification of knowledge.

[Insight-2] The asset orchestration process through DC promotes fusion and integration across different fields of specialization.

[Insight-3] The asset orchestration process through DC raises the level of organizational speed and practical capabilities to respond to emergent markets and disruptive technologies.

As shown in Figure 6.2, this book describes corporate systems that execute business by strategically and intentionally forming multi-layered, networked SC, the matrix for demonstrating DC both inside and outside of companies, as "the SC-based firm."

6.4 TOWARD THE STRATEGIC COMMUNITY-BASED FIRM TO BRING ABOUT DYNAMIC CAPABILITIES

In the age of mass production, companies were able to predict the environment. Hence, the greatest mission of the company was to provide customers with cheap, standardized products through top-down leadership that entailed analysis and rationalization strategies of top management teams. Later, as customer needs diversified, but as market change was slow, top management maintained their hierarchical organizations, and began introducing flexible organizational structures into their companies as required (such as cross-functional teams and project teams). Then, companies began to put more focus on the emergent strategies and actions of middle management leadership in workplace organizations to enable the company to follow environmental changes (e.g., Nonaka, 1988; Kodama, 2005). Here, the biggest mission of a company was to provide products to meet customer needs in a timely fashion, by constantly upgrading and improving products to respond to environmental changes. In these slow-moving environments, polishing OC to upgrade and improve products as best practice enabled a company to maintain its competitiveness for some amount of time.

In contrast, under conditions of dynamic change of recent years in industries like the ICT industry in which companies respond to the rapidly changing and unpredictable environments or create their own environments (markets), it's becoming more important to combine the diametrically opposed thinking and actions of strategy, planning and analysis with the thinking and actions of autonomy, improvisation and

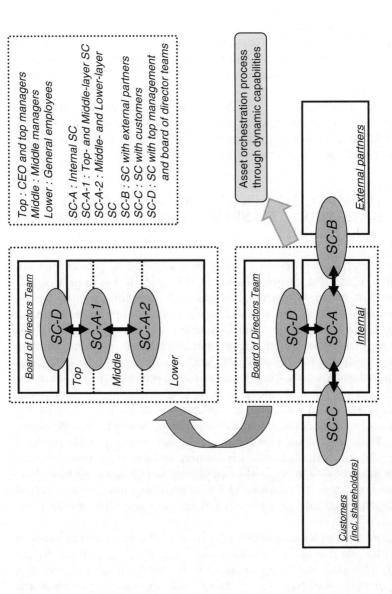

Top : CEO and top managers
Middle : Middle managers
Lower : General employees

SC-A : Internal SC
SC-A-1 : Top- and Middle-layer SC
SC-A-2 : Middle- and Lower-layer SC
SC
SC-B : SC with external partners
SC-C : SC with customers
SC-D : SC with top management
     and board of director teams

Asset orchestration process
through dynamic capabilities

Board of Directors Team

SC-D   SC-A-1   SC-A-2

Top   Middle   Lower

Board of Directors Team

SC-D   SC-A

Internal

SC-B

External partners

SC-C

Customers
(incl. shareholders)

*Figure 6.2   Generating dynamic capabilities with new corporate governance forming internal and external strategic
communities and networked strategic communities: the basic form of the strategic community-based firm*

creativity in all layers of management including top management (e.g., Kodama, 2003). For example, the management team at Apple centered on the late Steve Jobs used both strategic and improvisational thinking and action to launch the iTunes music distribution platform, and they combined iPod and iTunes to create a music distribution business, and later with the achievement of the iPhone and iPad, have gone on to expand contents and application services all around the world. Apple's integration of completely different capabilities, creativity for the new service innovations of iTunes and App Store, and the new product innovations of iPod, iPhone and iPad, with rationalizing, planning and making business processes efficient to expand markets around the world led to the success of its music distribution business and wide-ranging contents services. In other words, Apple succeeded in combining OC as processes with DC for innovation.

Hence, it is important in dynamically changing environments to integrate strategy-making processes and build organic networked collaborative organizations (Kodama, 2007a). As shown in the organizational structure image in Figure 6.2, it's important to form multi-layered SC and networked SC both in and out of the company that include customers, based on the formal, flat organizations at Apple discussed in Chapter 4. This is the basic form of a SC-based firm. Thus, leaders in a company are able to integrate (orchestrate assets) the new knowledge born through SC dispersed both in and out of the company. As new product innovation, Apple orchestrated co-specialized assets across boundaries between different industries to achieve its core iPod, iPhone and iPad products, and achieve its core iTunes and App Store service platforms to link together content such as music and applications, and so on.

The formation of SC and networked SC enables synergies through dialogue and practice between people, and are informal organizational systems where new knowledge is generated. However, SC and networked SC are not in opposition to formal networks. Instead, SC and networked SC include the management of routines and daily tasks with OC in formal organizations, and the management in SC and networked SC covering non-routine strategic actions such as problem solving and creative tasks with DC. CEOs, executives and organizational members, not only through the demonstration of ordinary capabilities by following basic rules and decision-making processes in formal organizations, but also through the demonstration of DC in SC and networked SC, they manage challenging, autonomous and decentralized organizational activities while at the same time coordinating SC and networked SC to expand them. In thinking about organizational management from the perspective of SC and networked SC, CEOs, executives and organizational members are released from the concepts of formal organizational management models and require perspectives on completely new management models. In other words, in dynamic contexts and changing environments, CEOs, executives and organizational members in formal organizations dynamically form and reform informal SC and networked SC across formal organizations, and flexibly change SC and networked SC to meet strategic objectives to execute the asset orchestration process.

In a SC-based firm, a formal organization does not mean the business-as-usual hierarchical bureaucratic organizations (the mechanistic organizational image). In SC-based firms, formal organizations have flat organizational structures in which rapid delegation of authority and decision-making is embedded. For example, flat formal organizations are composed of multiple business units overseen by executives, and executives and managers in a business unit collaborate with those of other business units in response to dynamically changing contexts, and form multi-layered, autonomous and decentralized SC and networked SC. SC and networked SC can include external partners and certain customers as required. SC-based firms simultaneously pursue existing business for short-term profit generation through thorough efficiencies, as well as pursue innovation for business creation over the long term (combining exploitation and exploration). SC-based firms aim to develop a new business by creating new environments at the same time as responding to dynamic and unpredictable environmental changes.

6.5   CONCLUSION

This chapter has discussed case studies analyzing details of R&D systems in the Japanese company Fujifilm, a company that successfully reformed itself and created new business through asset orchestration processes by demonstrating DC. The key to Fujifilm's business conversion with its new R&D and business strategies supporting its second founding was the triad model of SC to bring about DC.

On the other hand, even though Kodak promoted its existing business with OC maintained through its existing governance system, the company was unable to respond to new environmental change and retreated. The case of Kodak illustrates why companies need to bring about new DC by dynamically reforming structures and systems of governance to respond to changing environments (or create environments). For this, the required organizational platform is the formation of SC with a focus on non-routine strategic activities. This chapter has presented the SC-based firm, based on the principles of the DC view of the firm, which is a corporate model that enables the simultaneous pursuit of existing business aimed at generating short-term profits through thorough efficiencies, and innovation to create business for the long term (the combination of exploitation and exploration).

7. Successful and unsuccessful strategic innovation in the mobile telephone industry: the cases of NTT DOCOMO and SoftBank

Regarding mechanisms to accomplish continuous transformation to achieve strategic innovation in business, this chapter observes and analyses new business strategies in the extremely competitive ICT field. As a case study, from the perspective of negative interactions between capabilities (capabilities abrasion and friction), this chapter observes and analyzes the delay and retreat in the strategic actions of the formerly world-leading Japanese mobile telephone industry in response to the emergence of smartphones brought to the market by Apple and Google.

Japanese mobile phone manufacturers (NEC, Fujitsu, Panasonic, Sharp, and so on) including NTT DOCOMO and KDDI were slow to respond to the emergence of smartphones. According to existing research, it can be interpreted that the cause of this failure to respond to changes in the environment (markets and technologies) was the strong pull of habits built up over a long time and capabilities grown through experiences in their existing businesses (for example, competency trap (e.g., Levitt and March, 1988; Martines and Kambil, 1999), core rigidities (Leonard-Barton, 1992, 1995) or the innovators dilemma (Christensen, 1997)). However, looking deeply into the organizations in large corporations facing the need to change, it's clear that negative interactions (capabilities abrasion and friction) between the diverse capabilities within a large corporation are often the cause of the inability to respond with new potential technologies or products.

In contrast, SoftBank, a young player in the mobile telephone business and the only Japanese mobile telephone carrier that was not dragged down by negative interactions between its capabilities, was successful in its strategy transformation, as it demonstrated strategic innovation capabilities by executing capabilities congruence through configuration of its dynamic organizational forms both in itself and between it and other companies. This chapter analyses and describes in detail the negative interactions between capabilities that can hinder capabilities congruence (capabilities abrasion and friction), and presents theoretical and practical implications for successful strategic innovation.

7.1 INNOVATION BY NTT DOCOMO'S I-MODE: THE MOBILE INTERNET REVOLUTION

Japanese mobile telecommunications carrier NTT DOCOMO (DOCOMO hereinafter) led the world in the development and popularization of Internet and multimedia services with mobile communications. The i-mode innovation that was launched in Japan in February 1999, enabled data communications with mobile telephones, expanded the potential for using the Internet with mobile telephones, and had a big advance in mobile telephone usability. Technology that enabled Internet access from mobile telephones such as the DOCOMO i-mode has transformed mobile telephones from just simply being portable telephones to being information terminals. Around the year 2000, Japan was at least two to three years ahead of the West in regards to the use of mobile Internet. Also, American journalists pointed out that the mobile Internet services that Japan was so enthusiastic about had the potential to lead the world.

One of the factors of success of the i-mode development was the effect of positive interactions of the capabilities of Gateway Business Department (GBD) and those of existing organizations (capabilities abrasion, friction). Driving creative abrasion and productive friction, the new i-mode innovation was brought about by combining and prioritizing (coordinating with trade-offs) the positive collision and opposing elements of staff with their different viewpoints, knowledge, capabilities and strategic objectives. As a result of these processes, a diversity of friction was transformed into cooperation. This required understanding and sharing of strategic objectives (overall and partial) between GBD and existing organizations, clarified decision-making processes and open in-house discussions. Thus, by the formation of multi-layered strategic communities (SC) both inside and outside of the company, including with diverse partners, the achievement of asset orchestration of elements of dynamic capabilities was a major factor in the achievement of i-mode. This entailed the sharing of visions and building of trust relationships, and required co-specialization mechanisms to raise the level of the capabilities of DOCOMO and its partner companies (enhance strength and compensate weakness) using creative and productive friction to establish win–win relationships and hence motivate and uplift partners.

However, even though i-mode had been successful in Japan, the response to the Google and Apple iPhone and Android smartphones was sluggish

– these products hit Japanese mobile telephone manufacturers hard. At the time, nobody was able to predict such a dynamically changing environment (even the author, having worked as a project leader at DOCOMO).

7.2   NTT DOCOMO'S MOBILE MULTIMEDIA CHALLENGE: THIRD GENERATION MOBILE PHONE SERVICES

7.2.1   The Dynamic Capability Challenge through the Author's Actual Experiences in the Field

NTT East was formed with the split of NTT in June of 2000, and the author transferred to DOCOMO in December of the same year. The author was put in an organization involved with planning multimedia services called the Mobile Multimedia Division (MM division), and was charged with supervising a planning and development project for a mobile video service as a project leader. The aforementioned i-mode development GBD was also in the MM division, although the department the author was in was not GBD. Most of the organizational members of GBD were mid-career personnel head hunted from outside the department – not many of them were from NTT.

In contrast, staff outside GBD in the MM division, were mostly from NTT. Hence, the MM division consisted of staff who had the NTT organizational culture embedded in them, and mid-career staff in GBD who had a different culture. Naturally, clashes of these different cultures were unavoidable. Moreover, because GBD had succeeded with the new i-mode service, its members also had a lot of sway and political power in the company. Under this company environment, having been posted to DOCOMO from NTT East in December 2000, the author had to execute his mission to plan and develop a new service, while at the same time the author had to experience internal strife with GBD on a regular basis.

In planning and development work as a project leader, the author also uncovered and experienced a number of competency trap and core rigidity phenomena caused by the success of i-mode. For example, the number of subscribers grew with the mobile phone with built-in camera jointly developed by Sharp and J-PHONE, a competing mobile communications carrier at the time. At the same time, Sharp had also approached DOCOMO with a proposal for a mobile phone with a built-in camera. However at the time, DOCOMO was enjoying the height of market expansion for its i-mode mobile telephones, whose sales were rising day by day. As a priority service strategy at the time, DOCOMO's main theme was expanding the popularization of i-mode, and thought that adding a camera to a mobile phone would raise its price, making it less attractive. Moreover, DOCOMO predicted that users would mostly save photographs shot with the camera in the phone rather than send them using DOCOMO's packet communications lines. Hence, as a communications carrier, DOCOMO could see no advantage if images taken with these phones were not sent, because there would be no contribution to packet communications revenues. Accordingly, DOCOMO did not warm to Sharp's proposal.

Sharp aimed for a potential partnership with DOCOMO in the development of the mobile phone with built-in camera, but unfortunately this was not achieved at the time. DOCOMO also pointed out this reasoning at the time. Certainly, it became clear that after the spread of camera phones, there was a strong tendency for users to save the photographs they took for their own enjoyment without attaching them to emails and sending them. Nevertheless, after that, if a mobile phone did not have the camera accessory, it would no longer sell.

At the time, the following episode occurred in an in-house meeting that the author attended. This was a meeting of the sales directors from all around the country at headquarters to discuss problems and issues. Speaking with a sense of business crisis, one of these sales directors made the comment that J-PHONE's camera phones subscriptions were on the rise in the Hiroshima area, and that DOCOMO should also sell phones with cameras built-in. In response, one of the i-mode supervising executives asserted that camera phones were only a temporary fashion, and their growth would one day settle down – this assertion could also be said to be a trap caused by the successful experience of i-mode (competency traps and core rigidities).

Thus, lagging behind J-PHONE and au (KDDI), DOCOMO began selling camera phones through a collaboration with Sharp in June 2002. The i-mode organization (i-mode division) was not involved in the commercial development of DOCOMO's camera phones. Being carried out by the sales department at headquarters, this was an extremely unusual event for the company, one outside its normal business up to that time. The sense of crisis coming from the front line around the country received by the sales department at headquarters, causing it to act with a sense of urgency.

There were other similar examples. Around 2001, there were discussions in the company about including GPS functions with mobile telephones. However, the "i-area" simple mapping service for mobile phones was included as an i-mode application, and those in the company with the political power and sway asserted that the i-area function was sufficient, and that there was no need to incur extra costs by including GPS. Of course in hindsight, it goes without saying that these GPS and camera functions have been providing enormous value to consumers using mobile phones and smartphones.

In this way, it can be said that the "sensing" functions of dynamic capabilities to intuit or instinctively see through to the markets of the future can be dulled by the competency traps and core rigidities that arise from the experience of success. As discussed later, such an excessive inclination toward great successful experiences caused unproductive paranoia in the organizational leaders – they were strongly constrained by their experience of success, having initially achieved a radical innovation, but unable to move on to further innovations, which leads to the new proposition that having had success with radical innovation, these leaders have made the effort to transform it into simple incremental innovation with their own path dependencies.

In contrast, the multimedia service development organization (actually consisting of three departments) in the MM to which the author belonged experienced something largely opposite to that of GBD above. Initially, many project leaders, including the author, were taken up to plan and develop new (subsequent) services different from i-mode, and there were a few of these projects. One of these was the mobile video link project, for which the author served as project leader, and for which the mission was to plan and develop a new service to enable use of video with the 3G mobile telephones slated for commercialization two years later. Apart from this project, there were also a number of other projects that had been instigated, such as ITS/location information, broadcast and communications, music distribution, mobile EC and C2C services, and so on.

One of the major factors of conflict between GBD and the multimedia service development organizations was the compatibility of new service plans with i-mode (for example, cannibalization). In particular, in the strategic domain (in which GBD had in-house hegemony) with its focus on B2C/C2C services such as i-mode (in other words, content, applications and services for consumers), if the troop to which the author belonged (an organization related to multimedia service development) brought in a B2C/C2C plan, some friction or conflicts would arise, which is the case in many companies in the processes of planning and proposals for new business. These kinds of conflict and friction arise in all projects, including in the ones in which the author was involved.

Reflecting the successful performance of the i-mode, between July 2001 and July 2004 GBD boasted top status as a star department in the company as the independent "i-mode Business Division." During that time, the conflict and friction between the i-mode Business Division and the MM Business Division grew greater. This led to the MM Business Division being forced to aim most of the new services it had planned and developed as B2B rather than B2C/C2C. There was increased pressure and control from i-mode Business Division for control over service strategies.

The author continued with two service planning and development projects. The first of these was a live video delivery service, which had to be started up as a service initially restricted to B2B or a navigation site under the i-menu (also called "unofficial" sites at the time), because it would handle consumer-oriented content. As mentioned in Chapter 3, the other service was a multi point videophone service for mobile phones, but since it was not a consumer content service but a communications service, it could be provided as a B2C/C2C service.

Having to accept many constraints within the company, we proceeded with development in the direct face of a variety of friction and discord. Thus, not only the author as the project leader, but many of those under the author also had to engage in non-routine strategic business of which we had no previous experience, and so needed to demonstrate capabilities different to the ordinary capabilities discussed in Chapter 1 and 2. This led the author's project team to accumulate efforts to demonstrate dynamic capabilities through the processes in Domains I → II → III in the Capabilities Map described in Figure 1.1 in Chapter 1. Hence, to demonstrate dynamic capabilities, the members of this project had to learn from the successful i-mode development team. In other words, this was none other than the asset orchestration process – the integration of intangible assets through the formation of multi-layered SC involving customers and their needs, DOCOMO Group companies and the strategic partners.

7.2.2 Capabilities Abrasion/Friction: Unproductive Paranoia

From the perspective of dynamic capabilities, taking an objective view of the various events the author experienced at the time, the stronger the capabilities of organizations in the company that had clout and political power (including their dynamic elements), the greater negative interactions (the effects of capabilities abrasion and friction) between the respective capabilities of other organizations (including their dynamic elements). Depending on how the interactions between the organizations are perceived, in terms of common interests (Kodama, 2007c), they can have both negative and positive effects. The biggest factor regarding the degree of interaction, whether it be positive or negative, is conflicts arising from self-interest or stakeholder relationships, which are dependent on the excellence of capabilities and political power of individual organizations in a company (or in an industry).

Factors that originate in the self-interests and stakeholder relationships between different organizations ignite intentional political action in and between organizations (e.g., Ferris et al., 1989), and entail the wielding of power to control the advantageous resources of an organization (Bacharack and Lawler, 1980). This of course, means conflict is unavoidable. In all kinds of organizations, conflict is a natural and inevitable consequence and should have both positive and negative effects on capabilities congruence within a company. To have positive effects with capabilities congruence, it is necessary to promote productive conflict between organizations, which is also a factor that will raise the quality of decision-making in companies, stimulate organizational creativity and innovation, and drive dynamic capabilities.

Of particular concern is the existence of organizations that have had the experience of a major success in a company (in-house organizations that have forcefulness or clout). To drive business, these sorts of organizations consistently take strong actions above and beyond what is necessary to defend their strategic business territory, and show wariness and so forth toward any trivial problems or issues related to their own territory. Then, in cases in which the business context from other organizations infringes on the current (exploitation) business of the organization as well as its exploration for the future (boundary business, partial cross-over or cannibalization), it means overreacting to thoroughly eliminate the business of other organizations. If these kinds of exclusive organizational actions cause unproductive friction and conflict to arise between organizations, there is a good chance that the capabilities congruence of the entire company will be negatively impacted.

The greater the experience of success (performance) that an organization has, the greater the more prone the organization (and its leaders) will be to actions that bring about unproductive conflict and friction. The author calls these sorts of organization "unproductive paranoid organizations," but there are few cases of leaders in these organizations that have the converse elements of "productive paranoia" described in existing research (Collins and Hansen, 2011). Productive paranoia entails leaders always thinking about the worst case scenario for their company or organization, and engaging in thinking and action to raise safety margins by not neglecting to be prepared, fostering emergency measures, and creating mechanisms to mitigate attacks.

Former Intel CEO Grove, who said "only the paranoid survive," also asserted that since there will sooner or later be changes that overturn the foundations of business in an industry, it's necessary to distinguish the "strategic inflection points" and engage in strategy transformation (Grove, 1996). As a company that was impacted by attacks from Japanese companies in 1985, Intel withdrew completely from the semiconductor memory business, which has been its identity, and successfully surmounted that strategic inflexion point by shifting its business resources over to microprocessors. The way the company was steered at this inflexion point determined its future. Handling unforeseeable strategic inflexion points necessarily entails taking actions when there is no data at hand, solely by relying on one's intuition and judgment. In conventional methods and theories, attempting to overcome these issues can lead to the innovators dilemma (Christensen, 1997). Accordingly, managers and leaders must make use of the sensing function of their dynamic capabilities, polish their intuition, and distinguish a range of signals from the noise, so that only their useful paranoia will remain. Such productive paranoia has positive effects on the capabilities congruence of a company. In contrast, leaders in unproductive paranoid organizations are prone to legitimacy through rational self-dilution or defensiveness of one's self-interests. Such unproductive paranoia elements can drag down the capabilities congruence of an entire company. This is discussed in detail in Chapter 9.

In the DOCOMO case, to circumvent such negative interactions, in July 2004 the MM Business Division and the i-mode Business Division were merged to become the "P&S Business Division," with Enoki, who had been in charge of the i-mode development, serving as Executive General Manager. One might question the nature of the top management and governance at the time, as it was the role of those at the top to prevent conflict and contradiction between organizations such as these. Although the author can only discuss his own personal opinion, it is his interpretation that top management at the time fully knew that friction between similar business proposals (or cannibalization of existing services) from the projects in GBD (later the i-mode Business division) and MM Business Division could not be avoided, and to invigorate the company, maintained the stance of allowing organizational slack (Nohria and Gulati, 1996; Bourgeois, 1981) in the company as much as possible.

However, too much organizational slack can also be a cause of confusion in the development workplace. Also, MM Business Division was an organization that has the support of Tachikawa who succeeded Oboshi, the first CEO of the company. Tachikawa also gave the impression that he wanted to create new performance targets that were different from the i-mode (also an achievement of the previous CEO, Oboshi).

In contrast to DOCOMO, Apple's Jobs' pursuit of simplicity (discussed in Chapter 4) through productive paranoia in its in-house organizational structures, and its product and service systems, had positive effects on the capabilities congruence of the company as a whole.

7.3   CORE RIGIDITIES THAT SPREAD THROUGH JAPAN (AND THE WORLD) WITH CONVENTIONAL MOBILE PHONES

As discussed, although i-mode had been successful in Japan, the Japanese response to the Apple iPhone and Google Android smartphones was sluggish, and these products hit Japanese mobile telephone manufacturers hard. These environmental changes were also unpredicted. After the release of the iPhone in 2007, Tadashi Onodera, CEO of KDDI (au), which was the number two carrier in the Japanese market in September 2008, said the attraction of smartphones, including the iPhone, was inferior to the 10-key mobile telephone, as follows:

> Even looking at the total sales for smartphones, the attractiveness of these terminals is low. Mobile phones (conventional mobile phones devices) are still genuinely easier to use. Even for input, the 10-key input is a given for Japanese mobile users. Based on the assumption that Japanese language conversion is much easier on a 10-key device than the current smartphones, I thought iPhone might be a temporary boom, but questionable whether the general public would find these terminals attractive. I assumed this is what would happen. (KDDI meeting, September 17, 2008)

But the world moved in a different direction. Clearly the smartphone market grew after the release of the iPhone, even in Japan. Hence, the management team made a massive strategic mistake. In contrast, Japanese number three SoftBank Mobile's CEO Masayoshi Son adapted to a different strategy to that of KDDI or DOCOMO. Behind this strategy was the exchange below that Son had had with Jobs:[1]

> Masayoshi Son: That was two years before he introduced the iPhone. I called him up and went to see him. And I brought my little drawing of an iPod with mobile capability. Steve says, "Masa, don't give me your drawing. I have my own." He said, "You're crazy. We haven't talked to anybody, but you came to see me first. I'll give it to you." So I said, "Write it down and sign it for me." He said, "No, Masa, I'm not going to sign for you, because you don't even own a mobile carrier yet." I spent $20 billion doing that.

Here, Son's used his unique sensing abilities, one of the elements of dynamic capabilities, to buy the goodwill of the then Vodafone Japan to become a mobile communications carrier for the future. And then, he quickly got the rights from Jobs to sell iPhone exclusively in Japan. While SoftBank's dynamic capabilities are discussed in detail later, the company's current position as one of Japan's, and indeed the world's leading carriers, is due to the above exchange with Apple. Son's own entrepreneurial leadership is a necessary element of dynamic capabilities, and is the kind of CEO leadership required to make important strategic decisions about the future of a company, just like that of Jobs discussed in Chapter 4. In this way Son and Jobs are both equipped with the dynamic capabilities leadership needed to take action by themselves on matters too important to be left up to their subordinates.

Furthermore, another indication of the Japanese mobile telephone industry's failure to keep pace with smartphones at the time was its product and service strategies involved in the development and sales of the personal digital assistant (PDA) for businesses. In March of 2002, DOCOMO began offering its "infogate" portal site service for PDAs (mobile information terminals). DOCOMO positioned it as "i-menu" navigation PDA version of i-mode to provide information the company selected for mobile telephones. This was an offering of ASP services such as news and other information, and groupware for businesses (my project team also commercialized a PDA video distribution service as one of these infogate services).

However, DOCOMO put a stop to a range of PDA services with the closure of its infogate portal in June of 2005. This was due to a slowdown of growth of the PDA market in Japan. Even though some 220,000 info-gate subscribers remained, DOCOMO thought that the service could be supplemented to some degree by i-mode, and so shut it down. If there had been someone involved in development that had insight into the future, and could see how the PDA evolved into the smartphone and had acted with specific development initiatives, maybe the current strategic position of the Japanese mobile phone industry would be different.

As described above, it can be interpreted that as mobile phones in Japan advanced with i-mode, the more that market success was enjoyed, the more the industry fell into the trap of success. This means that while i-mode mobile phone technologies became a core capability of the Japanese mobile phone industry, it was a badly managed core capability that paradoxically also became a core rigidity. In other words, the company's strength was also its weakness (Leonard-Barton, 1995). The i-mode core capability deteriorated into a core rigidity, which instead of producing new knowledge which a core capability should, it interfered with the flow of knowledge.

The Japanese mobile phone industry, which had too heavily leaned toward the business models of the conventional mobile telephones (including i-mode), was unable to later respond to the smartphone business models like that of iPhone. In a different interpretation, the whole Japanese mobile phone industry of the time (mobile communications carriers and mobile phone manufacturers) became infused with unproductive paranoia, which entailed legitimacy through rational self-dilution and self-defense for the sake of profit. This had the effect of lowering capabilities congruence right across the industry, which was consequently unable to properly demonstrate the sensing functions of dynamic capabilities in response to the future smartphone market.

In contrast, new market entrant SoftBank did not become bogged in core rigidities, and its CEO Son demonstrated more than enough productive paranoia to firmly grasp the future smartphone trend, and with the demonstration of dynamic capabilities moved in to not only the Japanese market but now the American market as well.

7.4   CHAPTER SUMMARY

This chapter has described critical factors of the asset orchestration process enabled by NTT DOCOMO's dynamic capabilities, which brought about the successful i-mode mobile Internet service in Japan. However such an experience of success induced unproductive paranoia in the leaders and their organizations at the time, which entailed DOCOMO sticking to defense of its success and interests, which led to negative effects on the capabilities congruence of the entire company, and the entire industry.

In contrast, newcomer SoftBank with its entrepreneurial spirit was not bound by such core rigidities and CEO Son demonstrated more than enough productive paranoia, correctly grasping the trends and future of smartphones, oriented the company toward optimizing its internal capabilities congruence, and at the same time demonstrated the dynamic capabilities needed to succeed in both the Japanese and American markets.

NOTE

1. Masayoshi Son got the exclusive rights to sell the iPhone in Japan from Jobs. http://www.loopinsight.com/2014/03/13/softbank-ceo-how-i-got-steve-jobs-to-give-me-iphone-exclusivity-for-japan/ (accessed September 6, 2017).

8. Strategic innovation capabilities through capabilities integration: the cases of Qualcomm and TSMC versus Japanese semiconductor manufacturers

As a first discussion, this chapter presents the examples of the global semi-conductor businesses of Qualcomm and TSMC, and how these large corporations coordinate virtual and vertically integrated value chains through global partnerships with horizontal divisions of tasks in the semiconductor industry not only to drive their innovation activities, but also to offer new value for customer innovation. Skillfully using their semiconductor industry business models, the business strategies at both Qualcomm and TSMC are to configure modular organizations and networked modular organizations as dynamic organizational forms that include their customers and partner corporations. Thus, a business model through orchestration of co-specialized assets dispersed both in and out of the company is central to their organizational strategy.

Semiconductor design and mass production technology-related information sharing and joint development such as intellectual property with partners, libraries and electronic design automation (EDA) are the drivers of their open innovation. To achieve these kinds of business models, it is crucial that each company specializes its capabilities in a particular field (for example, the foundry capabilities at TSMC and the high-level design capabilities at Qualcomm) and engages in collaboration strategies enabled by configuring dynamic organizational forms with external partners.

In stark contrast to Qualcomm and TSMC, the second discussion looks at Japanese semiconductor manufacturer Renesas, Intel of the United States and the Korean Samsung, companies that have vertically integrated models involving integration and tight coupling of all functions within the company (technologies and organizations) as closed innovation business models that integrate their internal capabilities. However, why has the success of these closed innovation models at Japanese semiconductor manufacturers declined, and in contrast, why have Intel and Samsung maintained their competitiveness with these models?

This chapter observes and analyses these research questions from perspective of the three factors of capabilities congruence presented in Chapter 3, and describes how Qualcomm and TSMC redefine their corporate boundaries to maximize the success of their open innovation by executing capabilities congruence by configuring dynamic organizational forms to respond to dynamic changes in the environment. Contrasting that, the chapter also presents how standardized and regulated unified development, design and manufacturing brought about excessively inflexible intangible capabilities that hindered capabilities congruence at Japanese semiconductor manufacturers.

8.1 THE JAPANESE MANUFACTURE BUSINESS MODEL IN THE ELECTRONIC INDUSTRIES

In the golden age of analog technologies, most Japanese manufacturers built business units for each product or device area, and each of these units performed all tasks from product planning and development through to manufacture and sales, under vertically integrated organizational structures and business models.

However moving into the 21st century, Japanese consumer electronics and communications device manufacturers flattened the organizational structures of these conventional vertically integrated organizations (e.g., Kodama, 2007a), and have shifted to a new corporate model that entails skillfully absorbing the knowledge of their external partners while merging their own knowledge with that of other companies to bring about new knowledge. Currently, the first strength of Japanese consumer electronics and communications device manufacturers is their configuring of vertically integrated business model value chains that include everything from basic research, part and product development through to manufacture, sales, solutions and after service.

The Japanese electronics industry characteristically engages in digital and network technological development, achieving one-of-a-kind product developments with black-boxed core technologies, product development for a wide variety of types, cell production for manufacture reform, ICT development and use, business systems for global market domination and new solutions development. Core technical developments such as the black boxing, and the one-of-a-kind product technologies developed by Sharp, recently acquired by Hon Hai of Taiwan, are executed in-house, and know-hows are accumulated.

Furthermore, in discussions of the manufacturing process, Canon was a company that thoroughly sped up its manufacturing in its Oita factory, where the company produces its digital camera cells, to meet market demands for successive new products. As digital cameras have become increasingly more compact and higher performance in recent years, their component mounting has required higher levels of density. This has led to the emergence of a range of problems in assembly in the production of new products. For example, high levels of assembly know-how are required even to attach one small spring. Here, Canon developed new production methods in its headquarters production technology center using ICT, and combined the wide-ranging wisdom and experience of the production technology department charged with developing manufacturing equipment, produced original tools and assembly machines for new product production, which was relayed to the assembly department as know-how. This pursuit of speed and flexibility to respond in production technology is a competitive force for survival in the digital appliance market.

While it's true that embedded manufacturing methods as routines raise efficiency, in countries like America and Taiwan with their horizontally dispersed businesses, overemphasis on production efficiency will have negative effects on product innovation, and could bring about, in some sense, a "productivity dilemma" to the manufacturer (e.g., Abernathy, 1978). However, a common feature of manufacturing in Japan in its vertically integrated business model is its unified development and production processes. The thinking behind this unification is that advances in technology also have the effect of giving rise to new product innovations. New design rules impact on existing production rules. And in reverse, new production methods impact on existing design methods. Accordingly, developmental designers and production designers must dynamically and deeply share information and knowledge.

Digital appliance development in which cutting-edge technical elements are included, like those of Panasonic, entails the building of highly integrated organizational systems with vertical integration across the range of job functions and specializations (e.g., Wheelwright and Clark, 1992; Kodama, 2007b). This also ties in with Canon CEO Mitarai's assertion that development and manufacturing must be unified. Moreover at Canon, not only does the company integrate its digital camera development and production, but it also has its lens development and production organization in the same physical location to allow for synergies between development and production, as these are the common main components of a range of products including digital cameras, printers and copiers (Osono et al., 2006). Here, this unity, as integration across organizational and knowledge boundaries, is a trigger to inspire creativity in engineers required to advance new development and production rules. The above is also a characteristic of the electronic industry in Japan.

However, as discussed later, many of the large electronic companies in Japan have allowed the dynamic capabilities (DC) that they nurtured in the period of high growth after the Second World War to deteriorate to ordinary capabilities (OC), and have become unable to bring about new DC in the modern era.

8.2   CREATING NEW BUSINESS MODELS WITH VALUE CHAIN COORDINATORS

8.2.1   DC at Qualcomm

By having major partnerships with foundries and so forth, Qualcomm's technical strategy is that of a virtual IDM (Qualcomm calls this "integrated fabless manufacturing" (IFM)). Virtual IDMs have the advantages of the strength of a fabless company, and the fabrication capabilities of the manufacturer. One of the characteristics of Qualcomm's virtual IDM strategy is its promotion of close collaboration and coordination across the whole supply chain in the semiconductor development cycle by forming teams of boundaries (ToB) and networked ToB from the fabless company, EDA companies, IP and library companies, foundry companies, and assembly (after processing) companies and testing companies to bring about high performance, efficiency, low cost and shortened development periods to new products (semiconductor chipsets). At each juncture of the main semiconductor process, the Qualcomm virtual IDM has been shifting from the turnkey processes offered by foundries (in which the foundry managed everything from wafer manufacture to packaging and delivery to Qualcomm) to intervention and management of all processes, and manufacturing and shipping chipsets as complete products in response to the state of actual demands and orders. Hence, Qualcomm particularly must bring companies together through close coordination and collaboration with partners.

Second, virtual IDM strategies are characterized by standardized process technologies that enable building of a common platform for multiple foundry partners. This enables increases to the number of suppliers such as foundries with mass production capabilities (for example those in the United States, Taiwan, Korea, China and Singapore), and enables stable supply and cost reductions. To secure mid- to long-term line production capabilities while driving these characteristics, Qualcomm also pours efforts into new process development by investing in its main suppliers. For

Qualcomm, to achieve a virtual IDM like this, coordination and collaboration with partners is an extremely important factor. Thus, it's important for the company to form, maintain and develop ToB (and networked ToB), which are the organizational forms for bringing about DC between partners upstream and downstream in the supply chain. These ToB, and networked ToB, are the foundation of "networked modular organizations," which are discussed later.

8.2.2 DC at TSMC

TSMC's "platform solutions" is a platform that enables the manufacture of semiconductor products designed to satisfy customer needs with its strengthened customized services and special order specifications for a wide range of customers (designers and IDMs such as fabless companies and design houses). Put differently, TSMC's platform solution is also an environment that makes it easy for customers to use a foundry, and is replete with the unique functions (for example, LSI design and manufacturing services, turnkey services, ICT-based supply chain, and so on).

Dr Rick Tsai, TSMC CEO says:

> The most important event in the history of TSMC was the creation of the foundry business model in the semiconductor industry. For 20 years since establishment, we have consistently engaged in foundry business. Our success in the foundry business has resulted in the birth of many fabless semiconductor companies that don't have their own factories, in fact, the birth of the fabless industry itself. TSMC radically changed the semiconductor industry. Initially when TSMC was established, we only manufactured semiconductors under contract, but as well as gradually developing leading semiconductor process technologies, we began providing IP and a uniform design environment to customers. We believe that services expanded as a result of our continual and gradual development of technologies. By improving our manufacturing technologies and design capabilities we have been able to form close relationships with our customers and strengthen collaborative efforts. We currently have very strong bonds with our customers. (Tsai, 2007, pp.34–35)

The strong bonds with customers of which Dr Tsai speaks are enabled through the formation of ToB (and networks ToB) to bring about DC between the TSMC and its customers, and build relationships of trust.

Furthermore, TSMC has built a flat and flexible organizational structure by forming ToB (and networked ToB) as organizations to bring about DC within and between management layers in business strategy, R&D, manufacturing, and sales and marketing divisions. Thus, TSMC's in-house business processes are organically linked through these ToB and networked ToB, which gives rise to "internal integration capability" for TSMC's customer support services and semiconductor manufacturing. Furthermore, TSMC forms high-quality ToB and networked ToB with many partner companies to build a value chain that covers everything from design support and prototyping services through to mask manufacturing, wafer manufacturing, assembly and final testing. TSMC also brings about "external integration capability" through virtual, vertical integration with external partners. These internal and external integration capabilities bring about the DC needed for asset orchestration to keep TSMC sustainably competitive.

These TSMC DC draw in its partners, which are fabless companies, design houses, and IP, library and EDA vendors, and form ToB and networked ToB among these companies and build value chains as high added value virtual factories. Chenming Hu, TSMC's CTO says:

> We want to maintain win–win relationships with our partners and customers, and by further expanding market share, we want to further win our customers' trust. Our customer-oriented stance with a focus on services will not change going forward, and we will continue to provide excellence in technologies and production. We will grow with our customers. (Press conference, Tokyo, November 6, 2001)

Coordination and collaboration with various professional partners and these win–win relationships enable TSMC to provide diverse and customized LSI with a full return to its customers.

8.3   NETWORKED MODULAR ORGANIZATIONS FOR ACHIEVING A VIRTUAL IDM

As a characteristic of organizations in the semiconductor industry, TSMC and Qualcomm are classified as "modular organizations" that specialize in the individual professional functions of those in the value chains in the semiconductor market (Sanchez and Mahoney, 1996; Lei et al., 1996). Combining the resources and capabilities of modular organizations dispersed both within and outside of companies enables integration of a wide range of advanced and specialized technologies to provide products to meet a diverse range of customer needs. In particular, in fields in which standardized technology is embedded, or particular high-tech fields such as the PC and smartphone industries, industry structures are split up into these modular organizations with specialized functions. Apart from the existing capabilities of the company, the concept of orchestration to combine diverse external assets with the company's assets through the entrepreneurial spirit of top management is also important. This is an important element of DC.

As described in this case, while focusing on its foundry capabilities, TSMC has created a new foundry business model by perceiving external partners as modular organizations, skillfully bringing together these other capabilities of these modular organizations (such as EDA, IPA, library, after processing functions) by forming ToB and networked ToB, and engaging in coordination and collaboration (in other words asset orchestration, an element of DC). On the other hand, Qualcomm is a company that has specialized in semiconductor design capabilities, but does not have semiconductor production facilities, and perceives its external partners such as design houses, IP providers, foundries, assembly houses, and test houses as modularized organizations, and through the formation of ToB and networked ToB, engages in asset orchestration to provide the capabilities of these partners to its customers through its turnkey services. In this way, by raising the level of organizational modularity in these complex industrial structures, Qualcomm and TSMC are able to achieve optimal design of interfaces between the capabilities of these modular organizations, which enables them to maintain cost competitiveness in the midst of competitive environments and technical change.

In existing research (Schilling and Steensma, 2001), the level of coupling between modular organizations has been described as loosely coupled organizations (e.g., Orton and Weick, 1990) compared to tight and vertically integrated organizations (for example IDMs). If operational interfaces between all functions (between design in the fabless companies, manufacture in the foundry companies and assembly and testing) are standardized, or if technologies are matured (for example design and manufacturing process technologies from the previous generation), the interdependence between functions is weak, and the fabless, foundry, and IP provider companies are said to be modular organizations with weakly coupled functions. If activities are ordinary routines based on existing technologies, then best practices through OC centered on the communities of practice (CoP) described by Figure 2.1 in Chapter 2 are important between modular organizations as loosely coupled organizations. However, not all commercialized semiconductor products are reliant on existing technologies. In semiconductor developments where change of technical innovation is intense with high levels of advanced technological elements, the organizational forms are different to the "loosely coupled modular organizations." In other words, in these cases, the organizational forms are not same as the modular organizations that mainly demonstrate best practices through OC as simple (old, matured technologies) manufacturing contracting (e.g., Baatz, 1999; Holmes, 1986) and outsourcing of simple office work and routine work, and so on (e.g., Lepak and Snell, 1999; Belous, 1989; Davis-Blake and Uzzi, 1993). Here, fabless and foundry companies must shift to the business model of a virtual IDM with a strong interdependence between modular functions.

This is because in Qualcomm and TSMC, it's necessary to demonstrate DC as non-routine strategic activity, and have new meaning for contexts for technical solutions (either with existing technology, with a combination of existing technologies, upgrades of these or new technologies, and so on) to meet diverse customer needs (for quality, functionality, delivery, and so on), and coordinate and integrate highly specialized and dispersed technologies. For this reason, these companies have to dynamically share and integrate dissimilar knowledge in real-time (co-specialized assets orchestration) through virtual vertical integration (virtual IDMs) activities that are weighted toward the non-routine between these companies and their customers, and their external partners, and enabled by the formation of ToB and networked ToB. In this sense, Qualcomm and TSMC are considered as companies that demonstrate OC through loosely coupled modular organizations while demonstrating DC through tighter and closer relationships (coordination, an element of interdependencies) to design new products and develop new production processes, the author would like to call these organizational forms (the so-called virtual IDM form) "networked modular organizations." These networked modular organizations are based on the formation of ToB and networked ToB, and are a source of DC, which are the source of the strategic non-routine activities discussed in Chapters 2 and 3. Hence, as Qualcomm and TSMC simultaneously demonstrate both DC and OC, they can also be said to have characteristics of the "ambidextrous organizations" presented in Figure 2.6 in Chapter 2, which give rise to strategic innovation capabilities.

8.4 DYNAMIC CAPABILITIES BROUGHT ABOUT BY NETWORKED MODULAR ORGANIZATIONS

The following can be said about the networked modular organizations that Qualcomm and TSMC have built, from the perspective of DC. In Qualcomm and TSMC, DC, in part reside with individual managers and the top management teams (Adner and Helfat, 2003). At the important and decisive juncture of building a new business model in the semiconductor industry, the capability of the company CEO and its top management to recognize important developments and trends in technologies, propose responses, and lead the entire company forward is the most remarkable aspect of the DC that a company fosters (Teece, 2014).

Furthermore, the creation and embedding of new organizational value and culture, and capabilities to rapidly execute new business models as well as other reforms as an organizational and corporate system are factors that decide the quality of corporate DC. In an industry such as the semiconductor industry in which powerful companies like Qualcomm and TSMC are driving global competition and are jostling with each other for international market position or scale of business, as factors of success or failure, capabilities to link together dissimilar knowledge, and integrate and use (or create) it (in other words asset orchestration through DC) are increasingly required. This is because, in most cases, excellent knowledge and capabilities are rare, and it's difficult for third parties to imitate it. There are cases where knowledge and capabilities can be procured externally as explicit knowledge, but normally they have to be created. Clever asset orchestration (and co-specialized asset orchestration) of knowledge and capabilities requires entrepreneurial capabilities. It can be said that the management teams at Qualcomm and TSMC have these capabilities.

Decision-making by managers contributes to the formation of capabilities, and contributes to decisions about how those capabilities are to be used (Dosi et al., 2008). Asset orchestration, which is a core DC (Teece, 2007), is an entrepreneurial approach to bringing together wide-ranging resources for the purposes of developing new products, and pioneering new business models, and so on. By redefining their corporate boundaries, Qualcomm and TSMC configure dynamic organizations as networked modular organizations to respond to dynamic environmental changes (and to create new environments, see Figure 3.1 in Chapter 3), and bring congruence to their capabilities as shown in Figure 3.10 in Chapter 3, by orchestrating assets. Thus, TSMC and Qualcomm maximize the success of open innovation between their partners.

Furthermore, leading managers like those at Qualcomm and TSMC take both a creative and entrepreneurial approach to building networked modular organizations, which become the "signature processes" of the top management team as they become in-house routines (Gratton and Ghoshal, 2005). Signature processes are unique and deeply rooted in the company, and are born from company traditions that include past business behaviors, some kinds of irreversible investments and specific learning. Companies cannot easily copy a corporate culture from another company unless they have a common history. The knowledge underlying signature processes contains many tacit elements, which means there is a high possibility of them being possessed in de facto monopolies for considerable lengths of time. Not any company can simply adapt as Qualcomm or

TSMC. Signature processes can be an important source of heterogeneity for at least long periods (Jacobides and Winter, 2012).

As discussed by Teece (2014), a proposition extracted from the fact that VRIN resources including signature processes (the resource standards of "valuable, rare, imperfectly imitable, non-substitutable" that support sustainable competitive advantage) (Barney, 1991) are products of a company's traditions or the past judgments of practitioners, is that DC are created, difficult to copy and cannot be bought.

8.5   COLLABORATION STRATEGIES TO ACHIEVE OPEN INNOVATION THROUGH "ASSET ORCHESTRATION"

Qualcomm and TSMCs' business strategy is to skillfully use their semiconductor industry business models to build modular organizations and networked modular organizations, and to skillfully manage and integrate knowledge and capabilities distributed in-house and outside the companies through the asset orchestration process enabled by DC. The sharing and joint development of semiconductor design information such as IP, libraries, and EDA and mass production technology-related information such as semiconductor processes between partners are materials that drive open innovation through the demonstration of DC. To achieve these kind of business models, it is crucial that each company specialize its capabilities in a particular field (for example, the foundry capabilities at TSMC or the high-level design capabilities at Qualcomm) and engage in the asset orchestration process enabled by collaboration and coordination enabled by configuring external networks (ToB and networked ToB) with external partners.

Furthermore in 2008, TSMC first announced its open innovation platform (OIP) as an initiative to enable design across the entire industry. OIP cover entire supply chains and enable more efficient technological innovation, and are mechanisms in which newly generated income and profits can be shared, and include compatible ecosystem interfaces, jointly developed components, and design flows. Through its OIP, TSMC provides technical innovations based on its technology portfolio to the wider semiconductor design community and its ecosystem partners.

Foundries such as TSMC release these platforms to their ecosystem partners and the semiconductor design community, and many fabless companies flocked to TSMC's attractive platform. Hence, with multiple fabless companies designing according to the TSMC platform, it is becoming the de facto standard. As well as that, customers gather on these proposed platforms when they become a de facto standard. As a result, the operating efficiency of semiconductor production equipment increases, speedy depreciation of equipment is enabled, which in turn enables TSMC to use its profits to engage in joint development with semiconductor production equipment manufacturers and purchase that new equipment. By accumulating these processes over many years, TSMC's manufacturing technologies have taken the lead over other companies, which in turn has led to increasing numbers of fabless company customers gathering on TSMC's platform. As network externalities, this is the composition of a business ecosystem construction enabled through co-creation and co-evolution in win–win structures.

OIP is providing a full range of ecosystem interfaces and joint development tools developed and supported by TSMC, to effectively encourage innovation throughout the entire supply chain to share newly generated revenue and profitability. More than ever, OIP strategies involve even closer coordination and collaboration with external partners, and promote information sharing and joint development with partners to deeply share knowledge. Also, while simultaneously honing in-house design capabilities and after processing, these strategies promote knowledge integration through internal networks in in-house organizations (it's also asset orchestration). This concept entails a stance in which initiatives are taken to bring strongly interdependent elements of the functions (elements of closed innovation) into the open innovation-based combined capabilities of modular organization specializing in various fields, which implies a shift from modular organizations to networked modular organizations as virtual IDMs with strong levels of internal and external integration. This also indicates a trend of horizontally dispersed business models gradually changing in the vertical direction.

Through open innovation strategies such as OIPs, TSMC executes capabilities congruence by bringing about DC through asset orchestration of its co-specialized assets to bring about sustainable competitiveness. Behind this is the company's achievement of congruence between the corporate system and the environment (Insight-1), and congruence between individual capabilities within the corporate system (Insight-2) through congruence enabled by orchestration of co-specialized assets both inside and outside of the company (Insight-3). TSMC achieves congruence with changing environments by configuring a vertically integrated value chain enabled by orchestration of co-specialized assets between itself, its customers (fabless companies, design houses, IDMs, set manufacturers) and its partners (design houses, EDA vendors, IP/library vendors, back-end vendors, and so on), and by optimizing the vertical boundaries of the corporate system. As well as that, the company simultaneously dynamically orchestrates its co-specialized assets for the five main DC – strategy, technology, operational, organizational and leadership capabilities. As a result, the company creates virtual vertically integrated value chains through its standardized production technology platform, and at the same time, successfully creates win–win relationships between stakeholders, including customers, through the sharing of value and building of trust between the company and its partners.

8.6   THE FALL OF THE JAPANESE SEMICONDUCTOR INDUSTRY FROM THE DYNAMIC CAPABILITIES AND ORDINARY CAPABILITIES, TEAMS OF BOUNDARIES AND COMMUNITIES OF PRACTICE PERSPECTIVES

Japanese semiconductor IDMs such as Panasonic, Toshiba, Fujitsu and Renesas are in stark contrast to the modular organizations and networked modular organizations of Qualcomm and TSMC. Under a vertically integrated model, an IDM involves integration and tight coupling of all functions within the company (technologies and organizations), as a closed innovation business model to integrate internal capabilities and capabilities. With closed innovation, IDM develops all of its highly specialized technology in-house, and aims to provide solutions to customers by pursuing uniform in-house knowledge integration from design through to manufacture. Achieving this business model requires mastery in all of the company's areas of specialization with emphasis on coordination and collaboration between the company's internal organization networks.

Why have Japanese semiconductor manufacturers continued as IDMs with this vertically integrated model? This is because in consumer electronics manufacturers, design and manufacture are commonly integrated. LSI technology innovation has been rapid. Design and manufacturing rules for set (system) products such as appliances and smartphones have evolved many times so far, and LSIs have become advanced with more microfabrication, more miniaturization and lower power consumption to meet the high functionality and miniaturization requirements for these devices. Originally, Japanese semiconductor manufacturers commenced the semiconductor business in the vertical integration models, accumulated development, design and manufacture experience and knowledge over many years, developed new technologies through coordination and collaboration between development, design and manufacturing departments, and proactively trained engineers. Hence, Japanese semiconductor manufacturers were markedly characterized by accumulations of invisible assets such as tacit knowledge from the viewpoints of technical capabilities accumulation and personnel training as opposed to the sellout of unprofitable businesses and restructuring of personnel that accompanied digital technology innovation in the American model.

Being unique to Japanese manufacturing, tacit knowledge of manufacturing know-how is an important element of DC that is difficult for other companies to copy, and is also the "signature processes" mentioned earlier. However, over long periods of time, even signature processes can sometimes be mimicked by other companies. In fact, these unique Japanese signature processes have been imitated by successor industries in Korea (such as Samsung), which overtook the Japanese industry in the semiconductor and digital appliance fields around the beginning of the 2000s. In particular in the electronics industry, the shift from analog to digital technologies and from hardware to software brought about new design and manufacturing technologies. The digital industry is also characterized by product architecture modularization and division of job functions (e.g., Kodama, 2009b, 2010). The results of these structural changes in the industry gave rise to the fabless and foundry companies in the semiconductor industry, which are also EMS companies involved in electronics production. While some interdependent elements remain, the interdependent interfaces between design and manufacture that originated with specialized analog and hardware technologies became increasingly independent, because design and manufacturing technologies evolved independently with the emergence of digital and software technologies, and these interfaces have become explicit knowledge. Moreover, the development of the Internet dramatically reduced transaction costs between companies and organizations. These factors have simultaneously caused job functions to become even more horizontally divided. Accompanying these changes, the unique DC of the Japanese electronics industry have become obsolete, and reverted to OC as best practices.

Even though an example from another industry, the "Toyota production system" is a system that closely integrates all processes across the entire value chain from production design through to customer relations in the automotive industry, and since it has for several decades given the company a competitive edge, this system is spreading to other companies and industries through attempts by other companies to copy it (Womack et al., 1990). As Teece (2014) describes, there is even a possibility that similar things could happen with new drug development in which regulatory approval is a major concern. At the moment, many major pharmaceutical companies have well-developed and unique systems for managing approval processes. However, these systems could one day become standardized and become available from business service providers. When that happens, the past DC of the pharmaceutical industry will be downgraded to OC.

Nevertheless, OC have been described as achieving technical efficiency and "doing things right" in the three core business functions of operations, administration and governance (Teece, 2014). Much of the OC are fundamental to business operations, and can support competitiveness over the long term. While it could be said that having strong OC is a sufficient condition for competitiveness, they will only be effective until the competitive environment or situation a company is facing change, and similar to the experience of the Japanese electronics industry when it faced the massive changes of digitalization and development of Internet technologies, best practices based on OC downgraded from DC may hinder business.

High-quality product exports from the unique, vertically integrated manufacturing methods in the high-growth period of Japan in the 1970s and 1980s took other countries' industries, for example, the American electronics industry by storm. As tacit knowledge, Japanese companies' know-how was an important element of DC that were difficult for other companies to copy, and that were also signature processes. However as mentioned, these signature processes have been imitated by successor industries in Korea (such as Samsung), which began to lead in the semiconductor and digital appliance fields around the beginning of the 2000s. As well as that, the emergence of the new fabless, foundry and EMS business models have left the entire Japanese electronics industry, including its semiconductor manufacturers in a predicament. As discussed above, the rules of integrated design and manufacturing brought about excessively inflexible intangible capabilities, factors that hindered capabilities congruence at Japanese semiconductor manufacturers.

The fall of the unique DC of manufacturing technology brought about in Japan to OC can be interpreted in terms of organizational factors as described below. In this organizational theory, as SC demonstrating DC, the ToB (and networked ToB) between organizations forming the basis of integrated design and manufacturing, take on the characteristics of CoP in Figure 2.1 in Chapter 2 as their activities become routine and lose their substance. This phenomenon can be expressed as a "stagnant strategic community" or a "collectivized strategic community." CoP best organizational actions are mainly the demonstration of OC that are also learning and best practices. In contrast, by configuring and reconfiguring dynamic networked modular organizations based on the formation of ToB and networked ToB, Qualcomm and TSMC engage in asset orchestration and maintain and develop their DC (see Figure 8.1).

Apart from environments where competition is not so fierce, OC, including best practices, are generally not enough to establish sustainable competitiveness. This is because much of the knowledge behind OC is purchased from consultants, or is acquired through training by appropriate budgetary expenditure (Bloom et al., 2013). Since best practices can be learned, leveling occurs with best practices (OC), which makes these capabilities difficult to differentiate between competitor companies (Teece, 2014).

Hence, this means that companies must reform their OC at the same time as revise their signature processes (or reinvent them) as DC to maintain sustainable competitiveness. However, the Japanese electronics industry at the time did not continually or semi-continually revise their signature processes to produce new DC to suit the changes brought about by digital technologies, which is a factor in their current decline. In addition, by focusing on executing best practices, degraded to OC, for example, excessive upgrade and improvement activities to raise functionality and quality, and the fact that there seemed to be satisfaction with this organizational behavior were major factors in the defeat of companies in the Japanese electronics industry. In contrast, through the formation of ToB and network ToB as dynamic networked modular organizations, TSMC and Qualcomm demonstrated DC to uniquely orchestrate assets and achieved a new virtual IDM business model (see Figure 8.1).

As Teece (2014) discusses, whereas OC are capabilities to carry out things correctly, DC are capabilities to execute actions properly and timely through new product (and new process) development, unique asset orchestration processes of business people, strong organizational culture toward change, and predictive assessment of business environments and technology opportunities. Qualcomm and TSMC corporate executives can also be said to predict technical changes and business environments in the semiconductor industry, and to demonstrate context-specific, people-specific, timing-specific, and network-specific factors (Kodama, 2006). Whereas efficiency lies at the heart of OC, it is creativity based on adaptation, orchestration and innovation on which DC are centered. Companies like Qualcomm and TSMC that have strong DC are also able to respond to broader social objectives as they keep pace with markets and technological developments (Teece, 2014). Having strong dynamic capabilities does not only entail adjusting strategies and organizations to adapt to predicted changes in markets, technologies and business environments, but also importantly entails changes (reforms) to OC and routines that form the base of them (Teece, 2014).

However, are Intel and Samsung using their traditional IDM systems

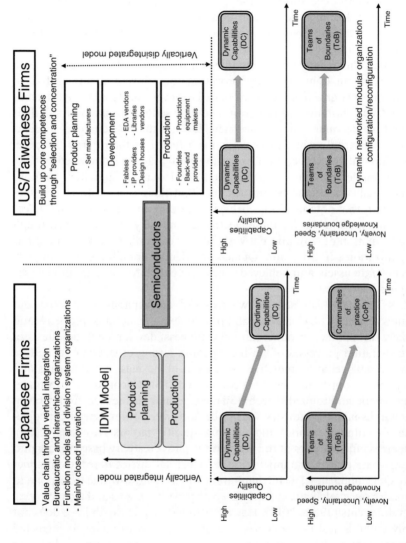

Figure 8.1   Dynamic capabilities and ordinary capabilities

to maintain their competitiveness? This question remains. Intel and Samsung have come to integrate design and manufacturing as a fundamental. Both Intel and Samsung are major corporations that make microprocessors and memory for personal computers respectively. Their market-dominating scale of production enables depreciation of their production line facilities. However, Intel and Samsung are also major foundry companies. Samsung's revenues from its semiconductor business have fallen into negative growth in recent years, although it has double the size of its foundry business, and currently holds the number three position globally. Intel is also proactive in its foundry business initiatives, for example Altera outsources production of its products to Intel. In this way, these major IDMs view parts of their own value chains as modular organizations, and similar to the TSMC business model, they achieve asset orchestration through the demonstration of DC with collaboration strategies with external partners (fabless and set manufacturer companies, and so on).

The Japanese semiconductor industry has a history of defeat with unprofitability, companies being swallowed up in price competition while pursuing excessive quality, such as the bankruptcies of the DRAMs of Elpida Memory (now Micron Memory Japan), and the microcomputers of Renesas Electronics that were chronically riddled with deficit. Hence, Socionext has jettisoned its production department with their expensive facility investments, and has specialized in design and development as a fabless company that aims to survive into the future although currently it is unclear whether it is on the road to success.

8.7   CONCLUSION

This chapter has presented Qualcomm and TSMCs' DC. These companies have orchestrated co-specialized assets by building networked modular organizations – dynamic organizational forms – that include partners and customers by coordinating virtual vertically integrated value chains with global partnerships, in horizontally dispersed industry structures. Through these, Qualcomm and TSMC have maximized the success of their open innovation by redefining their corporate boundaries and engaging capabilities congruence to respond to dynamically changing environments.

Contrasting with Qualcomm and TSMC, the chapter has presented the closed innovation business models of Japanese semiconductor manufacturers that integrate their internal capabilities through vertically integrated models enabled by integration and close linking of in-house functions (technologies and organizations). The rules of integrated developmental design and manufacturing brought excessively inflexible intangible capabilities, which is a factor that caused DC to decay into OC at Japanese semiconductor manufacturers.

9. Strategic innovation through sustainable capabilities congruence

Through the concept of capabilities congruence presented in the theoretical section in 9.1, and case analyses presented in the case research section in 9.2, this chapter presents new theoretical propositions and implications.

First, as implications related to the issues of the first points, the chapter deepens the discussion from the Capabilities Map perspective in contrast to Helfat and Winter (2011), who assert that it is impossible to draw clear boundaries between the two types of capabilities, that of dynamic capabilities (DC) and ordinary capabilities (OC).

Second, the chapter presents a model of the corporate system for sustainable capabilities congruence and sustainable growth enabled by the demonstration of continuous strategic innovation capabilities. Also discussed in Chapter 3, there is a necessity for practitioners to intentionally change business elements of capabilities of strategy, organizations, technologies, operations and leadership in corporate systems, to bring congruence to the boundaries between these capabilities so that corporations can adapt to changing environments (or ecosystems) (creating and executing environment adaption), or actively act on the environments (or ecosystems) to create new environments (creating and executing environment creation strategies).

This means that both the capabilities congruence between corporate systems and markets (ecosystems) (dynamic external congruence) (Insight-1) and capabilities congruence between capabilities in corporate systems (congruence between subsystems) (dynamic internal congruence) (Insight-2) are required. The functions that achieve capabilities congruence both in and outside of companies are strategic innovation capabilities brought about by asset orchestration through DC. Hence, this chapter discusses the "sustainable strategic innovation model" that achieves "external and internal congruence in capabilities" that lead to sustainable strategic innovation.

Third, the chapter presents new propositions on the boundaries vision of practitioners, which are also a cognitive capability as intuition to uncover the best intangible assets (and co-specialized assets). The chapter offers new propositions on four specific factors as elements of micro strategy practiced through the demonstration of boundaries vision to achieve optimal asset orchestration processes.

9.1   CLARIFYING THE BLURRY LINE BETWEEN DYNAMIC CAPABILITIES AND ORDINARY CAPABILITIES

Helfat and Winter (2011, p. 1245) assert that it is impossible to draw clear boundaries between the two types of capabilities, that of DC and OC. They reason that: (1) change is always occurring to at least some extent; (2) we cannot distinguish dynamic from operational (ordinary) capabilities based on whether they support what is perceived as radical versus non-radical change, or new versus existing businesses; and (3) some capabilities can be used for both operational (ordinary) and dynamic purposes.

In relation to this, Helfat and Winter (2011, p. 1245) mention "Heraclitus" and "Ecclesiastes," as follows:

> Nothing ever stays exactly the same, so "one does not step into the same river twice" (Heraclitus). Yet we often say that "there is nothing new under the sun" (Ecclesiastes). As Birnholtz, Cohen, and Hoch (2007: 316) put it, this is the "paradox of the (n)ever-changing world." If everything is changing all the time, what then is the basis of the impression that some things do not change at all? Part of the answer to this conundrum lies in one's perspective. If you examine small details close in, you see much more change than if you attend to large phenomena or high-level descriptions, or perceive from afar.

This is a classification of changing nature of capabilities in business organizations from a perspective on how people view things, and is described by the Capabilities Map so far discussed. The Capabilities Map clearly positions the weight to which DC and OC function in terms of the degrees of uncertainty and the speed of change inside and outside of the corporate organization which corporate organizations and the practitioners involved in them sense and recognize. Nevertheless, as Helfat and Winter (2011, p. 1245) identify grounds for ambiguity of the boundaries between DC and OC, in this section the author would like to discuss the nature of "dual-purpose and multiple-variant capabilities" that they identify from the perspective of the Capabilities Map.

9.1.1   Dual-purpose and Multiple-variant Capabilities

Helfat and Winter (2011) assert that some types of capabilities entail using both operational capabilities (or OC) and DC, further complicating the issue. There are capabilities with multiple variables (some operational-oriented, some dynamic-oriented), and capabilities that simultaneously satisfy both operational and dynamic objectives. In these cases, it is certainly difficult to draw clear boundaries between operational and DC as asserted by Helfat and Winter (2011, p.1248). Below is a discussion on "dual-purpose capabilities" and "multiple-variant capabilities" from the perspective of the Capabilities Map.

9.1.2   Dual-purpose Capabilities

Helfat and Winter (2011, p.1248) discuss capabilities providing "market access" in the cases of P&G and Microsoft. "Market-access capability" is the capability required for distribution, marketing and sales, and so on. In the case of P&G, brand development for new products is done through DC, while at the same time, established brands are managed through OC. Moreover, brand managers rely on OC in common corporate routines and processes to promote sales of both the old and the new, which means brand management is a capability with both DC and OC objectives. On the other hand, Microsoft formed a new ecosystem by establishing a new market through positive feedback formed using network externalities to expand sales of its new browser by demonstrating DC. At the same time, the company's OC elements with their "market-access capabilities" played the role of driving sales of the new-generation browser while maintaining sales of the existing browser, thus giving Microsoft a long-term competitive advantage.

With this market-access capability, in the processes in Domains I → II → III, brand managers simultaneously execute sales strategies in Domain III with existing OC sales routines for new product brands born through the demonstration of DC, and at the same time, execute sales strategies with existing OC in Domain III for the previous generation, and in Domain IV for several earlier generations of existing brand product lineups. Hence, "dual-purpose capabilities," or twin-objective market-access capabilities, are equivalent to the simultaneous demonstration of DC and OC in Domain III and OC in Domain IV.

9.1.3   Integrated Capabilities: Multiple-variant Capabilities

Helfat and Winter (2011, p.1248) assert that integrated capabilities can serve an operational purpose, for example by facilitating shared activities that produce economies of scope across stages of production or product lines. Integrated capabilities that make sharing activities simpler entail R&D using DC through the Domain I → II → III processes to develop new technical or production platforms and put them into practical use, while at the same time in Domain III, business divisions demonstrate OC to efficiently upgrade product lines and engage in production activities, or operational management, with new platforms such as these.

The execution of these integrated capabilities simultaneously achieves the development of new platforms by demonstrating DC mainly in R&D departments through Domains I $\rightarrow$ II $\rightarrow$ III processes, and operational efficiency through the demonstration of OC in development, production and sales divisions, and so on in Domain III using the results of the development. Integrated capabilities have different weights on DC and OC (some directed to dynamics, some directed to operations), and in the time frame of Domains I $\rightarrow$ II $\rightarrow$ III processes, enable communications and collaboration spanning organizations units across entire companies from R&D divisions through to production and sales departments.

In addition, as a different type of integrated capabilities, Helfat and Winter (2011, p.1248) assert that "Other types of integrative capabilities can make change possible, such as through the coordination of design and manufacture in new product introduction" (Iansiti and Clark, 1994, p.557). Specifically, this is equivalent to design and develop elemental technologies to develop new products or execute commercialization processes using new production technologies by different organizational systems (cross-functional teams (CFT), R&D departments, and so on) from existing organizations through the demonstration of DC in the processes of Domains $\rightarrow$ I $\rightarrow$ II $\rightarrow$ III. Thus, development design and production engage in close coordination to solve numerous problems and technical challenges.

In achieving new products, to develop elemental technologies based in basic or applied research, design and development of new products using the results of elemental technology development, and put production technology processes into practice in the processes of Domains I $\rightarrow$ II, R&D and related organizations must face many difficulties and overcome the so-called "valley of death." As DC are demonstrated in the processes of Domains I $\rightarrow$ II – many prototypes are developed and much commercialization testing done, and as R&D and related divisions overcome these hurdles, uncertainties of R&D projects success reduce, and commercialization in Domain III becomes closer. In the commercialization stage in Domain III, existing routines of operations management come into focus, OC are demonstrated at the same time as new products are introduced followed by product upgrades and improvements through the demonstration of DC and OC. In this way, in processes in Domains I, II and III, integrated capabilities can be both dynamic and operational depending on the types of capabilities used in each domain and their purpose.

Helfat and Winter (2011, p.1248) also argue that an integrative capability also may serve a dual purpose, such as its use in ambidexterity to manage both new and existing businesses (Tushman and O'Reilly, 1997). This is not just expanding sales with upgrades to existing competitive products in Domain III, or maintaining business with long sellers in Domain IV, but means also managing new business development with the shift from Domain III and/or Domain IV to Domain I. For this reason, as identified by O'Reilly and Tushman (2008), the ambidexterity is partially reliant on the DC of top management who perform the integration of new and mature businesses (Adner and Helfat, 2003). The important perspective here, as identified by Helfat and Winter (2011, p.1248), is that some types of capabilities enable ambidexterity (for example, the DC of top management) – the DC of managers can contribute to organizational level integrated capabilities in ambidexterity.

As described above, the concept of "dual-purpose and multiple-variant capabilities" can be explained from the perspective of the Capabilities Map presented in this book. The Capabilities Map can clearly position the weight to which DC and OC function in terms of uncertainty and the speed of change inside and outside of the corporate organization, and can clarify the intensity of ambiguous DC and OC boundaries.

9.2 CAPABILITIES CONGRUENCE INSIDE AND OUTSIDE OF THE CORPORATION THROUGH DYNAMIC STRATEGIC MANAGEMENT

As discussed in Chapter 2, in the view of strategic management as a dynamic process, corporate systems (management factors in a company such as strategies, organizations, technologies, operations and leadership) must change dynamically to adapt to dynamically changing environments surrounding corporations (for example markets, technologies, competition and cooperation, structures). The borders or corporate boundaries between environments and corporate systems define the relationships with environments and company business models. Changes in environments bring about changes in corporate boundaries and simultaneously affect individual elements of management in corporate systems. Conversely, changes to the individual management elements in corporate systems (either passive or active) bring about changes to the corporate boundaries of a company, and in turn also affect the environment.

Helfat et al. (2007) argue that in the activities of coordination and resource allocations by business persons, markets (or environments, ecosystems) form corporations, while in the same manner corporations form markets (or environments, ecosystems), and hence, there is a co-evolutionary relationship between corporations and markets (see Figure 3.1). Thus, good asset orchestration through technical fitting by business persons enables a company to create favorable external environments, which results in raising "evolutionary fitness" (Helfat et al., 2007).

Put differently, there is a necessity for business people to intentionally change business elements related to capabilities of strategy, organizations, technologies, operations and leadership in corporate systems, to bring congruence to the boundaries between these business elements so that corporations can adapt to changing environments (create and execute environment adaptive strategies), or actively create new environments (create and execute environment creation strategies). This means that both the capabilities congruence between corporate systems and markets (or ecosystems) (dynamic external congruence) and capabilities congruence between business elements in corporate systems (dynamic internal congruence, or congruence between subsystems) are required. The function that achieves capabilities congruence both within and outside of companies is DC (see Figure 3.1).

Good organizational capabilities and so forth form diverse DC, however, even if they are maintained, companies must consider the possibility of losing advantage when the environment changes if their capabilities become stable routines or patterns. In other words, as discussed in Chapter 2, companies have to unceasingly renew their resource bases by integration, alignment and realignment of their resources (capabilities) to change and reconfigure the capabilities in the corporate system ((1) strategy, (2) organizational, (3) technology, (4) operational and (5) leadership capabilities) through the demonstration of DC (sensing, seizing and transforming), in step with changes in the environment.

Regarding processes of change in environments and corporate systems, the important perspectives on executing sustainable dynamic strategic management are how practitioners sense and recognize changes in boundaries between environments and corporate systems, and changes in boundaries between individual business elements in corporate systems, and how they bring congruence to these boundaries. In rapidly changing environments, leading business practitioners need to execute processes of change in strategic management to achieve the aforementioned environment adaptive and environment creation strategies. Hence, by demonstrating DC (sensing, seizing and transforming), business practitioners have to dynamically bring congruence to the boundaries between environments and corporate systems, and bring congruence to the boundaries within corporate systems.

For a company to develop and grow sustainably, it's crucial to create new products, services and business models by practitioners demonstrating DC to bring about these processes (either gradual or rapid) of changing strategic management over time. Here, the concept and execution of capabilities congruence is pivotal (see Figure 3.2). Thus, observation and analysis focusing on the practical processes of business practitioners is required to understand the mechanisms of managing boundaries congruence (called "boundaries management"). As observed and analyzed in the case studies presented, this is specifically the process of bridging knowledge boundaries by forming human networks (in both real space and virtual space using ICT) across the boundaries of organizations and corporations, in addition to the activities of business practitioners in their formal organizations, both inside and outside of the company. Human networks are informal organizational forms such as the "strategic communities (SC)" mentioned in Chapter 2. Boundaries congruence comes about through business practitioners forming human networks, setting down and executing strategies through these practical processes. In dynamically changing environments, the way that business practitioners bring congruence to environments and business actions, and create and execute strategy on a wide range of knowledge boundaries inside and outside of corporations in dynamically changing environments is the essence of dynamic strategic management.

9.3   CONSTRUCTING A SUSTAINABLE STRATEGIC INNOVATION MODEL THROUGH DYNAMIC STRATEGIC MANAGEMENT

The case studies presented have placed importance on building business ecosystems through dynamic strategy management in high-tech companies in the ICT field such as Apple, Cisco, Fujifilm, NTT DOCOMO, SoftBank, Qualcomm and TSMC. In this section, the author would like to present a concept of a sustainable strategic innovation model as a factor of building a sustainable business ecosystem. In leader and follower corporations that play the central roles in the creation, development and growth of business ecosystems, as shown in Figure 3.1 in Chapter 3, dynamic congruence between the environment (the ecosystem) and corporate systems, and dynamic congruence with internalities of corporate systems are required.

Companies must constantly strengthen their strategic positions by actively changing their corporate governance and corporate boundaries in changing environments (or in environments that they themselves have created) (Kodama, 2009a). Research to date on corporate boundaries describes corporate governance structures and corporate boundaries decision-making as dependent on various factors in various perspectives such as transaction costs, capabilities, competences and identities. Thus, in building value chains as strategic objectives, decision-making about what type of business activity should be carried out within a company, or what type of resources should be accessed externally through agreements with the market are elements of corporate strategy that are important not only for large corporations but for ventures also (e.g., Pisano, 1991; Kodama, 2009a).

Santos and Eisenhardt (2005) describe four factors (efficiency, power, competence and identity) that determine corporate boundaries. In corporate activities, these four factors, those of cost (efficiency), autonomy (power), growth (competence) and consistency (identity) are basic business issues that managers must question, and are serious issues that determine corporate boundaries. Particularly, in reducing costs in recent years, determining corporate boundaries by strategic outsourcing has become even more prevalent as a way of making corporate activity more efficient. Also, the keiretsu networks typical of the auto industry, and rooted in long-term trust with contractor companies promote influence through power in corporate activities as well as autonomy for subcontractor companies.

In addition, the following can be said from research implications regarding competence identified by Santos and Eisenhardt (2005): In determining these corporate boundaries, new boundaries conception through the creativity views centered on leader companies drive self-creation for the creation of new business and expansion of business territory, and competitiveness (creative abilities), which ties in with the achievements of strategies for corporate creativity over the long term. Determination of these corporate (organizational) boundaries is an important business element to define the boundaries between the company (organization) and the environment to create, develop and grow new business ecosystems (Kodama, 2009a).

Furthermore the smartphone, mobile phone application, contents, and game (for example, Apple, Google, Microsoft, Amazon, Sony, Nintendo, and so on) and semiconductor production fabless (for example, Qualcomm) and foundry (for example, TSMC) business models are characterized by the creation of new environments as business ecosystems through co-evolution processes with stakeholders, which has massive impacts on the boundaries between many businesses and industries (e.g., Kodama, 2011). For all of these industries and stakeholders, the new boundary conception of the "dialectic view" centered on leader companies and main follower companies combines competition and cooperation (synergy of strategies), and through the formation of business communities such as SC (construction of community systems) brings about strategic innovation.

In executing corporate strategy, the important issue is how to consider consistency between the corporation and the environment in this way, dynamically change corporate boundaries and apply them to the ecosystem environments that have already been created (or create new ecosystem environments). In other words, this is the importance of dynamic consistency between environments (ecosystems) and corporate systems. Accordingly, companies have to define the strategic objectives of their sustainably competitive products, services and business models and optimally design their vertical boundaries (value chains to achieve the strategic objectives they defined) and horizontal boundaries (expansion and diversification of business domains) to achieve the strategic objectives they defined. To design corporate boundaries that are adapted environments – or ecosystems – it is necessary to optimize the design of the corporate system consisting of the aforementioned business elements of strategies, organizations, technologies, operations and leadership.

To optimize corporate systems, partial and overall optimization of each business element (strategies, organizations, technologies, operations and leadership) that makes up the system adapted to the environment or ecosystem (optimization of each business element such as strategy, organizations, technologies, operations and leadership in HQ, each division and each functional organization) must be carried out. Optimization of a corporate system as an organic system or congruence with ecosystems or environments in this way as "systems thinking" requires congruence in corporate systems. In other words, dynamic congruence between individual business elements in corporate systems is required (see Figure 3.2 in Chapter 3).

Achieving a new business model as a new ecosystem aiming for the concept of architecture thinking in a corporate system consisting of these individual business elements entails achieving an optimized sustainable strategic innovation model that includes all stakeholders. Corporate system architecture means a uniform structure between concepts in business, which thus represents a complex structure involving a wide range of business activities, such as relationships with stakeholders, products, services, organizations, business processes and ICT, which are objects of corporate strategic activities (the form of relationships and interdependencies between elements of business activities). "Architecture" is also a comprehensive concept that simultaneously considers congruence with environmental changes and congruence of business elements both in and out of corporate systems, and dynamic congruence through time.

Thus, companies must create a sustainable strategic innovation model as corporate systems (business elements in a company such as strategies, organizations, technologies, operations and leadership) adapted to the dynamically changing environments surrounding corporations including the ecosystems of leader companies and so on (for example, markets, technologies, competition and cooperation, structures). The boundaries or corporate boundaries between environments and corporate systems define the relationships with ecosystems and overall environments and company business models.

Changes in entire environments (and ecosystems) bring about changes in corporate boundaries and simultaneously affect individual business elements in corporate systems. Conversely, dynamic changes to the individual business elements in corporate systems bring about changes to the corporate boundaries of a company, and in turn also affect entire environments (ecosystems). The aforementioned dynamic strategic management entails not only adapting to environmental change (or ecosystem change), or developing appropriate strategies for the future to create new environments (or new ecosystems), but also optimizing the business elements that make up a sustainable strategic innovation model and executing optimization of entire corporate systems.

As illustrated by Figure 3.2, the sustainable strategic model consists of the business elements of strategy, organizations, technologies, operations and leadership. Hence, there has to be suitable congruence between these business elements to bring about congruence with environments, including ecosystems. Thus, in the view of the sustainable strategic innovation model as a dynamic process, both practitioners and academics must focus on dynamic changes in corporate systems (business elements in a company such as strategies, organizations, technologies, operations and leadership) adapted to dynamically changing environments surrounding corporations (for example markets, technologies, competition and cooperation, structures).

The aforementioned boundaries or corporate boundaries between environments and corporate systems define the relationships with environments and the form of company business models and ecosystems. Changes in environments (and ecosystems) bring about changes in corporate boundaries and simultaneously affect individual business elements in corporate systems. Conversely, changes to the individual business elements in corporate systems (either passive or active) bring about changes to the corporate boundaries of a company, and in turn also affect the environment (and ecosystems).

There is a necessity for companies to intentionally change business elements related to capabilities of strategy, organizations, technologies, operations and leadership in corporate systems, to bring congruence to the boundaries between these business elements so that companies can adapt to changing environments and ecosystems (creating and executing environment adaptive strategies), or actively create new environments or ecosystems (creating and executing environment creation strategies). The author calls the capabilities of companies (or organizations) to set down and execute these environment adaptive or environment creation strategies "adaption dynamic capability" or "innovation dynamic capability" respectively, as they are similar to the existing research described below (Dixon et al., 2014).

9.3.1   The Dynamic Capabilities Cycle by Dixon et al. (2014)

Regarding short- and long-term strategy and organizational reform, Dixon et al. present a theoretical framework of the "dynamic capabilities cycle" derived from an in-depth longitudinal case study on a Russian oil company. Conceptually, they cite two capabilities demonstrated by a company in processes deployed over the short and long terms. Here, the first capability is the ability of a company to regularly polish its extant knowledge (operational capabilities, and so on) to respond to environmental changes, and engage in "adaption dynamic capabilities" as exploitation activities to temporarily gain a short-term competitive edge. This corresponds to "DC and OC" demonstration in Domain III described by the Capabilities Map in this book. The second capability is the ability for "innovation dynamic capabilities" – exploration activities for a company to acquire long-term sustainable competitiveness through unique creative ideas and action. This corresponds to "DC" demonstration in Domain I and II described by the Capabilities Map in this book (see Figure 9.1).

Dixon et al. (2014) named these patterns of execution of strategy a "dynamic capabilities cycle" in which leading companies cycle these two different capabilities through time (both asynchronously and synchronously) (see Figure 9.2). In other words, the dynamic capabilities cycle entails DC theory for dynamic resources reconfiguration, divestment and integration to respond to changing environments (Teece et al., 1997). This theory is also a framework that considers capabilities for the achievement of innovation through new knowledge creation processes (Nonaka and Takeuchi, 1995) through exploration (March, 1991) and path creation (e.g., Kodama, 2007b). At the same time, this means that capabilities of companies to achieve the creation, development and growth of an ecosystem require "dynamic capability cycle" factors through these "adaption dynamic capabilities (exploitation)" and "innovation dynamic capabilities (exploration)" (see Figure 9.2). Hence, the capabilities of companies (or organizations) to set down and execute the aforementioned environment adaptive or environment creation strategies can be interpreted as the "adaption dynamic capability" or "innovation dynamic capability" respectively.

As shown in Figure 9.1, by integrating the Capabilities Map and strategic innovation capabilities presented in this book and the model of Dixon et al. (2014), in Domains I and II where DC is mainly demonstrated,

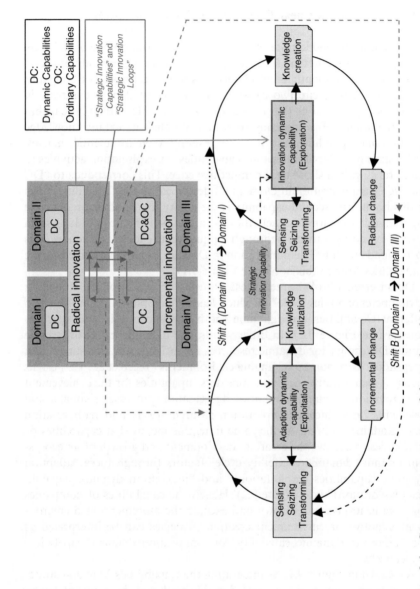

Figure 9.1   Strategic innovation capabilities through dynamic strategic management

innovation dynamic capabilities are demonstrated through the execution of environment creation strategies to create new knowledge through exploration (radical innovation). Furthermore, in Domain III where DC and OC are demonstrated mainly for rapid incremental innovation (including Domain IV where OC is demonstrated for slow incremental innovation), adaption dynamic capabilities are demonstrated through the execution of environment adaptive strategies to drive knowledge utilization through exploitation (incremental innovation). Moreover, the main elements of DC, sensing, seizing and transforming, function in these innovation and adaption dynamic capabilities (see Figure 9.1).

However, Dixon et al. (2014) do not provide details on how a company demonstrates adaption dynamic capabilities and innovation dynamic capabilities asynchronously or synchronously. Nevertheless, regarding dynamics in strategic innovation capabilities, as shown in Figure 9.1, it's clear from the Capabilities Map that these adaption dynamic and innovation dynamic capabilities are dynamically interlocked (either asynchronously or synchronously) in the shifting between Domains of Shift A (Domain III/IV → Domain I) and Shift B (Domain II → Domain III) (see Figure 9.1 and Figure 9.2). Thus, strategic innovation capabilities described in this book integrate adaption and innovation dynamic capabilities, which are connected with the achievement of the spiral innovation loop leading to sustainable growth of the ecosystem.

The companies presented in this book, Apple, Cisco, Fujifilm, NTT DOCOMO, SoftBank, Qualcomm, TSMC and so forth, are companies that have succeeded in creating, developing and growing ecosystems as sustainable innovation through ambidextrous corporate activities (e.g., Ahn et al., 2006; Gibson and Birkinshaw, 2004; Kodama, 2003; He and Wong, 2004), through which they have achieved sustainable strategic innovation by combining "adaption dynamic capability" and "innovation dynamic capability" as strategic innovation capabilities (and achieving strategic innovation loop), as shown in Figure 9.1.

9.3.2   The "Capabilities Lifecycles" by Helfat and Peteraf (2003)

Chapter 2 considered and analyzed the shift of capabilities through each Domain in response to changes in environments surrounding companies (speed, risk and uncertainty) and the dynamics of dynamic organizational forms, from the framework of the "Capabilities Lifecycles" of Helfat and Peteraf (2003). The capability lifecycle articulates general patterns and paths in the evolution of organizational capabilities over time. Thus, the capability lifecycle provides a foundational framework for the dynamic resource-based view of the firm. The capability lifecycle identifies three

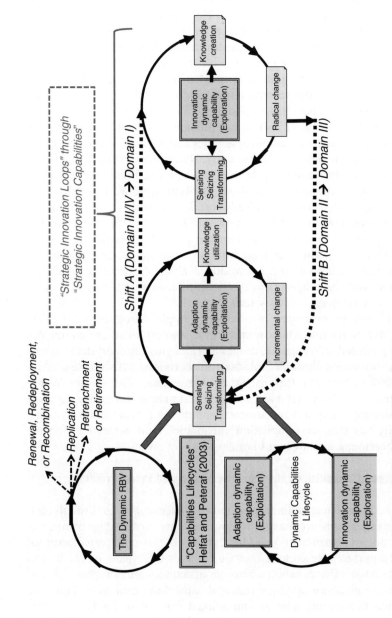

Source: Dixon et al., "Dynamic Capabilities Lifecycles,", 2014.

Figure 9.2 The "strategic innovation loop" through "strategic innovation capabilities"

initial stages of a capability lifecycle – founding, development, maturity – followed by possible branching into six additional stages.

Once the capability reaches the maturity stage, or even before then, a variety of events may influence the future evolution of the capability. The capability then may branch into one of at least six additional stages of the capability lifecycle: retirement (death), retrenchment, renewal, replication, redeployment, and recombination. These six stages may follow one another in a variety of possible patterns over time. Some of these branching stages also may take place simultaneously. Importantly, in each branch of the capability lifecycle, historical antecedents in the form of capability evolution prior to branching influence the subsequent evolution of the capability.

These capability lifecycles go through the stages of founding, development and maturity in each of the domains. Hence, from these six additional stages, as a new evolution system of capabilities, renewal, replication, redeployment, and recombination become shifts to subsequent domains, these capabilities lifecycles offer new knowledge on the "dynamic view of capabilities," a view that describes the evolutionary processes of diverse capabilities in domains and shifting between domains in companies.

In the case of Shift A (Domain IV → Domain I) in Figure 9.2, as threats encroached, companies well aware of the dangers and higher-order learning, and strategic collaboration through the formation of informal networks with differing areas of business (in other words, high-quality strategic non-routine activities) lead to the demonstration of strong DC to raise the potential for a shift to Domain I. This is a good example of strategy transformation through capability threats (Helfat and Peteraf, 2003). In addition, as Winter (2000) describes, organizations faced with threats are likely to be motivated to raise the level of their capabilities. When capabilities are renewed, new methods are sought out and developed, and a stage of new progression comes about. In some cases, companies also redeploy their capabilities in markets for different products. Redeployment is not the same as replication of the same products and services in a different regional market, but rather involves targeting markets for different products and services with a strong association. Furthermore, when companies transfer capabilities to different businesses, but ones that have strong linkages to their current business, there are often cases that involve recombining of capabilities with other capabilities instead of replication and redeployment (Helfat and Peteraf, 2003). As discussed in Chapter 6, the success of Fujifilm's new business development can also be thought of as the result of the processes of renewal, redeployment or recombination successfully functioning through strong DC.

On the other hand, an example of the shift from Domain III → Domain

I (Shift A (Domain III → Domain I) in Figure 9.2 is the case where environmental change is rapid, and competitors are locked in a fight to the death, in which uncovering "capability opportunities" is the idea behind the objective of new radical innovation. As described in Chapter 4, there are many cases of this, the most remarkable in the world being the case of strategy transformation through strong DC with Apple's radical innovation in its business shift from the PC to the music distribution and smartphone businesses. Apple succeeded in new business by moving from its in-house Mac development to orchestration of the best intangible assets both inside and outside of the company (co-specialized assets). This was the result of strong DC enabling processes of renewal, redeployment, or recombination to function well. The new Nintendo Wii and DS game concepts were also a radical innovation of gaming machines through redeployment to target customers in a completely different customer segment to the Sony PlayStation, a hugely popular product at the time (customers such as the elderly or housewives who had no previous interest in computerized games).

In contrast, the achievements of commercial development in Domain II that have overcome the "valley of death" as selection events move to the establishment of new product value chains with the shift to Domain III for renewal, replication, redeployment, or recombination enabled by the demonstration of new DC (see Figure 9.2 Shift B (Domain II → Domain III)). This shift from Domain II to Domain III is also triggered by "capability opportunities." In Domain III, further improvements and upgrades of new products accelerate renewal processes, and create the potential for "replication/redeployment" to duplicate, transfer or apply the results of commercial development in other business territories. As well as that, the possibilities for new products and services brought about by "recombination" of one's company's products or services and those of another through strategic alliances or M&A also increase.

As shown above, the framework of capabilities lifecycles according to Helfat and Peteraf (2003) can be integrated in the spiral strategic innovation loop through strategic innovation capabilities that integrate the adaption and innovation dynamic capabilities (see Figure 9.2).

9.4 THE FRAMEWORK OF THE SUSTAINABLE STRATEGIC INNOVATION MODEL

As shown in the case studies in this book of Apple, Cisco, Fujifilm, NTT DOCOMO, SoftBank, Qualcomm, TSMC and so forth, companies that create, develop and grow ecosystems as sustainable innovation achieved through ambidextrous corporate activities involving adaption and innovation dynamic capabilities, are cases of companies that simultaneously manage different contexts of five individual business elements of the corporate system (strategy, organizations, technologies, operations, leadership) and bring congruence among these internal elements.

As discussed above, regarding processes of change in environments and corporate systems, the important perspectives on executing dynamic strategic management are how practitioners sense and recognize changes in boundaries between environments and corporate systems, and changes in boundaries between individual business elements in corporate systems, and how they bring congruence to these boundaries. In rapidly changing environments, to achieve environment adaptive and environment creation strategies, it is crucial that practitioners execute processes of change in strategic management to bring congruence to the boundaries between corporate systems and the environment, and on the boundaries between the internal parts of the corporate system.

The theoretical framework of the "sustainable strategic innovation model" presented in Figure 9.3 aims to encompass the theories of the "positioning-based view" (e.g., Porter 1980, 1985), the "resource-based view" (e.g., Wernerfelt, 1984; Barney, 1991), the DC and OC of Teece (2007, 2014), the dynamic capabilities cycle of Dixon et al. (2014), and the "Capabilities Lifecycles" of Helfat and Peteraf (2003). For a company to develop and grow sustainably, practitioners must bring about processes to change strategic business (both incremental and radical processes) through time to create new business models. Thus, the sustainable strategic innovation model including the concept of "boundaries congruence" for dynamically integrating internal and external perspectives on corporate boundaries suggests that it can be expanded to strategic theories on business ecosystems that include diverse stakeholders.

Companies actualize these environment adaptive and creation strategies within the corporate system to grow existing business adapted to environmental change and realize new business aimed at creating environments, and so become able to establish a sustainable competitive edge. Figure 9.3 shows a strategy practice process framework for a company to continuously implement both an environment adaptive strategy to grow existing business through knowledge utilization and an environment creation strategy to build new market positions through knowledge creation aimed at achieving future strategic innovations and acquiring new knowledge.

The implementation cycle of the environment adaptive strategy adapts to a situation of environmental change (gradual or sudden progress, or a mixture of the two), and spontaneously synthesizes or separates deliberate strategy through daily commitment and organizational learning (improvement activities for daily tasks), and intentional emergent strategy through sensing, seizing and transforming with regard to strategy aims characterized by high motivation and hurdles. In the implementation cycle of the environment creation strategy, it is important for a company to implement intentional, contingent emergent and entrepreneurial strategies (Mintzberg, 1978) through sensing, seizing and transforming, thus creating its own sudden environmental change through innovative and strategic intent resulting from new emergence. As described below, these two cycles are not independent but interdependent.

The implementational shift from an environment adaptive strategy to a new environment creation strategy (Shift A in Figure 9.3) (Domain III/IV → Domain I) comprises action to enter completely new fields (and sometimes industries), and creates new business domains through new technologies emerging in the growth processes of existing businesses. The music distribution and smartphone businesses of Apple described in Chapter 4 and the move into the cosmetics business by Fujifilm described in Chapter 6 are examples of this strategy-making process.

Another example of strategy practice process is the case where the implementation of an environment creation strategy results in the redefining of newly emerging business domains as a company's core business, and a company achieves a sustainable environment adaptive strategy through committing to and investing new resources in this core business (Shift B in Figure 9.3) (Domain II → Domain III). This corresponds to venture companies (or established companies) with special technologies starting up from an environment creation strategy, and multiple rivals later entering the newly emerged markets, the competitive environments of the new markets steadily changing as they grow, and the expanded venture company (already grown to a medium-sized enterprise) (or established companies) changing toward an environment adaptive strategy.

Sony's game business through its corporate venture (subsidiary) Sony Computer Entertainment (SCE) (Kodama, 2007c), or Japanese Fujitsu's in-house venture Fanuc involved in the numerical computing market that was spun off from its parent (Kodama and Shibata, 2014a) are also examples of the strategy-making process in Shift B. These corporate venture startup companies built ecosystems as new markets, in which many competitors subsequently participated, hence, to adapt to the new competitive environment, these startup companies strengthened their environment adaptive strategies to become leader corporations in the ecosystem. This is a process which is equivalent to Shift B.

Moreover, in the sustainable growth of a business ecosystem, the renewal stage acting as the trigger creating new business (Shift A in Figure 9.3: Domain III/IV → Domain I) becomes a key condition for sustainable co-evolution with each stakeholder. Here, the leader companies within the business ecosystem set out a timely environment creation strategy and promote a shift from an environment creation to an environment adaptive strategy together with the stakeholders. Then the cyclic strategy stream flowing from environment creation strategy to environment adaptive strategy (Shift B in Figure 9.3: Domain II → Domain III) and back again (Shift A in Figure 9.3: Domain III/IV → Domain I) becomes the motive force behind the growth of a sustainable business ecosystem.

With recent corporate activities, the timespan for the effective functioning of the strategy has shortened while the focus–expand–redefine cycle of strategic activity has accelerated (Zook 2007). Accordingly, companies must pioneer and promote existing business growth and new business domains while implementing a spiral of sustainable strategy practice processes by achieving dynamic congruence of environment change and the corporate system, while skillfully managing environment adaptive and creation strategies.

Execution of these environment adaptive strategy through adaption dynamic capability and environment creation strategy through innovation dynamic capability hinges on congruence inside and outside of the corporate system ((1) strategies, (2) organizations, (3) technologies, (4) operations and (5) leadership). The dynamic capabilities cycles of the strategic activities of corporations in Figure 9.3 that integrate the cycle of adaption dynamic capability and innovation dynamic capability (asynchronously and synchronously) are their strategic innovation capabilities. The SC triad model shown in Fujifilm in Chapter 6 (Figure 6.1) is also an organizational form that enables ambidextrous strategy activities as this adaption dynamic capability and innovation dynamic capability, and promotes boundaries congruence both inside and outside of a company.

Hamel mentions that 21st century management innovation has to enhance both operational efficiency and the strategic aspects of adaptability (Hamel, 2008). This means that companies should sustainably implement the innovation streams of environment adaptive strategy. Hamel also talks about the importance of successively creating daring, rule-breaking innovations, saying "first picture the future, then create that future." Thus companies should sustainably implement the streams of environment creation strategy. In this way, "strategic innovation capabilities" also include and conceptualize Hamel's two assertions. Leading cases of "strategic innovation capabilities," including Apple, Cisco, Fujifilm, NTT DOCOMO, SoftBank, Qualcomm and TSMC also accord with these. These companies deliberately and simultaneously implement incremental innovation through sustainable improvement as an environment adaptive

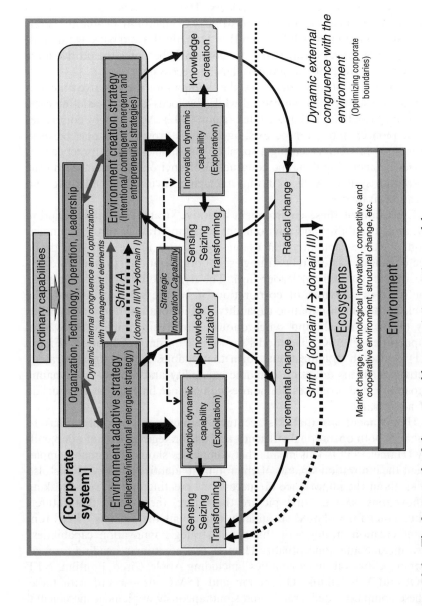

Figure 9.3   The framework of the sustainable strategic innovation model

strategy and radical innovation through innovative behavior as an environment creation strategy (see Figure 9.3).

Present-day business activities are complex, however, and the implementation of "strategic innovation capabilities" poses both a problem and a challenge. As Raynor (2007) points out, the future is uncertain, and it is unclear what strategies will succeed (cases abound where commitment to specific strategies that seemed sure to succeed in benefiting the whole company resulted in very little gain). This is truly a strategic paradox. However outstanding a technology appears to be, the value from the customer's point of view might be quite different. However, corporate dynamic strategic management with a sustaining strategic innovation model with embedded strategic innovation capabilities leads to the creation, development and growth of sustainable ecosystems.

9.5   ASSETS ORCHESTRATION PROCESSES AND MICRO STRATEGY PROCESSES: SENSING THROUGH BOUNDARIES VISION

In the knowledge economy, diverse human knowledge is the source of valuable products, services and business models that can give a company new competitiveness. Through convergence across different and diverse industries, co-specialized asset orchestration raises the potential to produce new products, services and business models that span wide-ranging boundaries, and value chains as new strategic models. Accordingly, for companies to configure new businesses, it's necessary to once again recognize the perspective of process-oriented management to create new intangible assets by transcending the organizational boundaries both in and between companies to dynamically share and integrate the intangible assets of people, groups and organizations. Thus, entire strategic processes must be optimized by dynamic assets orchestration on multiple organizational boundaries (which also means knowledge integration), through internal congruence in capabilities of the (1) strategy capabilities, (2) organizational capabilities, (3) technology capabilities, (4) operational capabilities, (5) leadership capabilities that make up the corporate system, and external congruence in capabilities with the environment.

For this, practitioners must use "sensing." Sensing functions to seek out, filter and analyze business opportunities, and is dependent on the cognitive capabilities of individual practitioners, such as members of leader organizations in management layers. In the process of R&D and selecting new technologies with innovation, the appropriate cognitive capabilities of management layers such as business opportunities are of extreme importance in responding to dynamic external environments.

In recent years, Helfat and Peteraf (2015) have discussed how differences (heterogeneity) in the cognitive capabilities of top manager teams bring about disparities in organizational performance in changing situations. According to their reviews of the theories of cognitive psychology, cognitive science, social psychology, cognitive neuroscience and behavioral decision theory, cognitive capabilities entail important aspects that are specific to certain contexts or areas. It has also been argued in existing research that these aspects can affect heterogeneity in cognitive capabilities (e.g., Ericsson and Lehmann, 1996).

Regarding cognitive capabilities underlying these mental processes, through research into management, Helfat and Peteraf (2015) assert that these cognitive capabilities are important attributes of managers at the top of organizations over many years, and present a number of cases of evidence such as research by Rosenbloom (2000) into NCR, and research by Tripsas and Gavetti (2000) into Polaroid. Furthermore, they also suggest that top managers should simultaneously strengthen "paradoxical cognition" (Smith and Tushman, 2005) to be able to pursue exploration and exploitation (March, 1991), and at the same time, warn that past empirical knowledge may adversely affect, from the many cases of failure caused by unwitting and inappropriate reliance on specialist knowledge of the past when companies search for new technologies and strategies (Miller and Ireland, 2005). As confirmed by existing research into the field of management, heterogeneity in the cognition of top management teams affects the heterogeneity of approaches to strategic change and their outcomes.

Nevertheless, the role of cognitive capabilities of leading practitioners, their intuition, is also significant, and much awareness and inspiration comes from intuition brought about by deep interactions with various stakeholders (customers, business partners, and so on). To demonstrate the cognitive capability of intuition, practitioners must have the capability of boundaries vision (Kodama, 2011; Kodama and Shibata, 2016) to be able to acquire new insights from complex and diverse boundaries. The concept of boundaries vision is a new proposition that entails dissimilar knowledge integration capability – the ability to orchestrate dissimilar intangible assets (knowledge integration), boundaries architecture – the ability to achieve corporate design for new business models by defining new corporate boundaries by integrating dissimilar boundaries, and boundaries innovation – the process of innovation across the boundaries between companies and industries (Kodama, 2009a) and so forth (Kodama, 2011).

In recent years, it has become necessary to engage in open innovation (Chesbrough, 2003) or hybrid innovation (Kodama, 2011) to bring in the best technologies from the outside to expand the breadth of the search for business opportunities through joint research systems between industry, government and academia that transcend the boundaries between corporate organizations, or to grasp customer needs through leading middle management and management layers cooperating with suppliers. In this era of convergence, important managerial considerations include new knowledge about the dynamic strategic processes of configuring new business models with "boundaries architects" using their boundaries vision to draw up grand designs for new boundaries architecture.

Business people and managers have to face these issues in their strategic thinking and actions focusing on wide-ranging boundaries to orchestrate different intangible assets (and co-specialized assets) to bring about innovations. Recently, the best core technologies of the world's cutting-edge businesses have become disbursed around the globe and are innovated all over the world. Accordingly, going forward in this era of convergence, in which valuable co-specialized assets bring about wealth, management that integrates in open systems multi-perspective intangible assets (assets orchestration) dispersed within and outside of organizations, and with customers, will become increasingly important. Thus, in knowledge economy, to create new products, services and business models, the concept of open innovation is extremely important to develop and accumulate competitive intangible assets in a company, at the same time, to orchestrate the company's intangible assets (and co-specialized assets) with those of other companies.

In the seizing process, boundaries vision is an extremely important cognitive capability or intuition of practitioners which enables them to uncover the best intangible assets (and co-specialized assets). Moreover, practitioners need to drive the four specific factors (context-specific, person-specific, timing-specific, network-specific) (see Kodama, 2006) to promote capabilities congruence with the environment and practice the asset orchestration process. Apple's foray into the music distribution and smartphone businesses described in Chapter 4, and Fujifilm's foray into the cosmetics business described in Chapter 6 are the results of this boundaries vision and these four specific factors.

10. Implications and future research issues: Schumpeter's view of innovation

Strategic innovation dynamically brings about strategic positioning through new products, services and business models, and is a dynamic view of strategy that enables a large corporation to maintain its competitiveness and establish sustainable growth. For these reasons, large corporations have to be innovators that can reinforce their existing positions (businesses) through incremental innovation, while at the same time constantly renew or destroy existing business through radical innovation.

From detailed reviews of existing dynamic capabilities theories, and further theories deeply related to the characteristics of corporate or organizational capabilities, this book presents a theoretical model of a strategic innovation system (and a sustainable strategic innovation model) as a corporate system capability to enable a large company to achieve strategic innovation. Furthermore, through several case studies, the book discusses the importance of strategic innovation capabilities to achieve a dynamic spiral of the two completely different ordinary and dynamic capabilities on the Capabilities Map, skillfully used and combined to achieve swift or slow incremental innovation as exploitation and radical innovation as exploration.

This final chapter presents implications gained from the theoretical framework of this book and a number of case studies, a conclusion, and future research issues.

10.1 IMPLICATIONS DERIVED FROM THE RESEARCH

As Hamel (1999) identified, the importance of "building silicon valley inside large traditional companies" is also an important proposition in the content of this book that aims to clarify the innovation process in large corporations in view of the essence of Schumpeter's (1961) assertion of "creative destruction" of the Mark I regime. It is well known that Joseph

Schumpeter held two different approaches to the innovative process. For Schumpeter, the main actor executing the innovation process is the "Entrepreneur (Unternehmer)," although the specific image of entrepreneurs in the Mark I regime (Schumpeter, 1961) and Mark II regime (Schumpeter, 1995) writings are markedly different.

In his first contributions, the emphasis was mainly on the role of new entrepreneurs entering niche markets. By introducing new ideas and by innovating, these entrepreneurs challenged existing firms through a process of "creative destruction," which was regarded as the engine behind economic progress (Schumpeter, 1912). Schumpeter Mark I is characterized by creative destruction whereby new firms play a major role in innovative activities and barriers to entry in technological activities are low. Around the time Schumpeter completed the Mark I regime writings, entrepreneurs driving innovation were assumed to be new companies rather than existing ones. Schumpeter asserts that the old themselves generally did not have the power to make new leaps forward (Schumpeter, 1961). Hence, as the source of original discoveries and ingenious inventions should be free and unbridled creative activities, such activities would be problematic under the bureaucratic control seen in large corporations. In this reasoning, those charged with creativity and originality should be small organizations rather than large ones, or further, left to individuals rather than organizations. Schumpeter asserts that entrepreneurs engage in free and creative activities (Schumpeter, 1912).

The "creative destruction" element in Schumpeter Mark I is equivalent to the cycle of innovation dynamic capability (exploration) for bringing about radical innovation presented in the sustainable strategic innovation model in Figure 9.3 in Chapter 9. In contrast, if the "creative destruction" element is put in the context of a large corporation, it will be equivalent to in-house ventures with the aim of "building a silicon valley inside the traditional company" or R&D activities through new organizations set up for new business etc. as alluded to by Hamel (1999).

However, Schumpeter (1942) mainly paid attention to the key role of large firms as engines for economic growth by accumulating non-transferable knowledge in specific technological areas and markets. This view is sometimes referred to as "creative accumulation." Creative accumulation is the main characteristic of Schumpeter Mark II, where large established firms play a major role in technological activities.

In this way, the "creative accumulation" element in Schumpeter Mark II is equivalent to the cycle of adaption dynamic capability (exploitation) presented in the sustainable strategic innovation model in Figure 9.3 in Chapter 9. Large corporations have the most powerful engines driving long-term expansion of economic progress, or general productivity, and in particular, some large companies engaging in incremental innovation (rapid or slow) even have dominating power over markets (monopolies). However, traditional companies that have experienced success have a tendency to lean toward "incremental innovation" as process innovation. Existing successful corporations can be fettered by the past, the experience of success or investments in existing facilities and so forth, and tend to concentrate on incrementally innovating to upgrade current products and improve production methods. As a result, there is a high probability that large corporations can become entrapped by "core rigidities" (Dougherty, 1992) in seeking out new market opportunities and bringing about radical innovations.

"Core rigidities" describes core capabilities, or a "creative accumulation of knowledge," that have been badly managed and paradoxically transformed into core rigidities. In other words, the company's strengths can simultaneously be its weaknesses as its core capabilities deteriorate into core rigidities, and instead of producing new knowledge like core capabilities should, core rigidities interfere with the flow of knowledge.

To acquire marketing knowledge from the viewpoint of the customer, organizational leaders must have points of view such as break away from existing mental models and experience in time and space where disparate and diverse knowledge intersect (Johansson, 2004), new ideas of strategic intent leveraging and stretching of existing resources and capabilities (Hamel and Prahalad, 1989), avoidance of "competency traps" (Levitt and March, 1988; Martines and Kambil, 1999) or core rigidities, destruction of information filter in organizations (Dougherty, 1992), destruction of power structures in organizations, creative destruction of resources, breaking away from organizational inertia (Hannan and Freeman, 1984), disposing of experience of success and promotion of future-oriented strategies (Ackoff, 1981). Moreover, it is also necessary for business practitioners with thought worlds (Dougherty, 1992) rooted in individual backgrounds and specialties to be consciously put off balance by the customer perspective. The practice of radical innovation does not only entail acquiring knowledge through regular organizational learning required for incremental innovation, but also requires that business people engage in challenging, transformative activities (Nelson and Winter, 1982). Moreover, leaders in organizations who are making precise decisions about carefully selecting a number of radical innovation strategies must also have a "disciplined imagination" (Weick, 1989).

For this, as the aforementioned Hamel (1999) identified, "creative destruction" must be promoted by organizations in large traditional corporations with the "silicon valley" mentality. For a company to acquire sustainable competitiveness through innovation, it must acquire the strategic innovation capabilities to practice both radical innovation through "innovation dynamic capability (exploration)" and incremental innovation through "adaption dynamic capability (exploitation)" and cycle through these in time (synchronously) (see the "sustainable strategic innovation model" in Chapter 9, Figure 9.3). In other words, this means practicing dynamic management to simultaneously engage in, combine and cycle through the "creative destruction" of Schumpeter Mark I and the "creative accumulation" of Schumpeter Mark II (synchronously).

Malerba (2002, p.253) had the following to say:

> Technological regimes and Schumpeterian patterns of innovation change over time (Klepper, 1996). According to an industry lifecycle view, Schumpeter Mark I pattern of innovative activities may turn into a Schumpeter Mark II. Early in the history of an industry, when knowledge is changing very rapidly, uncertainty is very high and barriers to entry very low, new firms are the major innovators and are the key elements in industrial dynamics. When the industry develops and eventually matures and technological change follows well defined trajectories, economies of scale, learning curves, barriers to entry and financial resources become important in the competitive process. Thus, large firms with monopolistic power come to the forefront of the innovation process (Utterback, 1994; Gort and Klepper, 1982; Klepper, 1996). On the contrary, in the presence of major knowledge, technological and market discontinuities, a Schumpeter Mark II pattern of innovative activities may be replaced by a Schumpeter Mark I. In this case, a rather stable organization characterized by incumbents with monopolistic power is displaced by a more turbulent one with new firms using the new technology or focusing on the new demand (Henderson and Clark, 1990; Christensen and Rosenbloom, 1995; Ehrnberg and Jacobsson, 1997).

In the perspective of the dynamic industry lifecycle view, patterns in the characteristics of technology innovation change cyclically (asynchronously) through time as Schumpeter Mark I → Schumpeter Mark II → Schumpeter Mark I. However as previously discussed, this means that to achieve sustainable growth through continual strategic innovations requires practicing dynamic management to simultaneously engage in, combine and cycle through the "creative destruction" of Schumpeter Mark I and the "creative accumulation" of Schumpeter Mark II (synchronously).

As discussed in Chapter 9, and shown in the case studies in this book of Apple, Cisco, Fujifilm, NTT DOCOMO, SoftBank, Qualcomm, TSMC and so forth, companies that create, develop and grow ecosystems as continual strategic innovation through dynamic strategic management achieved through ambidextrous corporate activities involving adaption dynamic and innovation dynamic capabilities, are cases of companies that simultaneously manage different contexts on five individual business elements of the corporate system (strategy, organizations, technologies, operations, leadership) and bring congruence among these internal elements.

Regarding processes of change in environments and corporate systems, the important perspectives on executing this kind of dynamic strategic management are how practitioners sense and recognize changes in boundaries between environments and corporate systems, and changes in boundaries between individual business elements in corporate systems, and how they bring congruence to these boundaries. In rapidly changing environments, to demonstrate adaption dynamic capability and innovation dynamic capability, it is crucial that practitioners execute processes of change in strategic management to bring congruence to the boundaries between corporate systems and the environment, and on the boundaries between the internal parts of the corporate system. The case of Edsel Ford that took place in 1957 is a lesson where "boundary congruence" could not be realized, and failure ensued (e.g., Drucker, 2009).

Also discussed in Chapter 9, to bring about radical innovation, the role of cognitive capabilities of intuition of practitioners is significant – much awareness, new meaning and inspiration comes from intuition enabled by deep communications and interaction with various stakeholders (customers, business partners, employees, and so on) (e.g., Nooteboom, 2009). To demonstrate intuition, in the process of sensing, practitioners must have the capability of boundaries vision (Kodama, 2011; Kodama and Shibata, 2016) to be able to acquire new insights from complex and diverse boundaries. Boundaries vision ties in with the cognitive capability of intuition that enables the discovery of the best intangible assets (and co-specialized assets).

Ford demonstrated "creative accumulation" in Schumpeter Mark II to demonstrate adaption dynamic capability (exploitation) through its conventional marketing strategies, but the release of the Edsel did not conform to the environment of a changing market. In contrast, with the later commercialization of the Thunderbird, Ford strengthened its sensing with boundaries vision to gain insights from complex boundaries of diverse customer psychologies to grasp and predict the changing market, and hence drove the "creative destruction" in Schumpeter Mark I. As a result, the company successfully drove innovation dynamic capability (exploration) to bring about new radical innovation.

10.2   CONCLUSION AND FUTURE RESEARCH ISSUES

In light of detailed existing research on dynamic capabilities, this book has presented a theoretical model of a "strategic innovation system" to achieve strategic innovation in a large corporation, and has presented the concept of "strategic innovation capabilities," which are the core factors that drive this system. This theoretical model has also been verified through many case studies (Apple, Cisco, Fujifilm, NTT DOCOMO, SoftBank, Qualcomm, TSMC). These case studies present a mechanism for executing "capabilities congruence" and "boundaries congruence" inside and outside of corporations through the asset orchestration process enabled by the dynamic formation of strategic communities (SC) as platforms for strategic non-routine activities in informal organizations.

In this book, although one end of the theoretical framework for strategic innovation capabilities is presented, numerous research issues remain. Specifically, theory on strategic innovation capabilities in large corporations at the macro and micro levels need to be further elaborated. First, there is the quest for both theoretical and empirical research at the macro level into achieving sustainable growth by bringing about strategic innovation systematically and continuously in large corporations. For this reason, from this perspective, research must be promoted of corporate and management systems that achieve sustainable growth.

For example, taking strategic innovation to mean "corporate system innovation," the individual subsystems that affect strategic innovation must be identified, and the characteristics of the subsystems, the interactive relationships between the subsystems (for example, organizations in charge of radical innovation versus organizations in charge of incremental innovation, new organizations versus existing organizations and their relationships), and the dynamically changing conditions of entire (corporate) systems and their individual subsystems (for example, individual business units) responding to changes in the environment (uncertainties and speed) must be deeply analyzed.

One of the analytical approaches to this is the Capabilities Map. This is because there are multi-layered, multiple and dissimilar Capabilities Maps for each individual enterprises within a large corporation, and it is the interactive relationships between these numerous Capabilities Maps that are the subject of analysis at the macro level. In short, there is a relationship between the Capabilities Map of the entire system of a large corporation, and Capabilities Maps of the subsystems – those of its individual enterprises (business units). How do these individual subsystem Capabilities Maps (capabilities in individual domains and strategic innovation capabilities) affect the Capabilities Map of an entire corporation (the entire system) and its strategic innovation capabilities?

The second research issue is theorizing the capabilities in each domain at the micro level that make up strategic innovation capabilities. First, what kinds of capability characteristics are required at the micro level? Second, is clarification (theorizing) related to the process of changing capabilities that accompanies shifts in domains in response to factors of dynamically changing environments (uncertainty and speed). In particular, large corporations that achieve sustainable growth through strategic innovation are run by a multi-layered "strategic innovation loop" enabled by acquiring new capabilities.

However, how are strategic innovations capabilities achieved and changed within and between (including shifts) the domains, and what changes should be made to organizational structures and strategic actions at the micro level both inside and outside organizations? Furthermore, what is the optimum pattern for acquiring capabilities to achieve strategic innovation? Regarding organizational forms in particular, there are very deep relationships with the SC described in the book. Therefore, more detailed research at the micro level into strategic innovation capabilities from a theoretical, empirical and practical standpoint should be promoted, including relationships with organizational forms.

The third research issue is the approach from the knowledge-based theory of the firm (Nonaka and Takeuchi, 1995; Grant, 1996). Companies that achieve sustainable strategic innovation can be said to be implementing a new knowledge creation (or integration) chain through a layered strategic innovation loop. However, research is required into "knowledge integration dynamics" that asks such questions as how strategic innovation capabilities can change or realize this knowledge integration process occurring within and among domains (including shifts), how strategic behavior and organizational structure change, and what patterns form the optimal knowledge integration process for realizing strategic innovation. This research, which needs to progress from a theoretical, to an actual and practical viewpoint, forms the true theme of this book.

References

Abernathy, W.J. (1978), *The Productivity Dilemma: Roadblock to Innovation in the Automobile Industry*. Baltimore, MD: Johns Hopkins University Press.

Ackoff, R.L. (1981), *Creating the Corporate Future*. New York: Wiley.

Adner, R., and Helfat, C.E. (2003), 'Corporate effects and dynamic managerial capabilities', *Strategic Management Journal*, 24(10), 1011–1025.

AFP. (2013), Apple still has "magic," innovation, says CEO Cook. February 12, *afp.com*. Retrieved September 6, 2017 from: http://www.globalpost.com/dispatch/news/afp/130212/apple-still-has-magic-innovation-says-ceocook-0.

Ahn, J.H., Lee, D.J., and Lee, S.Y. (2006), 'Balancing business performance and knowledge performance of new product development. Lessons from ITS industry', *Long Range Planning*, 39(6), 525–542.

Allen, T.J. (1977), *Managing the Flow of Technology*. Cambridge, MA: MIT Press.

Amabile, T., and Khaire, M. (2008), 'Creativity and the role of the leader', *Harvard Business Review*, October, 100–109.

Amasaka, K. (2004), 'Development of "Science TQM", a new principle of quality management: effectiveness of strategic stratified task team at Toyota', *International Journal of Production Research*, 42(17), 3691–3706.

Amburgey, T., Kelly, D., and Barnett, W. (1993), 'Resetting the clock: the dynamics of organizational change and failure', *Administrative Science Quarterly*, 38(1), 51–73.

Ancora, D., and Backman, E. (2010), It's not all about you. Retrieved November 29, 2014 from *Harvard Business Review*: https://hbr.org/2010/04/its-not-all-about-me-its-all-a.

Anderson, K. (2013), What makes collaboration actually work in a company? Retrieved November 29, 2014 from *Forbes*: http://www.forbes.com/sites/kareanderson/2013/02/02/what-makes-collaboration-actually-work-in-a-company/.

Augier, M., and Teece, D.J. (2009), 'Dynamic capabilities and the role of managers in business strategy and economic performance', *Organization Science*, 20(2), 410–421.

Baatz, E. (1999), 'How purchasing handles intense cost pressure', *Purchasing*, 126, 61–66.

Bacharach, S.B., and Lawler, E.J. (1980), *Power and Politics in Organizations*. San Francisco, CA: Jossey-Bass.

Barney, J. (1991), 'Firm resources and sustained competitive advantage', *Journal of Management*, 17(1), 99–120.

Bechky, B.A. (2003), 'Sharing meaning across occupational communities: the transformation of understanding on a production floor', *Organization Science*, 14(3), 312–330.

Belous, R.S. (1989), 'Human resource flexibility and equity: difficult questions for business, labor, and government', *Journal of Labor Research*, 10(1), 67–72.

Benner, M., and Tushman, M. (2003), 'Exploitation, exploration, and process management: the productivity dilemma revisited', *Academy of Management Review*, 28(2), 238–256.

Birnholtz, J.P., Cohen, M., and Hoch, S.V. (2007), 'Organizational character: on the regeneration of Camp Poplar Grove', *Organization Science*, 18(2), 315–332.

Blodget, H. (2009), Google announces layoffs (GOOG). *Silicon Valley Insider*. Retrieved May 15, 2009 from: www.businessinsider.com/2009/1/google-announces-layoffs-goog.

Bloom, N., Eifert, B., Mahajan, A., McKenzie, D., and Roberts, J. (2013), 'Does management matter? Evidence from India', *Quarterly Journal of Economics*, 128(1), 1–51.

Bourgeois, L.J. (1981), 'On the measurement of organizational slack', *Academy of Management Review*, 6(1), 29–39.

Branscomb, L.M., Auerswald, P.E., and Chesbrough, H.W. (2001), *Taking Technical Risks*. Cambridge, MA: MIT Press.

Brown, J.S., and Duguid, P. (1991), 'Organizational learning and communities-of-practice', *Organization Science*, 2(3), 40–57.

Brown, J.S., and Duguid, P. (2001), 'Knowledge and organization: a social-practice perspective', *Organization Science*, 12(6), 198–213.

Brown, S.L., and Eisenhardt, K.M. (1995), 'Product development: past research, present findings, and future directions', *Academy of Management Review*, 20(2), 343–378.

Bruch, H., and Ghoshal, S. (2004), *A Bias For Action: How Effective Managers Harness Their Willpower, Achieve Results, and Stop Wasting Time*. Boston, MA: Harvard Business Press.

Buckman, R. (2003), *Building a Knowledge-Driven Organization*. New York: McGraw-Hill.

Burgelman, R.A., and Sayles, L.R. (1988), *Inside Corporate Innovation*. New York: Simon & Schuster.

Burns, T.E., and Stalker, G.M. (1961), *The Management of Innovation*. London: Tavistock.

Burrows, P. (2004), 'The seed of Apple's innovation', *Businessweek*, 12.

Cappelli, P. (1999), *The New Deal at Work: Managing the Market-Driven Workforce*. Boston, MA: Harvard Business Press.

Carlile, P. (2002), 'A pragmatic view of knowledge and boundaries: boundary objects in new product development', *Organization Science*, 13(4), 442–455.

Carlile, P. (2004), 'Transferring, translating, and transforming: an integrative framework for managing knowledge across boundaries', *Organization Science*, 15(5), 555–568.

Chandler, A. (1962), *Strategy and Structure: Chapters in the History of American Enterprise*. Boston, MA: MIT Press.

Chandler, A. (1990a), *Scale and Scope: The Dynamics of Industrial Capitalism*. Cambridge, MA: Harvard University Press.

Chandler, A. (1990b), 'The enduring logic of industrial success', *Harvard Business Review*, 68(2): 130–140.

Chesbrough, H. (2003), *Open Innovation*. Boston, MA: Harvard Business School Press.

Chesbrough, H. (2006), *Open Business Models: How to Thrive in the New Innovation Landscape*. Boston, MA: Harvard Business School Press.

Christensen, C.M. (1997), *The Innovator's Dilemma: When New Technologies Cause Great Firms to Fail*. Boston, MA: Harvard Business School Press.

Christensen, C.M., and Rosenbloom, R.S. (1995), 'Explaining the attacker's advantage: technological paradigms, organizational dynamics, and the value network', *Research Policy*, 24(2), 233–257.

Cisco. (2011), Cisco announces streamlined operating model. Retrieved November 27, 2014 from *Cisco*: http://newsroom.cisco.com/press-release-content?&articleId=752727.

Collins, J., and Hansen, M.T. (2011), *Great by Choice: Uncertainty, Chaos and Luck: Why Some Thrive Despite Them All*. New York: Random House.

Collins, J., and Porras, J. (1994), *Built to Last: Successful Habits of Visionary Companies*. New York: HarperCollins.

Collis, D.J. (1994), 'Research note: how valuable are organizational capabilities?', *Strategic Management Journal*, 15(S1), 143–152.

Collis, D.J., and Montgomery, C.A. (1998), *Corporate Strategy: A Resource-Based View*. New York: McGraw-Hill.

Danneels, E. (2002), 'The dynamics of product innovation and firm competences', *Strategic Management Journal*, 23(12), 1095–1121.

D'Aveni, R.A. (1994), *Hypercompetition: Managing the Dynamics of Strategic Maneuvering*. New York: Free Press.

Davis-Blake, A., and Uzzi, B. (1993), 'Determinants of employment externalization: a study of temporary workers and independent contractors', *Administrative Science Quarterly*, 195–223.

Day, G., and Schoemaker, J. (2005), 'Scanning the periphery', *Harvard Business Review*, 135–148.

Dewar, R.D., and Dutton, J.E. (1986), 'The adoption of radical and incremental innovations: an empirical analysis', *Management Science*, 32(11), 1422–1433.

Dixon, S., Meyer, K., and Day, M. (2014), 'Building dynamic capabilities of adaptation and innovation: a study of micro-foundations in a transition economy', *Long Range Planning*, 47(4), 186–205.

Dosi, G., Faillo, M., and Marengo, L. (2008), 'Organizational capabilities, patterns of knowledge accumulation and governance structures in business firms: an introduction', *Organization Studies*, 29(8–9), 1165–1185.

Dougherty, D. (1992), 'Interpretive barriers to successful product innovation in large firms', *Organization Science*, 3(2), 179–202.

Drucker, P.F. (2009), *Managing in a Time of Great Change*. Boston, MA: Harvard Business Press.

Easterby-Smith, M., and Prieto, I.M. (2008), 'Dynamic capabilities and knowledge management: an integrative role for learning?', *British Journal of Management*, 19(3), 235–249.

Ehrnberg, E., and Jacobsson, S. (1997), 'Indicators of discontinuous technological change: an exploratory study of two discontinuities in the machine tool industry', *R&D Management*, 27(2), 107–126.

Eisenhardt, K., and Martin, J. (2000), 'Dynamic capabilities: what are they?', *Strategic Management Journal*, 21(10–11), 1105–1121.

Eisenhardt, K., and Sull, D. (2001), 'Strategy as simple rules', *Harvard Business Review*, 79, 106–116.

Ericsson, K.A., and Lehmann, A.C. (1996), 'Expert and exceptional performance: evidence of maximal adaptation to task constraints', *Annual Review of Psychology*, 47(1), 273–305.

Ettlie, E., Bridges, P., and O'Keefe, D. (1984), 'Organization strategy and structural differences for radical versus incremental innovation', *Management Science*, 30(6), 682–695.

Ferris, G.R., Russ, G.S., and Fandt, P.M. (1989), 'Politics in organizations', *Impression Management In The Organization*, 143(170), 79–100.

Floyd, S., and Wooldridge, B. (1999), 'Knowledge creation and social networks in corporate entrepreneurship: the renewal of organizational capability', *Entrepreneurship Theory and Practice*, 23(3), 123–142.

Gawer, A., and Cusmano, M.A. (2004), *Platform Leadership*. Boston, MA: Harvard Business School Publishing.

Gibson, C.B., and Birkinshaw, J. (2004), 'The antecedents, consequences, and mediating role of organizational ambidexterity', *Academy of Management Journal*, 47(2), 209–226.

Goold, M., and Campbell, A. (2002), *Designing Effective Organizations: How to Create Structured Networks*. San Francisco, CA: Jossey-Bass.

Gort, M., and Klepper, S. (1982), 'Time paths in the diffusion of product innovations', *The Economic Journal*, 92(367), 630–653.

Govindarajan, V., and Trimble, C. (2005), *Ten Rules for Strategic Innovations*. Boston, MA: Harvard Business School Press.

Grant, R.M. (1996), 'Toward a knowledge-based theory of the firms', *Strategic Management Journal*, 17(winter special issue), 109–122.

Gratton, L., and Ghoshal, S. (2005), 'Beyond best practice', *MIT Sloan Management Review*, 46(3), 49–57.

Green, S., Gavin, M., and Aiman-Smith, L. (1995), 'Assessing a multi-dimensional measure of radical technological innovation', *IEEE Transactions on Engineering Management*, 42(3), 203–214.

Greenwood, R., and Hinings, C. (1993), 'Understanding strategic change: the contribution of archetypes', *Academy of Management Review*, 36(5), 1052–1081.

Griffin, D.R., and Sherburne, D.W. (eds) (1929/1978), *Process and Reality: an Essay in Cosmology*. New York: Free Press.

Grinyer, P., and McKiernan, P. (1994), 'Triggering major and sustained changes in stagnating companies', in H. Daems, and H. Thomas (eds), *Strategic Groups, Strategic Moves and Performance*. New York: Pergamon, 173–195.

Grove, A.S. (1996), *Only the Paranoid Survive: How to Exploit the Crisis Points that Challenge Every Company and Career*. New York: Currency Doubleday.

Hacklin, F., Marxt, C., and Fahrni, F. (2009), 'Coevolutionary cycles of convergence: an extrapolation from the ICT industry', *Technological Forecasting and Social Change*, 76(6), 723–736.

Hagel III, J., and Brown, J.S. (2005), 'Productive friction', *Harvard Business Review*, 83(2), 139–145.

Hamel, G. (1999), 'Bringing Silicon Valley inside', *Harvard Business Review*, 77(5), 70–84.

Hamel, G. (2008), 'The future of management', *Human Resource Management International Digest*, 16(6), 12–18.

Hamel, G., and Prahalad, C.K. (1989), 'Strategic intent', *Harvard Business Review*, 67(3), 139–148.

Handy, C. (2002), 'What's a business for?', *Harvard Business Review*, 80(12), 62–70.

Hannan, M., and Freeman, J. (1984), 'Structural inertia and organizational change', *American Sociological Review*, 49(2), 149–164.

Hargadon, A. (2003), *How Breakthroughs Happen: The Surprising Truth about How Companies Innovate*. Boston, MA: Harvard Business School Press.

He, Z., and Wong, P. (2004), 'Exploration vs. exploitation: an empirical test of the ambidexterity hypothesis', *Organization Science*, 15(4), 481–494.

Hegar, K.W. (2011), *Modern Human Relations At Work*. New York: Cengage Learning.

Helfat, C.E., and Peteraf, M.A. (2003), 'The dynamic resource-based view: capability lifecycles', *Strategic Management Journal*, 24(10), 997–1010.

Helfat, C.E., and Peteraf, M.A. (2015), 'Managerial cognitive capabilities and the microfoundations of dynamic capabilities', *Strategic Management Journal*, 36(6), 831–850.

Helfat, C.E., and Winter, S.G. (2011), 'Untangling dynamic and operational capabilities: strategy for the (n)everchanging world', *Strategic Management Journal*, 32(11), 1243–1250.

Helfat, C.E., Finkelstein, S., Mitchell, W., Peteraf, M.A., Singh, H., Teece, D.J., and Winter, S.G. (2007), *Dynamic Capabilities: Understanding Strategic Change in Organizations*. Oxford: Blackwell.

Heller, T. (1999), 'Loosely coupled systems for corporate entrepreneurship: imaging and managing the innovation project/host organization interface', *Entrepreneurship, Theory and Practice*, 24(2), 25–31.

Henderson, R. (1993), 'Underinvestment and incompetence as responses to radical innovation: evidence from the photolithographic alignment equipment industry', *The RAND Journal of Economics*, 248–270.

Henderson, R., and Clark, K. (1990), 'Architectural innovation', *Administrative Science Quarterly*, 35, 9–30.

Hill, C., and Rothaermel, F. (2003), 'The performance of incumbent firms in the face of radical technological innovation', *Academy of Management Review*, 28(2), 257–247.

Holland, J. (1975), *Adaption in Natural and Artificial Systems*. Ann Arbor, MI: University of Michigan Press.

Holmes, J. (1986), 'The organization and locational structure of production subcontracting', in A.J. Scott and Michael Storper (eds), *Production, Work, Territory: The Geographical Anatomy of Industrial Capitalism*. London: HarperCollins, 80–106.

Iansiti, M., and Clark, K.B. (1994), 'Integration and dynamic capability: evidence from product development in automobiles and mainframe computers', *Industrial and Corporate Change*, 3(3), 557–605.

Imai, T. (2015), *Practice Corporate Governance Code Preparation Handbook* (in Japanese). Tokyo: Bunsho-do.

Isaacson, W. (2011), *Steve Jobs*. New York: Simon & Schuster.

Jacobides, M.G., and Winter, S.G. (2012), 'Capabilities: structure, agency, and evolution', *Organization Science*, 23(5), 1365–1381.

Jantsch, E. (1980), *The Self-Organizing Universe*. Oxford: Pergamon Press.

Johansson, F. (2004), *The Medici Effect*. Boston, MA: Harvard Business School Press.

Kanter, R. (1985), 'Supporting innovation and venture development in established companies', *Journal of Business Venturing*, 1(1), 47–60.

Kanter, R.M. (2001), *Evolve! Succeeding in the Digital Culture of Tomorrow*. Boston, MA: Harvard Business School Press.

Kaplan, S., Murray, F., and Henderson, R. (2003), 'Discontinuities and senior management: assessing the role of recognition in pharmaceutical firm response to biotechnology', *Industrial and Corporate Change*, 12(4), 203–233.

Katz, R., and Allen, T. (1982), 'Investigating the not invented here (NIH) syndrome: a look at the performance, tenure, and communication patterns of 50 R&D project groups', *R&D Management*, 12(1), 7–12.

Kennedy, A. (2000), *The End of Shareholder Value: Corporations at the Crossroads*. New York: Perseus Books Group.

Kim, W.C., and Mauborgne, R. (2005), *Blue Ocean Strategy*. Boston, MA: Harvard Business School Publishing.

King, A., and Tucci, L. (2002), 'Incumbent entry into new market niches: the role of experience and managerial choice in the creation of dynamic capabilities', *Management Science*, 48(2), 171–187.

Klepper, S. (1996), 'Entry, exit, growth, and innovation over the product life cycle', *The American Economic Review*, 562–583.

Kline, S.J. (1985), 'Innovation is not a linear process', *Research Management*, 28(4), 36.

Kodama, M. (2003), 'Strategic innovation in traditional big business', *Organization Studies*, 24(2), 235–268.

Kodama, M. (2004), 'Strategic community-based theory of firms: case study of dialectical management at NTT DoCoMo', *Systems Research and Behavioral Science*, 21(6), 603–634.

Kodama, M. (2005), 'Knowledge creation through networked strategic communities: case studies in new product development', *Long Range Planning*, 38(1), 27–49.

Kodama, M. (2006), 'Knowledge-based view of corporate strategy', *Technovation*, 26(12), 1390–1406.

Kodama, M. (2007a), *The Strategic Community-Based Firm*. London: Palgrave Macmillan.

Kodama, M. (2007b), *Knowledge Innovation – Strategic Management As Practice*. Cheltenham, UK and Northampton, MA, USA: Edward Elgar Publishing.

Kodama, M. (2007c), *Project-Based Organization in The Knowledge-Based Society*. London: Imperial College Press.

Kodama, M. (2007d), 'Innovation and knowledge creation through leadership-based strategic community: case study on high-tech company in Japan', *Technovation*, 27(3), 115–132.

Kodama, M. (2009a), 'Boundaries innovation and knowledge integration in the Japanese firm', *Long Range Planning*, 42(4), 463–494.

Kodama, M. (2009b), *Innovation Networks In Knowledge-Based Firms: Developing ICT-Based Integrative Competences*. Cheltenham, UK and Northampton, MA, USA: Edward Elgar Publishing.

Kodama, M. (2010), *Boundary Management: Developing Business Architecture for Innovation*. Germany: Springer.

Kodama, M. (2011), *Interactive Business Communities*. Fanham: Ashgate Publishing.

Kodama, M. (2012), *Competing Through ICT Capabilities*. London: Palgrave Macmillan.

Kodama, M. (2014), *Winning Through Boundaries Innovation: Communities of Boundaries Generate Convergence*. London: Peter Lang.

Kodama, M. (ed.) (2015), *Collaborative Innovation: Developing Health Support Ecosystems* (Vol. 39). London: Routledge.

Kodama, M. (2017), *Developing Holistic Leadership: A Source of Business Innovation*. London: Emerald.

Kodama, M., and Shibata, T. (2014a), 'Strategy transformation through strategic innovation capability: a case study of Fanuc', *R&D Management*, 44(1), 75–103.

Kodama, M., and Shibata, T. (2014b), 'Research into ambidextrous R&D in product development – new product development at a precision device maker: a case study', *Technology Analysis & Strategic Management*, 26(3), 279–306.

Kodama, M., and Shibata, T. (2016), 'Developing knowledge convergence through a boundaries vision: a case study of Fujifilm in Japan', *Knowledge and Process Management*, 23(4), 274–292.

Kodama, M., Tsunoji, T., and Motegi, N. (2002), 'FOMA videophone multipoint platform', *NTT DoCoMo Technical Journal*, 4(3), 6–11.

Kogut, B., and Zander, U. (1992), 'Knowledge of the firm, combinative capabilities and the replication of technology', *Organization Science*, 5(2), 383–397.

Kutaragi, K. (2005), Sony admits losing out on gadgets, January 21, *Washington Post*, E05.

Lashinsky, A. (2012), *Inside Apple: How America's Most Admired – and Secretive – Company Really Works*. London: Hachette.

Lave, J., and Wenger, E. (1990), *Situated Learning: Legitimate Peripheral Participation*. Cambridge: Cambridge University Press.

Lawrence, P., and Lorsch, J. (1967), *Organization and Environments: Managing Differentiation and Integration*. Cambridge, MA: Harvard Business School Press.

Learned, E.P., Christensen, C.R., Andrews, K.R., and Guth, W.D. (1965), *Business Policy: Text and Case*. Homewood, IL: Irwin.

Lei, D., Hitt, M.A., and Goldhar, J.D. (1996), 'Advanced manufacturing technology: organizational design and strategic flexibility', *Organization Studies*, 17(3), 501–523.

Leifer, R., McDermott, M., O'Connor, C., Peters, S., Rice, M., and Veryzer, W. (2000), *Radical Innovation: How Mature Companies Can Outsmart Upstarts*. Cambridge, MA: Harvard Business School Press.

Leonard-Barton, D. (1992), 'Core capabilities and core rigidities: a paradox in managing new product development', *Strategic Management Journal*, 13(2), 111–125.

Leonard-Barton, D. (1995), *Wellsprings of Knowledge: Building and Sustaining the Source of Innovation*. Cambridge, MA: Harvard Business School Press.

Lepak, D.P., and Snell, S.A. (1999), 'The human resource architecture: toward a theory of human capital allocation and development', *Academy of Management Review*, 24(1), 31–48.

Levitt, B., and March, J.B. (1988), 'Organization learning', in W.R. Scott, and J. Blake (eds), *Annual Review of Sociology*, 14, Palo Alto, CA: Annual Reviews, 319–340.

Lindkvist, L. (2005), 'Knowledge communities and knowledge collectivities: a typology of knowledge work in groups', *Journal of Management Studies*, 42(6), 1189–1210.

London, M. (2011), *The Oxford Handbook of Lifelong Learning*. Oxford: Oxford University Press.

Maccoby, M. (2000), 'The human side: understanding the difference between management and leadership', *Research-Technology Management*, 43(1), 57–59.

Malerba, F. (2002), 'Sectoral systems of innovation and production', *Research Policy*, 31(2), 247–264.

March, J. (1991), 'Exploration and exploitation in organizational learning', *Organization Science*, 2(1), 71–87.

March, J. (1996), 'Continuity and change in theories of organizational action', *Administrative Science Quarterly*, 41(2), 278–287.

Markham, S.K. (2002), 'Moving technologies from lab to market', *Research-Technology Management*, 45(6), 31–36.

Markides, C. (1997), 'Strategic innovation', *Sloan Management Review*, 38(1), 9–23.

Markides, C. (1999), *All the Right Moves: A Guide to Crafting Breakthrough Strategy*. Boston, MA: Harvard Business School Publishing.

Markides, C. (2001), 'Strategy as balance: from "either-or" to "and"', *Business Strategy Review*, 12(3), 1–10.

Martines, L., and Kambil, A. (1999), 'Looking back and thinking ahead: effects of prior success on managers' interpretations of new information technologies', *Academy of Management Journal*, 42(3), 652–661.

McDermott, C.M., and O'Connor, G.C. (2002), 'Managing radical innovation: an overview of emergent strategy issues', *Journal of Product Innovation Management*, 19(6), 424–438.

Merrifield, B.D. (1995), 'Obsolescence of core competencies versus corporate renewal', *Technology Management*, 2(2), 73–83.

Miles, R., and Snow, C.C. (1984), 'Designing strategic human resources systems', *Organizational Dynamics*, 13(1), 36–52.

Miles, R., and Snow, C. (1994), *Fit, Failure, and the Hall of Fame: How Companies Succeed or Fail*. New York: Free Press.

Miller, C.C., and Ireland, R.D. (2005), 'Intuition in strategic decision making: friend or foe in the fast-paced 21st century?', *The Academy of Management Executive*, 19(1), 19–30.

Miller, D., and Le Breton-Miller, I. (2005), *Managing for the Long Run: Lessons in Competitive Advantage From Great Family Businesses*. Boston, MA: Harvard Business Press.

Mintzberg, H. (1978), 'Patterns in strategy formation', *Management Science*, 24, 934–948.

Nadler, D., Gerstein, M.S., and Shaw, R.B. (1992), *Organizational Architecture: Designs for Changing Organizations* (Vol. 192). San Francisco, CA: Jossey-Bass.

Nelson, R. and Winter, S. (1982), *An Evolutionary Theory of Economic Change*. Boston, MA: Belknap Press.

Nire, S. (2013), *'Like' Breaks Society* (in Japanese). Tokyo: Shintyou-sya.

Nisbett, R. (2003), *The Geography of Thought*. New York: Free Press.

Nohria, N., and Gulati, R. (1996), 'Is slack good or bad for innovation?', *Academy of Management Journal*, 39(5), 1245–1264.

Nonaka, I. (1988), 'Toward middle-up-down management: accelerating information creation', *Sloan Management Review*, 29(3), 9–18.

Nonaka, I., and Takeuchi, H. (1995), *The Knowledge-Creating Company*. New York: Oxford University Press.

Nooteboom, B. (2009), *A Cognitive Theory Of The Firm: Learning,*

Governance And Dynamic Capabilities. Cheltenham, UK and Northampton, MA, USA: Edward Elgar Publishing.

O'Connor, C., and Rice, P. (2001), 'Opportunity recognition and breakthrough innovation in large established firms', *California Management Review*, 43(2), 95–116.

O'Connor, G. (2008), 'Major innovation as a dynamic capability: a systems approach', *Journal of Product Innovation Management*, 25(2), 313–330.

O'Connor, G., and DeMartino, R. (2006), 'Organizing for radical innovation: an exploratory study of the structural aspects of RI management systems in large established firms', *Journal of Product Innovation Management*, 23(2), 475–497.

O'Connor, G., Leifer, R., Paulson, P., and Peters, P. (2008), *Grabbing Lightning: Building a Capability for Breakthrough Innovation.* San Francisco, CA: Jossey-Bass.

O'Reilly III, C., and Pfeffer, J. (2000), *Hidden Value: How Great Companies Achieve Extraordinary Results with Ordinary People.* Boston, MA: Harvard Business School.

O'Reilly, C., and Tushman, M. (2004), 'The ambidextrous organization', *Harvard Business Review*, 82(4), 74–82.

O'Reilly, C., and Tushman, M.L. (2008), 'Ambidexterity as a dynamic capability: resolving the innovator's dilemma', *Research in Organizational Behavior*, 28, 185–206.

Ohtsubo, F. (2006), 'Interview (in Japanese)', *Voice*, 11, 153–158.

Orr, J. (1996), *Talking about Machines: An Ethnography of a Modern Job.* Ithaca, NY: ILP Press.

Orton, J.D., and Weick, K.E. (1990), 'Loosely coupled systems: a reconceptualization', *Academy of Management Review*, 15(2), 203–223.

Osono, E., Kodama, M., Yachi, H., and Nonaka, I. (2006), *Practice Theory of Innovation Management* (in Japanese). Tokyo: Hakuto Shobo.

Osterlof, M., and Frey, B. (2000), 'Motivation, knowledge transfer, and organizational forms', *Organization Science*, 11(3), 538–550.

Pennings, J.M. (1987), 'Structural contingency theory: a multivariate test', *Organization Studies*, 8(3), 223–240.

Penrose, E.T. (1959), *The Theory of the Growth of the Firm.* New York: Wiley.

Peters, T., and Waterman, R. (1982), *In Search of Excellence.* New York: Harper & Row.

Pfeffer, J., and Salancik, G. (1978), *The External Control of Organizations: A Resource Dependence Perspective.* New York: Harper & Row.

Pisano, G.P. (1991), 'The governance of innovation: vertical integration and collaborative arrangements in the biotechnology industry', *Research Policy*, 20(3), 237–249.

Pisano, G. (1994), 'The governance of innovation: vertical integration and collaborative arrangements in the biotechnology industry', *Research Policy*, 20(3), 237–249.

Porter, M. (1980), *Competitive Strategy: Techniques for Analyzing Industries and Competitors*. New York: Free Press.

Porter, M. (1985), *Competitive Advantage*. New York: Free Press.

Porter, M. (1996), 'What is strategy?', *Harvard Business Review*, 74, 61–78.

Rafols, I., and Meyer, M. (2010), 'Diversity and network coherence as indicators of interdisciplinarity: case studies in bionanoscience', *Scientometrics*, 82(2), 263–287.

Raynor, M. (2007), *The Strategy Paradox: Why Committing to Success Leads To Failure*. Anderson, IN: Broadway Business.

Ricci, R., and Wiese, C. (2011), *The Collaboration Imperative: Executive Strategies for Unlocking Your Organization's True Potential*. San Francisco, CA: Cisco Systems, Inc.

Richardson, G.B. (1972), 'The organisation of industry', *The Economic Journal*, 82(327), 883–896.

Roberts, J. (2006), 'Limits to communities of practice', *Journal of Management Studies*, 43(3), 623–639.

Rosenbloom, N. (2000), 'Leadership, capabilities and technological change', *Strategic Management Journal*, 21, 1083–1103.

Rumelt, R. (1984), 'Toward a strategic theory of the firm', in R. Lamb (ed.), *Competitive Strategic Management*. Englewood Cliffs, NJ: Prentice Hall, 556–570.

Rumelt, R. (2011), *Good Strategy/Bad Strategy: The Difference And Why It Matters*. New York: Crown Business.

Sanchez, R., and Mahoney, T. (1996), 'Modularity, flexibility, and knowledge management in product and organizational design', *Strategic Management Journal*, 17(winter special issue), 63–76.

Santos, F.M., and Eisenhardt, K.M. (2005), 'Organizational boundaries and theories of organization', *Organization Science*, 16(5), 491–508.

Schilke, O. (2014), 'Second-order dynamic capabilities: how do they matter?', *Academy of Management Perspectives*, 28(4), 368–380.

Schilling, M.A., and Steensma, H.K. (2001), 'The use of modular organizational forms: an industry-level analysis', *Academy of Management Journal*, 44(6), 1149–1168.

Schumpeter, J.A. (1912), *The Theory of Economic Development*. New Brunswick, NJ: Transaction Publishers.

Schumpeter, J.A. (1942), *Creative Destruction. Capitalism, Socialism and Democracy*. London: Routledge.

Schumpeter, J.A. (1961), *The Theory of Economic Development: An Inquiry into Profits, Capital, Credit, Interest, and the Business Cycle* (trans. by Redvers Opie). Boston, MA: Harvard University Press.

Schumpeter, J.A. (1995), *Capitalism, Socialism and Democracy*. New York: Harper Perennial Modern Classics.

Shannon, C., and Weaver, W. (1949), *The Mathematical Theory of Communications*. Urbana, IL: University of Illinois Press.

Siggelkow, N. (2001), 'Change in the presence of fit: the rise, the fall, and the renaissance of Liz Claiborne', *Academy of Management Journal*, 44(4), 838–857.

Simon, H.A. (2002), 'Near decomposability and the speed of evolution', *Industrial and Corporate Change*, 11(3), 587–599.

Sirmon, D.G., Hitt, M.A., and Ireland, D. (2007), 'Managing firm resources in dynamic environments to create value: looking inside the black box', *Academy of Management Review*, 32(1), 273–292.

Smith, S., and Tushman, M. (2005), 'Managing strategic contradictions: a top management model for managing innovation streams', *Organization Science*, 16(5), 522–536.

Spender, J.C. (1990), *Industry Recipes: An Enquiry into the Nature and Sources of Managerial Judgement*. Oxford: Basil Blackwell.

Teece, D.J. (1980), 'Economies of scope and the scope of the enterprise', *Journal of Economic Behavior and Organization*, 1(3): 223–247.

Teece, D.J. (1986), 'Profiting from technological innovation', *Research Policy*, 15(6), 285–305.

Teece, D.J. (2000), *Managing Intellectual Capital: Organizational, Strategic, and Policy Dimensions*. Oxford: Oxford University Press.

Teece, D.J. (2007), 'Explicating dynamic capabilities: the nature and microfoundations of (sustainable) enterprise performance', *Strategic Management Journal*, 28(13), 1319–1350.

Teece, D.J. (2012a), 'Next-generation competition: new concepts for under-standing how innovation shapes competition and policy in the digital economy', *Journal of Law, Economics and Policy*, 9(1), 97–118.

Teece, D.J. (2012b), 'Dynamic capabilities: routines versus entrepreneurial action', *Journal of Management Studies*, 49(8), 1395–1401.

Teece, D.J. (2014), 'The foundations of enterprise performance: dynamic and ordinary capabilities in an (economic) theory of firms', *Academy of Management Perspectives*, 28(4): 328–352.

Teece, D.J., Pisano, G., and Shuen, A. (1997), 'Dynamic capabilities and strategic management', *Strategic Management Journal*, 509–533.

Thompson, J.D. (1967), *Organizations in Action*. New York: McGraw-Hill.

Tripsas, M., and Gavetti, G. (2000), 'Capabilities, cognition, and inertia: evidence from digital imaging', *Strategic Management Journal*, 1147–1161.

Tsai, R. (2007), 'NE interview: what is the future of foundry? (in Japanese)', *Nikkei Electronics*, 963, 34–35, October 22.

Tushman, M. (1977), 'Special boundary roles in the innovation process', *Administrative Science Quarterly*, 22, 587–605.

Tushman, M., and Nadler, D. (1978), 'Information processing as an integrating concept in organizational design', *Academy of Management Review*, 3(3), 613–624.

Tushman, M., and O'Reilly, C.A. (1997), *Winning Through Innovation*. Cambridge, MA: Harvard Business School Press.

Tushman, M., and Romanelli, R. (1985), 'Organizational evolution: a metamorphosis model of convergence and reorientation', *Research in Organizational Behavior*, 7(2), 171–222.

Utterback, J. (1994), *Mastering the Dynamics of Innovation*. Boston, MA: Harvard Business School Press.

Utterback, J., Vedin, B.A., Alvarez, E., Ekman, S., Walsh Sanderson, S., Tether, B., and Verganti, R. (2006), 'Design-inspired innovation and the design discourse', *Design-Inspired Innovation*, 154–186.

Van Mieghem, J.A. (2008), *Operations Strategy: Principles and Practices*. Belmont, MA: Dynamic Ideas.

Vanhaverbeke, W., and Peeters, N. (2005), 'Embracing innovation as strategy: the role of new business development in corporate renewal', *Creativity and Innovation Management*, 14(3), 246–257.

Verganti, R. (2009), *Design-Driven Innovation: Changing the Rules By Radically Innovating What Things Mean*. Boston, MA: Harvard Business School Publishing.

Vogel, S. (2006), *Japan Remodeled: How Government and Industry are Reforming Japanese Capitalism*. Ithaca, NY: Cornell University Press.

Von Hippel, E., and Katz, R. (2002), 'Shifting innovation to users via toolkits', *Management Science*, 48(7), 821–833.

Weick, K.E. (1989), 'Theory construction as disciplined imagination', *Academy of Management Review*, 14(4), 516–531.

Wenger, E. (1998), *Community of Practice: Learning, Meaning and Identity*. Cambridge: Cambridge University Press.

Wernerfelt, B. (1984), 'A resource-based view of the firm', *Strategic Management Journal*, 5(2), 171–180.

Wheelwright, S.C., and Clark, K.B. (1992), *Revolutionizing Product Development: Quantum Leaps in Speed, Efficiency, and Quality*. New York: Simon & Schuster.

Winter, S. (2000), 'The satisficing principle in capability learning', *Strategic Management Journal*, 21(10–11), 981–996.

Winter, S. (2003), 'Understanding dynamic capabilities', *Strategic Management Journal*, 24(10), 991–995.

Womack, J.P., Jones, D.T., and Roos, D. (1990), *Machines that Changed the World*. New York: Simon & Schuster.

Yano, K. (2006), 'Interview (in Japanese)', *Voice*, 11, 159–164.

Young, H.P. (2001), *Individual Strategy and Social Structure: An Evolutionary Theory of Institutions*. Princeton, NJ: Princeton University Press.

Zahra, S.A., Sapienza, H.J., and Davidsson, P. (2006), 'Entrepreneurship and dynamic capabilities: a review, model and research agenda', *Journal of Management Studies*, 43(4), 917–955.

Zollo, M., and Winter, G. (2002), 'Deliberate learning and the evolution of dynamic capabilities', *Organization Science*, 13(3), 339–351.

Zook, C. (2007), 'Finding your next core business', *Harvard Business Review*, 85(4), 66–75.

Index